FORSAKEN
The Making and **Aftermath** of
Roger Corman's
The Fantastic Four

WILLIAM NESBITT

*Forsaken: The Making and Aftermath of
Roger Corman's* The Fantastic Four
© 2019 William Nesbitt. All Rights Reserved.

The Fantastic Four and associated characters, their distinctive likenesses, and related elements are TM and © Marvel Characters, Inc. All rights reserved.

No part of this book may be reproduced in any form or by any means, electronic, mechanical, digital, photocopying or recording, except for the inclusion in a review, without permission in writing from the publisher.

Published in the USA by:
BearManor Media
1317 Edgewater Dr. #110
Orlando, Florida 32804
www.bearmanormedia.com

Hardcover: ISBN 978-1-62933-504-9
Paperback: ISBN 978-1-62933-503-2

Printed in the United States of America.
Cover Image courtesy of Chris Walker *(See Page 88)*.
Book design by Brian Pearce | Red Jacket Press.

Table of Contents

Foreword by Mark Sikes 7
Preface. 9
Introduction 13
A Note About Stan Lee 17
Lloyd Kaufman 19
President and Co-Founder
of Troma Entertainment
Craig J. Nevius. 33
Screenplay — *Part I*
Chris Gore 47
On-Set Journalist for *Film Threat*
Mick Strawn 53
Production Design, Miniatures
Creator, Director: Miniature Unit
Pete Von Sholly. 69
Storyboard Artist
Chris Walker III 77
Effects, *Fantastic Four* (2005/2007)
Chris Walker 81
Director of Animation
Everett Burrell. 93
Special Effects Makeup
John Vulich 107
Special Effects Makeup
Mark Parry. 119
Director of Photography
David Wurst & Eric Wurst 127
Music
Oley Sassone. 133
Director
Carl Ciarfalio 149
The Thing
Jay Underwood. 161
Johnny Storm/The Human Torch

Rebecca Staab 171
Susan Storm/The Invisible Girl
Michael Bailey Smith 195
Ben Grimm
Kat Green. 213
Alicia Masters
Alex Hyde-White 221
Reed Richards/Mister Fantastic
Joseph Culp 231
Victor Von Doom/Doctor Doom
David Keith Miller. 247
Trigorin
Robert Alan Beuth 253
Dr. Hauptman
Glenn Garland 261
Co-Associate Producer, Film Editing
Craig J. Nevius. 267
Screenplay — *Part II*
Mark Sikes 279
Casting Assistant
Roger Corman 305
Co-Executive Producer
Bernd Eichinger 315
Co-Executive Producer
Ivan Kander 329
Lucky 9 Studios
Stan Lee 337
Co-Creator of the Fantastic Four
Conclusion 345
Who Created the
Fantastic Four? 359
A Brief History of *The
Animated Fantastic Four*. . . . 361
Index. 363

*This book is dedicated to my grandfather
James Eldred Brady, my own superhero.
I always felt safe with him.*

Foreword
by Mark Sikes

"How many movies did Roger Corman make and never release? One."

That's a quote from the documentary I produced, *Doomed!: The Untold Story of Roger Corman's The Fantastic Four*. I know the line well because I said it. And it's true. So why did Academy Award-winning producer Roger Corman develop, cast, shoot, and finish a feature film that cost $1 million only to decide not to release it?

Was it so bad that the producer of *Humanoids from the Deep* and *Boxcar Bertha* thought he couldn't sell it? Was it ever even intended to be released, or was it just a way to maintain the option for future productions? Exactly who made the decision to shelve the film and destroy all official copies? Surely it took an evil mind that would rival that of even Victor Von Doom, no?

The answers are all right here in this book. William has interviewed more people than we did on *Doomed*, and you will see longer versions of all their stories. We only had ninety minutes to tell our story as a documentary. William's book would translate into hours and hours of interview footage. What a great resource. It belongs on every comic book fan's and film buff's bookshelf. And if you love a great mystery, this is one of the best in all of movie history.

I am writing this foreword for William's book, *Forsaken: The Making and Aftermath of Roger Corman's The Fantastic Four*, for a number of reasons. As the executive producer of *Doomed*, I guess that qualifies me right there. My producing partner, Marty Langford, and I became bona fide experts on the film over the four years it took us to interview actors and crew from the original film, and, of course, I worked on the film back in 1992 and 1993. But I think there is an even better reason, and here it is.

I am a fan of the Fantastic Four. Not just Corman's ill-fated film, but the comic book series as well. I've been collecting them since the 1970s, and in the early 1990s I had the thrill of working on the very first live-action film ever made. If you are unaware of this film, this book will be even better because it's a new story to you. If you are a longtime fan like so many of us, sit back and get ready to learn some new stuff.

Stan Lee and Jack Kirby must be mentioned here because without these creative geniuses there would be no Fantastic Four and no movie. We finally had to bid a fond farewell to Stan "The Man" last year and we lost "The King" way too soon, many years ago, but their legacy lives on and no doubt will for many more years.

I am a huge fan of our film. I love the cast. I love the director. I think that Roger Corman's version of the property is still the best version despite incredible budgetary restrictions. Director Oley Sassone and writer Craig J. Nevius are the only ones so far who have gotten it right, proving all the money in the world doesn't beat an amazing writer and a resourceful director.

My wish is that one day Marvel decides to put the fans first and officially release this lost gem. Anything this first film lacks in CGI is no more than the later films lack in concept and script. My film *Doomed* began to tell the true, untold story of Roger Corman's *The Fantastic Four*. This book is the rest of the story and an essential part of the film's history.

Excelsior!

Mark Sikes
January 2019

Preface

Because it is not bound by the time and length constraints of a documentary, this project goes deeper and further in some ways than *Doomed*. However, you should start with *Doomed*. Besides giving an excellent overview of the entire saga that is *The Fantastic Four*, you'll get a sense that no book can give you of the people involved in making the film. A book is bound to stationary words and fixed photographs. Not a film. In *Doomed*, you can see what everyone looks like, watch their body movements and body language, look them in the eye, hear them talk, and learn the sounds and rhythms of their voices.

As the interviewer, I ask most of the questions. However, the interviewees generally have a few of their own. The most common question I was asked was some variation of how I came I up with this project.

Part of the answer is that it began as part of a much larger project, and if I hadn't been involved with that project, this one would not have happened. About two years ago, Stephen Armstrong, my colleague and friend from graduate school contacted me and Robert Powell, another colleague and friend from graduate school, about working on a series of interviews about New World Pictures and Roger Corman (that project, by the way, should appear around the same time as this one). Although that wasn't at the top of my area of scholarly expertise, I'm up for about anything, and it sounded exciting. I worked my way through finding and contacting interview subjects, interviewing them, transcribing the interviews, and editing them into a mutually agreeable final form. I ended up with interviews from Barry Schrader, Durinda Wood, Sid Haig, Alex Hajdu, and Grace Zabriskie. It was a lot of work and a lot of fun. I still had some time left, so I cruised through Corman's filmography one more time to see if anything caught my eye.

I became intrigued with *The Fantastic Four* for several reasons. It's about a comic book, and it's unreleased. While *The Fantastic Four* is not a New World Pictures film, it is a Roger Corman film. The idea was to include an interview about it as an appendix. What I decided to do was ask two to four people involved with the film a series of questions and compile everything for a roundtable interview. The ideal final length was about 4,000 words. I started contacting people, and to my amazement I received prompt yesses from all four. For the other project, I contacted twenty-one people and conducted interviews with five, so my success rate for that was slightly less than 25%. Now here I was batting a thousand. I realized maybe I had something larger on my hands.

Everyone I contacted knew about Mark Sikes and Marty Langford's documentary *Doomed!: The Untold Story of Roger Corman's The Fantastic Four* and they said, "You gotta talk to Mark. You gotta talk to Mark." I started corresponding with Sikes and found out that he is not only a wealth of information but also *inspiration*. In the midst of e-mailing back and forth one night, he convinced me that there was enough here for a book. With the blessing of my friends, I broke *The Fantastic Four* idea off from that book and started working towards this book. One of my hesitations in doing so was the fear of having too much for the roundtable interview but not enough for a full book and then becoming stranded somewhere in between. The two to four interviews became twenty-seven and the 2,000 to 4,000 words became over 110,000 after the editing the interviews for length and clarity. Additionally, I cut about eighteen pages, and this is without any other parts but the interviews themselves. People weren't just willing to talk, they were *eager* to talk and many of them — especially Sikes and director Oley Sassone — put me in touch with other people. Good people like Craig J. Nevius, Mick Strawn, and Everett Burrell further helped me by letting me use previously unseen photographs they took. Chris Walker III even supplied the cover image based on some personal work he did after the film.

I've heard people talk about projects having a life and an energy of their own, as if the musician or artist or writer was more channeling energy than creating it. I've had moments like that, but not many pieces of writing that gave me that feeling from start to finish and, certainly, nothing of this length. This project feels like that, like it gave birth to itself, willed its way into the world, and I was just lucky enough to come along for the ride.

The other part of the answer explaining how I came to be involved with this project is that I love comic books. This is my twentieth year teaching English and literature at the college level. Among other classes, I designed and taught a graphic novel class (the 220 in the LIT 3220 prefix and course number is a tribute to my grandfather who was born on February 20 and bought me a lot of comics). I've been into reading and writing for almost as long as I can remember. *Almost.* There was a very early time in my life when reading held no great appeal to me. I just didn't see why it might be enjoyable. But the bright, vibrant covers of comic books started getting my attention. At that time, comics were less mainstream, yet more visible. You could find them at the checkout lane of a supermarket, in the magazine aisle, or — my favorite — in those revolving racks at convenience stores. I became curious and I started recognizing some of the same characters from the various cartoons I was watching. I wanted to know what was going on. I wanted *in.*

Things changed one summer in the early 1980s. I think the first comic book I got was either an *Iron Man* or *The Brave and the Bold* issue from around that time (*Fantastic Four* wouldn't be far behind). Either way, once I got into reading, I got into reading. I was reading at grade level, but when I returned for the fall, I jumped three grade levels in reading.

Music, my other great love, wouldn't come to me for another decade. In the meantime, I visited dedicated comic book shops such as The Old Book Shop in Jacksonville, Florida; newsstands like Thomasville, Georgia's The Smokehouse on its Broad Street location, and used media outlets like Atlanta's Book Nook, where you could buy unorganized back issues five for a dollar (I once found a somewhat used *Tales of Suspense* #80 there that I still have). My grandfather kept me supplied with comics from trips we made together to The Smokehouse and the corner convenience store with its spinning comics rack up the street from my grandparents' house.

That passion for reading eventually took me to a Ph.D. in English at Florida State University and the story comes full circle. Reading, writing, and teaching have sustained me, taken me around the world, and given me a great life and almost everything worth having.

All of it began with comic books.

Introduction

Marvel comic books have always been big business. Marvel comic book movies? Not so much. The 2000 *X-Men* was Marvel's first big success. It wasn't their first big-budget attempt, however. *Howard the Duck* (1989) had a budget of $37 million and did little more than break even. Marvel had other lower-budget adventures that were mostly made-for-television such as the first version of Doctor Strange, *Dr. Strange* (1978). Since 2000 Marvel has experienced more success than DC, but originally it was the other way around. Other than *The Amazing Spider-Man* television series of the 1970s, which lasted two seasons and did well in the ratings but was ultimately cancelled, and *The Incredible Hulk* series of the late 1970s and early 1980s, Marvel was just not well-represented on either the small or the big screen in terms of live-action movies. There were other mixed attempts at live-action material, such as *Captain America,* and also cartoons, and while these productions have their own importance and place in history, few remember or talk about them in the same way as the movies from 2000 to today.

DC, on the other hand, did much better. They had their 1950s *Adventures of Superman* and 1960s *Batman* television series. They created theatrical releases as well including the four *Superman* movies, a *Swamp Thing* (1982) flick that as a kid I thought was pretty good, and a forgotten *Supergirl* (1984) film. The first two Superman movies made a mark. They brought performed wonderfully in the box office and the first *Superman* received three Academy Award nominations and received a Special Achievement Award for Visual Effects. Winning an Academy Award and generating over $400 million at the box office on a $35 million budget, *Batman* (1989) was the second part of the one-two DC cinema punch. Fans bought over $750 million in merchandise. It even had two soundtracks: one by Danny Elfman and one by Prince. POW! BAM! ZAP! indeed. Three successful sequels followed prior to the *Batman Begins* (2005) reboot.

There was money to be made at the box office with comic book movies if you knew how to do it. This is where Bernd Eichinger and Roger Corman enter the story. Eichinger was a German producer with Neue Constantin, a film production and distribution company. In 1986 Eichinger bought the option to make a *Fantastic Four* film for $250,000 (almost $600,000 in 2019). By today's standards, that figure seems absurdly low. Considering the lack of profitability of Marvel films and that the industry was still learning what these films were supposed to be about and how to make them, coupled with adjustments for inflation, $250,000 looks like a fair deal for both sides in retrospect. Eichinger had difficulty securing the big funding and big studio to make the huge movie he envisioned. With time running out on his option, Eichinger began to talk with lower-budget studios that could make the movie both inexpensively and quickly as his option was set to run out. He may have had some discussion with Lloyd Kaufman and Troma Entertainment but ultimately settled on Corman and Concorde-New Horizons.

Corman was the mastermind behind New World Pictures, which he co-founded in 1970. He had sold the company in 1983 and formed Concorde-New Horizons. Concorde-New Horizons was poised to capitalize on the booming video market of the 1980s. While the delivery model was financially successful, many Concorde-New Horizons movies didn't make it to the big screen and, in general, the New World Pictures films are held in higher regard. Still, Concorde-New Horizons maintained a Hollywood presence and the ability to produce movies quickly, profitably, and on tight budgets.

Corman was not entirely unacquainted with comic book movies. In 1982, Corman had the option for *Spider-Man* and was working with Orion Pictures. He enlisted Stan Lee to write for the movie and they made enough headway that the basic plot and ending were fleshed out. Unable to come to mutually agreeable terms — possibly over the budget — and begin filming, production kept getting pushed back until the option expired and Cannon Films, who made the disastrous *Superman IV: The Quest for Peace*, picked it up for $225,000 in 1985 (this is just one anecdote from the complicated film history of *Spider-Man*). In an August 5, 2015 interview with Aaron Sagers of *Syfy Wire*, Corman explains that they had a first draft of the script completed, but Orion Pictures failed to renew the option.

Keeping his library and production staff, Corman sold New World Pictures in 1983. He formed a new company named Millennium that he later renamed as Concorde Films. Although he ended up suing New World Pictures in 1985 when they reneged on their distribution deal with him, he most likely kept up with what they were doing. Interestingly, New World Pictures got involved in making live-action comic book movies. *The Incredible Hulk Returns* (1998) was produced by New World Television, a division of New World Pictures, and Bixby-Brandon Productions. *The Trial of the Incredible Hulk* (1989) was produced by New World International, another division of New World Pictures, and Bixby-Brandon Productions. However, both were only intended for television. *The Punisher* (1989) was produced by New World Pictures and starred Dolph Lundgren and Louis Gossett Jr. (Nicole Kidman was also cast). It received a theatrical release, though the release was limited in the United States. Despite the star power and a $9 million budget, the film was not a success.

With the Fantastic Four franchise, Corman had another shot at trying to use a big property and a low budget to turn a profit, and he may have learned something from his former company's adventures with live-action comic book films. This one might even make it into theaters and get a wide release. A trailer was later made and shown. Stan Lee didn't write the script for this one and Eichinger was running out of time, so Corman may have had considerable input into the overall shape and feel of the film. Filming began in late December of 1992, just before the option was set to expire, and ran about three weeks or so. Later on, actors Michael Bailey Smith and Alex Hyde-White traveled and promoted the film using materials provided by Corman such as posters and stills. The two hired a publicist out of their own pockets. *The Hollywood Reporter* and *Film Threat* put *The Fantastic*

Four on their covers, and *Film Threat* listed Labor Day as a release date. Theaters were showing trailers. Various events such as San Diego Comic-Con were showing clips of the film. An announcement was made that the world premiere would take place at the Mall of America in Minneapolis, Minnesota on January 19, 1994. On the outside, at least, everything suggested that this film would be released.

On the inside, strange things were happening. Resources were disappearing. After principal photography concluded, director Oley Sassone had few resources to finish the film with and resorted to having footage snuck in so that he could edit it. The film was never released. Corman called Sassone and told him the film would not be coming out. The actors were told to stop promoting it. Eventually, Eichinger's big-budget version of the Fantastic Four appeared as the 2005 *Fantastic Four*. It cost $100 million dollars and Eichinger made it with Fox.

What happened?

Was this an elaborate conspiracy designed just to keep Eichinger's option from running out? If so, who knew what when? Did Corman know? Did Sassone know? Did the actors know? Did anyone working on the film know? What about Stan Lee and producer Steve Rabiner? What was the original plan for the movie, and did it change? Were there any negotiations between or among Eichinger, Fox, and/or Marvel? Was *The Fantastic Four* a million-dollar bargaining chip or bluff? Was releasing the 1994 movie plan A or plan B? Did Eichinger even know for sure what he wanted to do with it? Was the movie simply too bad to be released?

No one seemed to know anything for sure. Some didn't even want to talk about it at all. This book is an attempt to answer those questions and discover the truth behind the unreleased *The Fantastic Four*.

A Note About Stan Lee

Late into this project, Stan Lee passed.

If you kept up with Stan Lee's final years and months, you know that he was not doing well. I completed these interviews before his passing, but he was often a topic of conversation. Though his passing was not a complete surprise, obviously no one knew he was going to go when he did. Looking back, I am especially glad people shared their memories of him. Although I was not able to interview him directly, he does have his own interview, his own voice, and he also has a place in this book through other people's recollections and thoughts about him.

An unexpected and fortunate occurrence happened as I was close to finishing the first draft of the conclusion. When I started the project, I looked around for various materials about the film. "Fantastic Faux!" is a very well-written and comprehensive article about *The Fantastic Four* composed by Robert Ito for *Los Angeles* magazine in 2005 right around the release of the big-budget *Fantastic Four*. This, for example, is the source for the famous anecdote about Avi Arad saying that he burned the film.

As I moved into writing the part of the conclusion concerning Stan Lee, I revisited Ito's article one more time. In the second-to-last paragraph Ito writes that Stan Lee and Jack Kirby watched the movie. I wondered how he knew this information. Was it speculation (which I doubted)? A secondhand tidbit from elsewhere? Did Stan Lee tell Ito this himself? It was important because if Stan Lee watched the movie it meant he had a certain interest or curiosity in it, and he probably wasn't embarrassed by it if he admitted to seeing it. This information would help settle the longstanding question of what Stan Lee really thought about the movie because, as we know, he was positive on the set but later distanced himself from the film. I decided to contact Ito.

Ito responded and told me he knew Stan Lee saw the movie because Stan Lee told it to him. The quotes from Stan Lee weren't quick quotes or stock lines handed off to him quickly or by someone else. Ito had actually sat down with Stan Lee and interviewed him in person. If you read, for example, the third paragraph of the article, Ito describes not just the sound of Stan Lee's voice but the image of him "peer(ing) out from behind his sunglasses." I asked Ito if he had a transcript for the interview. He did. I asked him if it was published. It wasn't. I asked him if I could publish it for this project. I could. So that is how I managed to include an interview with Stan Lee about both the low-budget and big-budget versions. Since Eichinger is quoted in the article, I asked Ito the same question about Eichinger that I asked about Stan Lee — do you have an unpublished transcript of the interview that I can publish? — and received the same answers, so I have that previously unread interview here, too, thanks to Ito. I did a little more smoothing out of Eichinger's answers than Stan Lee's since Bernd is native to Germany and his English is sometimes imperfect. I did leave a few examples of that in, though, to give readers a sense of how he actually spoke.

Both interviews are so rich in material for this project because Stan Lee and Eichinger both seem to think the main purpose of the interview is talk about the 2005 version because of the timing but instead both interviews discuss more of the 1994 version than either of them probably anticipated.

Lloyd Kaufman
President and Co-Founder of Troma Entertainment

You said in the *Doomed!: The Untold Story of Roger Corman's the Fantastic Four* documentary that Bernd Eichinger approached you about making *The Fantastic Four* on a low budget and you had several conversations with him about it. He was with Constantin Film also referred to sometimes as Neue Constantin, New Constantin, Constantin Film, and Constantin Film AG. Do you recall when you had those conversations?
No, I do not recall.
What was his pitch?
We were at a high school party and he pushed me down on the bed and put his hand over my mouth. No, no, no. That's the Supreme Court justice. I got it all mixed up.

He called me in. I'm from New York but I was out in Los Angeles for some reason anyway. I go out there often. I went to his office and we discussed the project. Obviously, he was doing it with a low budget.

I remember Stan Lee and I were working on a superhero called Congressman. This was after *Sgt. Kabukiman N.Y.P.D.* It might have been around 1989 or 1990.

Do you remember anything else about the conversations that you had with him?
He was in a rush. He wanted to do something quickly.
Do you recall if he told you much of the movie he had to make or get finished?
I don't recall that. No.

We had done *The Toxic Avenger*, *Class of Nuke 'Em High*, *The Toxic Avenger Part II*, *Kabukiman*, so Troma in those days was the east coast Roger Corman. Not as successful, obviously. Not nearly as successful.

Why do you think he came to you before Roger Corman?

I don't know that he did. Who said he came to me before Corman?

Well, that seems to be the prevailing assumption and it fits the timeline. Since Corman made the film, Bernd would have come to you before him.

I can't imagine he would go to me before Corman. Maybe Roger wanted more money and he went to me because he thought I'd be cheaper. I don't know. I can't say that he called me up before Corman.

It's possible that although Bernd ended up making a deal with Roger, he may not have had an uninterrupted series of conversations with him. He could have been talking with you — or others — in between there. So maybe he could have gone to Roger or even some other studio first. Now, I can see that possibility. I was assuming monogamy during negotiations. So much for assumptions.

In the documentary you mentioned your relationship with Stan Lee and suggest that one of the reasons you didn't go forward with the project was concern about alienating him. Can you tell me more about that?

It's not just Stan Lee; it's our fans. For me to make a low-budget movie of Stan Lee's property would do a disservice to Stan Lee. I've known Stan Lee for fifty years. I started a friendship and we wrote more than one script together among other things. Part of it was I didn't want to do something that was going to be cheap and that might hurt his franchise. He wasn't the Stan Lee then that he is now. I don't think he had as much money and I don't think he had as much fame. He was a friend, so I didn't want to do something that would be low-budget that might hurt his mainstream standing.

And he's very into mainstream. Stan was always telling me that my projects were too underground, too controversial, and that I should try to do something more mainstream. His favorite Troma movie is almost a mainstream movie: *Sgt. Kabukiman N.Y.P.D.*

So I certainly didn't want to do something that might hurt his valuable creation, and, also by that, time Troma had fans. I didn't want to do a shitty movie that would piss off our fans. I didn't want our fans to think I was selling out.

As I remember the fee was not very good. I don't remember being offered a very decent fee. I don't even recall what it was. If I remember correctly...Honestly, I don't want to say a number because it wasn't enough, obviously. If he talked about a decent fee, maybe I would have gone to Stan and said, "Hey, I've got an opportunity to make some money here. Would you mind if I went ahead with this?" I don't think Stan and I ever discussed it. If we did, I don't remember it. So I didn't want to piss our fans off, right?

Yes. That makes sense.

We already had an experience along those lines with a movie that I directed call *Troma's War*, which is a Troma masterpiece but the MPAA, the Motion Picture Association of America, which is the name for scum, for scumbags. They use the rating system not to protect the public but to protect the Rupert Murdochs of the world against competition. They took out all the good stuff in *Troma's War*. They removed punches. They removed funny things. Our movies are cartoons, basically. They're not scary and the violence is cartoon-violence. They totally disemboweled *Troma's War* unfairly because *Die Hard* had just come out before that and was full of serious violence. When *Troma's War* finally made it into the movie theaters around 1987, it looked like a G rated movie.

Our fans were pissed off. They thought we were selling out. Then there's the small number of old men who went to see *Troma's War* thinking it was going to be a hard-hitting action film and instead it was this crazy, lacking in action movie. To get the R rating the MPAA totally destroyed the movie. Richard Hefner, the guy who was president of the MPAA, told my partner Michael Herz that our movie was NFG — No Fucking Good. The MPAA is not supposed to give you any opinions about your movie. They're just supposed to give you an idea of where the movie needs to be disemboweled so that you can get the R rating and get into theaters. In those days you couldn't get into theaters of any note without the R rating.

So I didn't want to piss our fans by doing *The Fantastic Four* and doing something that was selling out and not get a lot of money for it, and I didn't want to upset Stan Lee.

You said in the documentary that there didn't seem to be very much in it for Troma to make the movie, that it wasn't

exciting or interesting enough. What would it have taken for you to have done *The Fantastic Four***?**

A huge fee and Stan Lee's okay. Stan's a good guy. He probably would have let me do it.

In those days the movie industry was different. You didn't have to be part of a giant international media conglomerate or one of the vassals of a giant devil-worshipping international media conglomerate in order to make any revenue. Today, if you are truly an independent film studio, you can't make any money. Do you know of any other independent film studios that are doing what Troma does? There are none left. Tell me I'm wrong. We are the last one. We are the last independent studio. We're forty-four years old. It is impossible now, but in 1989 we were successful because we had good commercial movies and because the rules to prevent monopoly were still in force. We could *compete*.

Now, the rules that used to prevent monopoly have all been done away with. That's why you have a small number of these giant conglomerates and Netflix and Amazon that control all the sources of revenue. No independent movie studio is able to survive and prosper except for Troma unless they are tied in with a vassal of one of the conglomerates like Fox Searchlight or Sony Classics or the Independent Film Channel or the Sundance Film Festival.

Also, in those days we were building Troma and I didn't want to make a movie that somebody else would own. I wanted to own all our movies. Troma owns all these movies we've made and produced. We own all the negatives. We have hundreds of movies, maybe a thousand different properties in our library. At least half of them we own entirely. The other half we distribute and some of them go on forever, eternity. We wanted to own whatever we made. I didn't want to do a work for hire unless there was a huge fee. Apparently, there wasn't. Do you know what the fee was for directing?

There have been different numbers discussed and speculated about. My understanding is Roger had a million dollars to make the film with and he got a payoff of half a million when it didn't get released. All of the figures I have come across are pretty close to those. I've heard $750,000 to $2 million for the budget and $500,000 to $1 million for the buyout.

I don't think we got that far in our conversation about Troma making *The Fantastic Four*. I may have wanted Troma to distribute it. I have some vague recollection of talking about that with Bernd because Troma had always distributed its own movies. My recollection was the fee he offered was *much* less than that.

You said in the documentary that the profit wasn't there and have talked about that with me. I was going to ask how you saw the numbers and the money (e.g., costs versus profits) working out, but, if I'm understanding you correctly, you're telling me that the conversation may not have gotten that far.

No, we never got that far. No. I think that I was probably at that time angling for distribution or something and he had something to do with Fox. I think I may have pushed a little bit on trying to get Troma involved in the distribution.

What would a version of *The Fantastic Four* made by Troma be like? Had you given any thought to what you would do with the movie if you had accepted it for production?

No, I didn't give any thought to it. I like comedy, so probably I would have tried to go in that direction. I haven't seen the film. I've only heard that it's very good. I'm sure I would have made it funny. Or funnier. Maybe it is funny. Most of those kinds of movies are kind of cartoony, and that's what I do. Our movies tend to be very controversial, cartoony type movies with lots of sex and violence, but nobody gets scared when they see *The Toxic Avenger* and our special effects are extremely low-budget. Now, they're making R rated superhero movies. But the original *Toxic Avenger* superhero movie is still much more violent than any of the mainstream superhero movies. Akiva Goldsman, this bigtime producer in Los Angeles, and others have been trying to make a mainstream version of *Toxic Avenger*. I was a superhero creator. Superhuman beings like The Toxic Avenger, Dolphin Man, Master-Bater, Sgt. Kabukiman, The Vibrator, and others all reside in Tromaville. Maybe that's why Bernd called me.

I'm just speculating here based on what you've said. If you had done *The Fantastic Four*, it would maybe have had more comedy in it and you talked about how sex and violence are keystones of many Troma releases. Do you think

that you could have gotten those elements into the movie or would Troma have had to make a different and unfamiliar movie lacking humor, sex, and violence?

There was no way I could have done *The Fantastic Four* because the fans would be pissed off. There's no way I would have been permitted to make it as intense as our movies. Now with *Deadpool* they talk about Troma. James Gunn, the director for *Guardians of the Galaxy*, worked for us. He wrote *Tromeo and Juliet* for Troma and worked for us for a couple of years. Twenty-five years later they're making movies that have a lot of Troma's graphic and controversial elements. In those days, I don't think I would have wanted to make a *Fantastic Four*, which would have had to have been, I guess, a PG kind of a movie. It would have really looked bad to our fans.

On the other hand, if Bernd would have said to me, "You can take $500,000 as a fee," I would have had to think about that very very carefully, especially at that time when $500,000 was probably the equivalent of over a million today. We never got that far. I know that Michael Herz would have wanted me to do it. I know I never heard any number like $500,000. I have some recollection that it was $50,000. I could be wrong because I had a few other offers along the way for shitty horror movies and stuff.

I respect Bernd. His body of work is excellent. He made very good movies. I did not think that he was a schlock producer. That was not...

...part of your reasoning behind not making it.
Exactly.

Did you make the right decision passing on it?
I'm not sure I was in a position to pass on it. Bernd may have been talking to both of us as the same time. I'm glad I didn't spend...Probably it would not have ended up right because I would have wanted to make it more in the Troma style and probably the producers would have wanted to make it more mainstream. It would probably would have resulted in fights.

In fact, when we made *Sgt. Kabukiman N.Y.P.D.*, which was 1989, our partners were a company called Namco, the company that created Pac-Man. The man who owned the company was a billionaire. He wanted to create a superhero for his small theme parks in Japan. Stupid me, I didn't hear him, so we did a co-production where I was pushing to have Troma-style things like people eating worms and babies being killed with a samurai sword. Namco wanted to do something mainstream. They put in half the money, and we put in half the money. The movie was about a million dollars. Stupid me, we ended up with something that wasn't what Namco wanted, and it also wasn't what I wanted. It was a middle of the road kind of things. It's a good movie, an excellent movie. In fact, they just ran it again in New York last night. It was a full house. The theater was packed. They had standing room only. It's a very entertaining movie.

The Namco people were wonderful. They were great. We never had any fights. They just didn't quite understand why I had to have the protagonist eat a handful of live earthworms. Why did I have to have other elements like that? They were very nice, and we did compromise. I regret that I didn't do 100% what they wanted or 100% what I wanted. Back then, I was more of a — how shall we say it? — fighter. I wanted my way. It's art. It's an art form. I've never made a movie for anybody else, except the *Kabukiman* experience. We own the movie, but we had partners, so I've never made a movie on assignment. That's mainly because I've only been offered shit scripts and shitty fees. There's not enough in it for us, and we want to own all our negatives.

Charlie Chaplin died a rich guy, right? Charlie Chaplin was blackmailed, blacklisted, accused of pedophilia, kicked out of the United States — you name it. But he died a very rich man because he owned his negatives. Buster Keaton was a genius and as brilliant as Chaplin but died penniless. He was ruined by this because he was a studio contract director. In fact, all his negatives were almost lost. So when I was coming along at Yale, I read a lot of film history, and that was a big deal for me. I want to own my negatives — that's our model for Troma — so it would have taken a lot for me to do another movie in a situation like *Kabukiman*.

Let me clarify a little bit. I'm getting the impression that when you talked with Bernd, he never exactly laid everything out and made you an offer. It sounds more like both parties were talking about *The Fantastic Four* and didn't get

too far into the conversation before you realized it wasn't going to be right for Troma. Is that correct?

I think we had two meetings, but we definitely never got to any kind of proposal. Probably, he was reading me and probably knew or got the sense that I'm a bit crazy — that would be my guess. Also, I think if I made it pretty clear or I may have come out and said that I wanted to talk to Stan about it. Did anybody talk to Stan about it when it was made? Was he involved?

Stan knew about it, but I don't think he was involved in the actual making of the movie.

Stan and I have been friends since 1969. We wrote a script together after I got out of Yale called *Night of the Witch*, which actually got optioned by Cannon, among others. He's a very good buddy. I assume he would have wanted *The Fantastic Four* to be done in a mainstream, big-budget way. My impression was that Bernd wanted to do this thing on a Troma budget. Since I never did the project, I don't know that I ever talked to Stan about it, but I think I did tell Bernd at some point that I'm buddies with Stan and I should talk to him about it.

Stan showed up to the set for some of the filming. People remember him there. He was supportive, but after the movie was made he seemed to distance himself and Marvel from it.

It just didn't seem like it would do anything for Troma or me at the time other than piss people off and disappoint the fans of the Fantastic Four, Troma fans, and Stan Lee — all in one fell swoop *(laughs)*.

Did you ever talk with Stan or Roger about the movie after it was made? Did it ever come up as a topic of conversation?

Not that I recall.

You never saw the finished version, correct?

I have not seen it.

Have you see any of the big-budget versions?

No, I'm sorry to say. But I've heard very good things — like really good things — about the bootleg version of Roger's movie. By the way, I'm a good buddy of Roger Corman. I discovered his movies when I was at Yale. I'm a huge admirer of his films, and, in fact, movies like *X: The Man with X-Ray Eyes* and *Attack of the Crab Monsters* and the Poe movies were shown at the Yale Film Society and they were a major motivation, major proof for me when I was deciding to become a moviemaker, that one could indeed make very low-budget movies with good scripts and good acting and provocative themes. That was a big deal for me and informed my decision *not* to move to Hollywood but to stay in New York and make low-budget movies as an "auteur."

Corman's a big influence on me, and the movies he directed are wonderful. Every one of them. I remember revisiting *The Trip* when I was in London. They showed a brand new 35 mm print of *The Trip*, which was written by Jack Nicholson. They showed it in a festival or something with a Troma movie. I had seen it a long time ago, but this new print was a masterpiece. The same with the Poe things. They're beautiful. They look like Claude Chabrol. Corman was a big influence on motivating me to start Troma with Michael Herz. He's a good guy. I know him, his family, and his kids pretty well. One of his kids had a sleepover over in New York with our kids a long time ago. We're pretty friendly. He's the best, absolutely the best. So I'm not surprised that he did a good job with *The Fantastic Four* under whatever the difficult circumstances were. From what I'm hearing it's a very good movie.

It is. If you ever get curious, you can find it on YouTube. You can get a DVD off of eBay for about ten bucks. It's around. It's not straight from the negative, but that's what there is. I don't know where *Doomed* got its footage, but what is in the documentary looks a lot better and gives you a more accurate idea of what the film actually looks like.

Oh, so it's easy to find. I should look at it. It's on YouTube, really?

Yes. If you watch it there, it's sort of low-quality because it's dubbed off something else, probably VHS, but if you look at the trailer, the trailer was finished and it gives you a sense of what the rest of the film looks like in its best form.

What happened to it?

The story is it didn't come out and Marvel made a deal with Bernd so that the 2005 big-budget version could come out.

Right, that's what I heard.

Roger gets paid for it. The movie just never gets released. Oley Sassone, the director, tries to finish it up as best he can. The negative disappears. Presumably, Marvel confiscates it.

So Roger didn't direct it?

No. He was an executive producer along with Bernd. They used his studio, his equipment, and all of that in California. This is post-New World Pictures. This is the Concorde-New Horizons era.

Well, that probably is the other reason I passed on doing it because I'm sure that I would have insisted on making the movie in New York. I would have insisted on shooting on location. I am heavy on location filming. My guess is that I would not have wanted to film in a studio.

Some of the shooting was on location — although nowhere near New York — but most of it was in a studio.

Some people have speculated that the movie was never going to be released. It was just a way for Bernd to hold onto the rights because those right were due to expire. Did Bernd ever give you an indication that this was not going to be a real film or that it wasn't going to be a film that would be released?

No. Not that I recall. (*laughs*) Then I definitely would have turned it down. I'm pretty sure that I let him know that we had to be involved in distributing it. By the time we got through, I think he knew what Troma's business model was. I would have had to direct it, for sure. I would have had to have some kind of control over it. I think he probably knew that might not be the best relationship. Again, I have total respect for him and his body of work. I regret...Especially if half a million bucks was involved. That's a lot of dough.

Did you just finally tell him Troma wasn't going to do the film or how...

No. I just never heard from him again.

So you had your first and maybe second conversation and he just never...

I think he realized...I can't say I turned it down. But when he first approached me, he sounded like he wanted me to do it. Then, I think my frame of mind and Troma's business model, shooting in the East, and shooting on location, and Troma having to be involved in distribution, were all factors. If we couldn't get what we wanted on that level, I certainly wasn't going to do it, and in my head it sounded like it was going to be a shitty fee, a bad experience, I would piss off Stan Lee, and I would piss off the Troma fans.

Let me see if I've got this right. What it sounds like is that you never told him no and he never told you no. After the first or second conversation he just never called you back or followed up, but, if he had, it's very likely you would have pulled out anyway because it didn't seem like...

Well, I did think he asked me if I was interested in doing it. I mean he called me in because I think he thought he wanted me to do it. I don't recall him ever offering me the job, but he made it sound like he was an admirer and that he wanted me. I don't know if that's before he talked to Roger Corman or after he talked to Roger Corman. He was probably shopping like everybody does. He's a businessman.

I see what's you're saying. He might have had a conversation or two with you, and then he talks to Roger Corman, works out a deal with him, and that's why he never gets back in touch with you.

That's probably it. And I probably really didn't get very interested. I really wasn't interested for the reasons I've told you. It wasn't that I called him; I don't believe I ever called him back. In fact, I'm certain I never called him back. We had a couple of meetings. We had a couple of discussions. If he wanted me, he could have called me back. I think it was pretty clear that I would be a little bit difficult and that I wouldn't fit. It wasn't a good fit.

So Bernd didn't pursue the conversation but neither did Troma.

Exactly.

Those are pretty much all my questions, but if you have anything else that you want to add or expand on, let me know.

It sounds like a fascinating book. It's really original. I think film students, film fans, and the general public will be interested in it. It's important for film history because Roger Corman is one of the giants, and it's an important part of his career. And it's an important property. The Fantastic Four is huge.

What do you feel the theme of the book will be? What's the narrative arc? I've written seven books, so I'm always interested in this stuff.

Well, the way I'm going to structure it is not by putting the interviews in the book in the order in which I've conducted them. I'm starting with the crew and some of the people like you who were involved in the pre-history, pre-production, and early phases of the movie. Then, I'm moving to the actors and actresses. After that, there will be interviews with some of the producers like Roger Corman and people like Mark Sikes who did the documentary on the film and has a long view of the movie and has investigated what happened after the movie was made and ditched.

I'm trying to structure it so that it reads as a narrative and progresses and builds up. Instead of the interviews being like cards in a deck, they will be more like strands in a web or links in a chain.

Roger's interview will be next to last. There's a young director, Ivan Kander, who does some independent work and has put out a couple of interesting short films using Marvel characters including one that focuses on Doctor Doom, so I'm ending with him.

Why do you end it with him if nobody's ever heard of him?

I thought it would a different way to end because he is relatively unknown and has a perspective completely outside of the film. He might have the most objective viewpoint of all of us — maybe even including me since I will have talked to a lot of people by the time I am through — but he also knows a lot about film and comic book characters, so it's an informed viewpoint. I thought, too, it would be a way to kind of move to the next generation of filmmakers.

Yeah, that makes sense.

Also, quite frankly, some of the people connected with the movie are upset with Roger over it not coming out and hold him responsible to some degree. I thought it might sit better not to let him have the last word by having his interview as the final one. Instead, the book will end by focusing on the future with Ivan's interview.

I didn't know about all of that history. I get it now. Yeah.

How did the guy who made the documentary know that I was approached by Bernd?

Mark Sikes and Marty Langford did the documentary. Mark was assistant casting director for the movie, receptionist — he did like eight jobs for Corman. He was very involved and on the scene for the making of the film. He's actually in the movie doing some late shots because Carl Ciarfalio who is in the Thing suit had moved on to his next project, so they needed somebody to fill in.

He knew that I had spoken to Bernd?

He knew you were connected somehow because, of course, you're in the documentary.

Somebody must have been with Bernd in his office. That's interesting. (*laughs*) That's fascinating. It's a good documentary. I saw it at Comic Con. It was very well done. The movie looked good, too. The clips they showed look like a lot of fun.

I'll tell you something else. I think Roger Corman certainly would have been a better director for this particular project than Lloyd Kaufman without a doubt. He's much more mainstream than I. He's well-educated and funny. He's a very, very good director. I always thought he directed it. For what the needs were, he would have been a better director. I think the film would have been a bigger hit with him directing it than with me.

Let's hope it comes out.

Craig J. Nevius
Screenplay
Part I

How were you chosen to write the screenplay?
I had done a couple projects for Corman. Steve Rabiner started off in casting, which is where I got to know him. He was a casting director and also one of Roger's attorneys. Eventually, he became a producer. One of these first things, one of the bigger ones was going to be *The Fantastic Four*.

The movie I had done right before or maybe once removed from *The Fantastic Four* was *Stepmonster*, which is the one that I think qualified me in Roger's mind to do *The Fantastic Four*.

How so?
It was a horror family comedy about a boy whose dad was going to take a new wife who would be the boy's stepmother and he wasn't over the perceived death of his real mother. There's a comic book thread throughout the movie. Comic books are blamed for a twelve-year-old boy's overactive imagination. Ultimately the secret to the stepmother's vulnerability and how to kill the monster is within a comic book. There are lots of comic book references. I don't really know that qualified me to write *The Fantastic Four*, but it certainly demonstrated an awareness of comic books. The comic book theme gave the movie a nice tone and through-line that stuck in both Steve Rabiner's mind and Roger Corman's mind. I was endorsed by them. Bernd Eichinger would still have to approve me, which in hindsight is kind of funny because there's the guy with the preconceived plan.

What do you mean?
He was never going to release this. This was being made to keep the rights. So it's kind of funny that there was this song and dance, this kind of jumping through hoops that I would

have to do get his approval since it didn't matter who was going to write it.

But that's my other theory, too. This is pure speculation on my part. I think that in order not to be sued for breach of contract or for bad faith by Marvel who I think wanted the rights back, it had to look legitimate. Marvel had just made their X-Men deal with 20th Century Fox and had a whole vision that we've all seen come to fruition since. They had a plan. Maybe it was Avi Arad. I think Marvel wanted the rights back. They'd be idiots not to want the rights back. They were hoping the contract with Constantin would lapse. I think they would have taken any opportunity had there been a realistic one to take the rights back, but Bernd was smart enough to know he had to go to somebody who was legitimate, who was known.

Is that why he went to Troma Entertainment first?

I don't think that's Troma. That whole thing was news to me. I don't know Lloyd's recollection is entirely accurate. Think about it. You go to Troma before you go to Roger Corman? Don't forget that Eichinger already had a relationship with Corman. Ehhhh...I question it.

I question Lloyd's involvement or point of view. Perhaps he knew about it as it was going on. I don't buy that he turned it down. I don't. I could be absolutely wrong. I'm not trying to defame him. I'm not trying to say he's a liar. Maybe he's not remembering correctly. I just have a hard time buying that. His explanation in the documentary is "We had our own characters. Why would we want somebody else's?" Really? Toxic Nuclear Guy, Toxic Mess Man, or whatever his name is?

The Toxic Avenger.

You're going to turn down *The Fantastic Four* because of the Toxic Nuclear Avenger? Because you already had a character or a couple of characters? Karaoke Cop or Sambooki Samurai Cop or whatever the name is?

Kabukiman from *Sgt. Kabukiman N.Y.P.D.*

It didn't ring accurate to me. I think Eichinger was smart enough to know that Marvel was certainly not as powerful as they became but was big enough, established enough, and probably had the resources to take him to court if they had to for fraud, for breach of contract, for bad faith. Otherwise they might claim that you're not really making this movie. You're not really doing this. You're paying this lip service in order to retain the rights, which would allow you remake rights and sequel rights in perpetuity.

As a parallel, the James Bond movie *Thunderball* was in the courts for years. There was an additional writer or producer besides Albert R. Broccoli and Harry Saltzman, the other guy who produced half of them and left.

Fleming came to Kevin McClory who was an aspiring screenwriter and/or producer about producing the first Bond film. He and some other people started writing about a different version of Bond. Later, Fleming tried to get him out of the film, but he used the draft of a screenplay McClory had written for his *Thunderball* novel. McClory got attached to the whole thing. Kevin McClory and his attorney said, "Well, that gives me certain rights and options. I can remake this if I want to even though I'm not with Broccoli, Saltzman, and Eon Productions." So Kevin McClory for years said, "I can do a sequel to *Thunderball* if I want to." I'm not sure that was granted but they were in a court battle that must have lasted a decade or more with several reversals and this, that, and the other.

I'm looking this up and what I see says that legal disputes began in 1961 and went on until 2006 in some form or another.

Eventually he got a ruling that said that he could remake a movie that he was one of the creators of. The rights would be limited. He couldn't, for example, bring in other characters from other Bond novels, but he could remake what was in *Thunderball*. Hence it became *Never Say Never Again* and it was Sean Connery's return to the role after he had left some years ago. It was around the time Roger Moore did *Octopussy*, so that summer you had two competing bonds for the first and only time. Moore was in the official line of 007 movies and Connery came back and did *Never Say Never Again*, which was a remake of *Thunderball*.

The situation with *The Fantastic Four* is similar. Not the same. With the McClory situation the argument was put together after the fact when McCrory wanted to get his hands back on the 007 franchise in some way. The point is that Eichinger as per the Marvel contract could, I believe, remake the movie and do sequels. He would be attached in perpetuity to the Fantastic Four if they went into production on a movie. If he had gone to Troma and spent $250,000, Ehhhh…I think Marvel may have called bad faith. Roger Corman is a different story.

There is a brand difference between Troma and Corman. Using Roger Corman legitimizes it more.

That's exactly right. Spending a million dollars or maybe slightly more is not an insignificant amount of money for a theatrical release. By today's standards it's a joke. Back then it was still a low number but not one that a judge or jury would say, "This is fake." They say it was more than a million. Constantin was putting up a million. This is the usual practice especially in television movies; the actual physical producer would match it. That money might be in services. It's a little bit of an accepted con, but it goes on all the time and everybody knows it. If it went to court, I'm sure the argument would have been it was $1.5 or $1.7 million from Constantin and $750,000 from Roger or whatever the number would be.

The argument is that it wasn't hard cash that Roger was putting up. He was putting up his team, his people, me, casting, his facilities. Roger's money was his name, his team, his equipment, his ability to do this quickly and legitimately — even if not by mainstream standards. This is the man who gave Ron Howard his directing start, who gave Jonathan Demme his directing start, who gave De Niro one of his first roles, who gave Stallone one of his first roles. The list goes on and on and on. Coppola is in there somewhere.

James Cameron.

There are so many. Corman is legitimate. He was given an honorary Oscar a few years ago. He's a maverick. He's outside the system, absolutely, but he's legitimate. You know his name. A million dollars plus the Corman investment of name, reputation, team, talent, facilities.

The credentials, and that means something.

That's enough. Could a judge or jury say this is a fake? No. Maybe Eichinger considered making the movie with Troma.

But didn't pursue it.

Kaufman knew Roger. Kaufman knew Eichinger. Maybe Kaufman was present for a conversation over lunch or something. I think that was enough to get his face in the documentary. Lloyd jumped on this. I'm not saying it's bad. I'm not sure his memory is exactly accurate, though.

So to clarify: Bernd always presented this as "We're going to make this movie and it's going to be released?"

Yep. And Roger did, too. He acted as if it was going to be released. I don't think that was an accident on Roger's part.

Eichinger was brilliant. I say that as a reluctant compliment, but he was. If he told Roger, "Look, buddy, this is the plan" there's a good chance that Roger would have told Steve Rabiner who was his attorney and his trusted creative producer at the time. Or maybe he would have told somebody else. That kind of information would get passed around and would echo back at some point. And that would be a problem for Eichinger if Marvel said, "Is this a sham?" But again you got a legitimate name in Roger Corman. You got the million dollars. You got the title. You've got the facilities, the studio. I was an established writer. Jay Underwood had a career. Rebecca Staab was working. Joseph Culp was the son of a terrific actor, Robert Culp — they all had careers. There's enough there to say, "Gosh, if we sue for breach of contract, it would be he said versus he said. There's enough here that it seems legitimate." The best way to guarantee that is not to tell anybody.

Craig J. Nevius with *The Fantastic Four* backdrop. PHOTO COURTESY OF CRAIG J. NEVIUS

Let me jump back to one thing I didn't quite finish in terms of how I got the job. I'm a big believer in visual presentation when it comes to pitching. In the past I've used drawings of things. I sold a wonderful project to ABC that did not get made called *Action Heroes Inc.* about three aging television heroes who are so typecast by the roles they once played that they can't get other work so they end up being spokesheroes for a commercial endorsement of a struggling detective agency run by a girl who may or may not be one of their daughters. The crazy night owls who watch late night shows and see their infomercials come to the detective agency wanting Captain Kirk, the Six Million Dollar Man, and Jonathan Hart — not those literal names — to take their cases. My agent set up the meeting at ABC who initially didn't want to hear it. They said, "It's a clever cute idea, but you're never going to get William Shatner, Lee Majors, and Robert Wagner to do that." My agent says, "We've already got them. They're coming to the meeting." I walked in with those three guys and sold it in the room. That was the easiest easy pitch I ever made, but it was also a reflection of my earlier pitch of *The Fantastic Four*.

Roger and Steve were behind me. Roger and I had lunch with Bernd Eichinger at the restaurant directly downstairs from Roger's office. I had to talk about my take on *The Fantastic Four*. When I did the *Action Heroes Inc.*, pitch I used Shatner, Majors, and Wager as my living action figures. What I brought to the meeting with Roger and Bernd were my action figures, the Mego dolls of the 1970s.

I remember those. I think I had Spider-Man and Batman.

I had every single one of them: the Fantastic Four, Batman, Superman, Batgirl, Supergirl. I've still got them. They're sitting in my closet in plastic. They're pretty beaten up, but they're worth about 300 bucks a piece now. I love them. I brought them to the meeting in my briefcase and I took out the four Fantastic Four dolls, set them up on the table in front of Eichinger, and said, "This is why I'm the guy to write the Fantastic Four." I explained that I did not go out and buy these. These are not new. They were mine as a kid. This is why I'm your guy. I saw in his eyes that it was a done deal as soon as I set up those dolls. Roger just sat there grinning. This is why I was one of his go-to guys. Roger was confident I would sell Eichinger. He didn't give much thought to how and didn't know I was going to do that.

Thank you for backtracking and telling that story because it's really, really good.

I've done a couple of interviews and I've never told that story.

Did you have source material that you referred to or kept in mind while writing the screenplay?

The *Batman* series wasn't an influence on *The Fantastic Four*, but it certainly was an influence in that it's what got me into superheroes and comic books. I did like comic books, bu I was less into the actual comic books then I was the film depictions of them. Adam West's series was my first love. Both it and *Star Trek* premiered the year I was born. They were two of the first series to utilize color the way they utilized it. By today's standards *Batman* is corny and silly, but it was brilliant and innovative even ten years later when I started watching it. The tilted angles of the villains, the bam and zap. It was a comic book come to life. Certainly any filmmaker, whether TV or movie, would rather die than to have a comic book come to life. It has to be dark and gritty. It was the first show

Craig J. Nevius' Fantastic Four Mego dolls. PHOTO COURTESY OF CRAIG J. NEVIUS

that was ever on two times in one week. It had a cliffhanger. When I watched it as a kid, I didn't get that it was funny, but I loved the good versus evil, the costumes, the Batmobile, and the villains.

Batman brought me into the world of comic books. However, there was not a direct tonal influence on *The Fantastic Four*. In terms of source material, my inspiration was action figures, which I set up on my desk as I wrote the screenplay, and the original issues of the *Fantastic Four*, which I had bought reproductions of.

Who wrote the treatment?

Stan Lee wrote the treatment for Constantin, which was the first issue but told in his voice with a few added details. I do vaguely recall an epilogue where a silver streak appears in the sky signaling that there is something yet to come (in a sequel). I think the treatment ended with the written question: "Could that be...the Silver Surfer?" I cut that for three obvious reasons: 1) Budget 2) Taking up screen time to explain or hint at a new character in the final sixty seconds of the movie that may confuse movie fans as opposed to hardcore Marvel fans and 3) A sequel was not guaranteed.

The treatment was written in Stan's voice just like the "Bullpen Bulletins" he wrote. So my inspiration was the comic, the dolls, and Stan's treatment, which was about two and a half pages.

Kevin Rock is also credited with writing the screenplay. What was his involvement?

I want to say it's a sore subject, but these things happen sometimes. Roger has key things he wants to see in his movies depending on which movie it is. If it's an action movie, he'll want a certain amount of explosions and fights. He also likes humor. This was the first time he had done this, at least with me. Even after scripts have been written for the *Black Scorpion* series, he sometimes would then put the scripts through what he would call a joke writer. I don't think it worked so well in *The Fantastic Four*. And to co-credit somebody for putting in some jokes? I don't know.

Do you have an example of one of those jokes?

A couple of those jokes I forgot about but I was reminded of them when I watched the movie a couple of months ago. When it comes to mind, I just shudder, and it's in my favorite scene about strengths and weaknesses. After Alex's dialogue comes the Kevin Rock line spoken by Jay, which is, "Holy Sigmund Freud, Batman." I want to vomit. I still want to vomit.

It undermines the scene and washes away that emotional layer.

It's not funny. For our *Fantastic Four* to reference the Adam West *Batman* series commits what is a mortal sin to many people. You have a Marvel movie referencing a DC character. Kevin Rock did a lot of stuff like that. He did some editing and streamlining and some of that was good.

There's another joke that I think made it in. "I don't think we're in Kansas anymore." Really? Has that never been said in 500 other movies? Is that funny or is that just saying we're going to rely on clichés that reference other movies? That's not as bad as the Sigmund Freud one, but it's certainly not funny and it's not original. There was a lot of stuff like that. There may have been some good jokes in there but I don't remember them. I had no power to excise the jokes because that came from Roger. He's the boss. I never met Kevin. Never spoke to him. I'll leave it at that.

At what point did he become a part of the process?

I did three drafts and a polish on it, basically four drafts. He may have come in after the third draft and done the jokes, but I think he must have come in after my polish. I don't know how they may have relabeled drafts. Sometimes they changed or removed title pages through the development process to help control what an outsider might know.

The one I have just has your name. It says, "1st draft October 9, 1992."

Were you involved in the writing process from start to finish, or did you enter and exit at a different time?

I was the first one hired other than Roger. Rabiner contacted me first and said Roger wants to talk to you about this project. I went in and talked to Roger. He said, "You have to sell Eichinger." I was involved from start to finish. I was on the set. I wasn't editing as much as I was on projects after. Once or twice I came into editing and I got a copy of it as soon as it was "done." I didn't work at Roger's office. I didn't work in the studio. I went to the head office for meetings with Roger to talk about scripts, notes, changes, and casting.

Did Stan Lee have any involvement in the drafting process?

If he did, it came through Eichinger. Not directly. Stan was on the set, holding court in a fun way, and was complimentary. Eichinger had very few notes as I recall.

What was Roger Corman's involvement in the drafting process?

He always had notes. His role was no different than what it always is. Some of his notes are very specific and some of his notes are broader. Sometimes it's a matter of a line. He didn't like that line or wondered whether a character should say something different. Are we getting this point across? Sometimes it's we need something bigger; we need more action. We need to blow something up. This isn't necessarily specific to *The Fantastic Four*. He's the father. He's the patriarch. He's the last word.

In the screenplay, but not the film, Reed and Sue get engaged in space during the pivotal flight that gives them their powers.

I remember the proposal in space. I really liked that scene but don't remember why. I think it may have been the dialogue. There were some turns of phrases that I thought were clever. It was not quite a romantic comedy but I thought it was romantic.

There's a tenderness about it.

And then suddenly they're married at the end of the version we did without really setting it up beyond what we already know, which is that they like each other. I liked the setup. I liked the proposal in space a lot just from a playwriting and acting standpoint. Whether it was Eichinger or Roger who wanted it cut I can't remember. Maybe it was Rabiner. Keep it moving. Keep it moving. Keep it moving.

Those are the things that immediately leap to mind. If you have anything else specific, you can ask me. I'm not sure if I'll remember.

I'm curious about a couple of other things. Comparing the October 9, 1992 version to the final film, I note that the overall shape of the story seems to be more or less the same, but there are a number of small to medium changes. What can you tell me about each of these?

In the screenplay Doom is a professor, but in the film he is a student.

I kind of liked Von Doom as the professor. It seemed like more of a betrayal, but the changes we made with them both being students and friends worked, too. I'd also like to point out that there was a bond between Alex and Joseph as performers and as people.

In the screenplay we see the Mole Man, but in the film he becomes the Jeweler. My understanding is that everyone found out that Eichinger's rights to the Fantastic Four had specific limitations and that they renamed the Mole Man because they did not have the rights to him. This draft would indicate that was a fairly late discovery.

The Mole Man was not in Stan's treatment. I wanted/thought we needed a secondary villain (since we had four heroes) and I saw a way of using an underground criminal/kingpin to not only steal the diamond needed for the rocket (and later the laser) but also be able to offer a haven to Ben/Thing as he was now an outcast as well. Both that conceit and the diamond as a refracting lens were both my creations. I never understood why we were not legally allowed to use the Mole Man since the Constantin contract with Marvel said that they (and therefore "we") could. If Marvel didn't want the movie to be made and was purposely trying not to be helpful and perhaps was throwing out roadblocks, this would explain why we suddenly couldn't use him.

It's strange, too. Did they think they were going to make a series of standalone films about him? "Sure you can use Doctor Doom, but we draw the line at the Mole Man." Of all the characters to restrict usage of why the Mole Man?

The screenplay includes the Lord of Latveria, but the film drops him.

I don't remember the Lord of Latveria.

He's Victor's father.

Yes, yes. I vaguely remember that, so I must not have missed it. I don't know why we excised it.

The movie eliminates this sequence: When Dr. Hauptman tells them about their powers, Ben confirms that Reed can indeed stretch any part of his body and jokes to Reed that he should "try this out on Susie in the sack."

That was a cheap joke *(laughs)*. At the time I probably thought it was funny. In hindsight maybe it's not so funny.

It's honest. It's probably something people have wondered. I had a student once speculate that Spider-Man's spider-sense made him a "minute man." I've always wondered if the Human Torch can shoot fire from his behind. These things are a little crude, but the mind does touch on them.

The movie cuts some screenplay material in which Doom reveals he been funding Reed's research and tells him that "scientists are always used as puppets of the government."

The scientists think they're doing research to help mankind but the government wants to use those things as weapons, or a professor using his students. With Reed and Doom we have a very similar situation here, don't we, if Doom is the money man? We have the financial interest of Constantin in using the creative people as puppets.

That's a really good parallel.

I wish it had ended up in the movie. Boy, that was the first thing I thought of when the news trickled in. I said, "What is going on?" Per the original draft, I thought we were the Fantastic Four. We were Reed. We were duped. We were being used by the government, the larger powers that be whose mechanisms we don't always see. We were working with our hearts toward one goal in order for those funding it to use our work for another goal that was contrary to what we thought we were doing. I loved that theme. I haven't seen it in any other Marvel movie, and I'm surprised I haven't.

Why was that cut from the final version?

It was too heavy, too talky. Eichinger or Roger, probably Roger, wanted it to be a little more big print than fine print. Broader strokes. Keep it moving, less talk. I think it was in my first draft. I was never a big *X-Men* comic book fan, although I became one with the movies. So I didn't know I was hitting on a theme that was so prevalent in the early *X-Men*, maybe all of them. The Fantastic Four were looked at as freaks in my first or second draft. They were ostracized. I think they made a monument or something to them when they were thought to be dead from a space accident. When they reemerged at a press conference, their powers came out. I think the monument was changed from the Fantastic Four to the Freaky Four. That's not why it was taken out though. Again, the big picture was Good versus Evil. This was too much fine print. This is action. This is sci-fi. Let's not go so dark. I was sad to see that go especially when I saw the first couple of *X-Men* movies which are about ostracizing those who are different. When I saw those, I knew I was on to something.

I'm flipping through the first draft and it's in there.

The movie cuts Alicia's art exhibition and her initial meeting with Ben Grimm while he is playing football.

What's the context? Is she kidnapped at the exhibit? Wait, Ben is her work of art, right?

He's either her work of art or people see him and start talking about him like he's a work of art even though he's not.

I barely remember the scene, but as we're talking about it, I'm liking it. I don't remember how it was executed or what the point was.

It reads as pretty funny.

I'm looking back at the script at the gallery scene. There's a part where the husband is looking at the Thing and says, "Well, I don't know about that but it is a brilliant thematic variation on man's frequent..."

...inhumanity toward man *(laughs)*. I remember it as you're saying it.

That sounds like one of those things that you said was maybe a little too heavy.

Exactly. A little too thoughtful.

In the screenplay Doom vaporizes himself activating a laser instead of falling from his fortress and disappearing as he does in the film.

The version of his death that we went with was easier to execute and less cliché. It had something to do with the idea that Colossus is in them all.

The screenplay says, "He presses the button. It channels his cosmic cells into the charging laser beam." This implies that his death is purposeful.

Oh yeah, so he uses himself because he can't use the Fantastic Four. He's so bent on revenge or seeing his plot through that decides to sacrifice himself, essentially.

The screenplay says, "He smiles twistedly and salutes Reed," which suggest that he knows that this process with the laser is going to kill him. Von Doom says, "Long Live

Latveria! The professor screams hellishly as his body goes through a series of mutations. He reverts back to his original self for a split second before vaporizing." So it implies that it's a self-sacrifice that he enters into aware and willingly in order to fulfill a larger plan.

Yes, that's exactly right. It was a more original way to go. It was an unusual way to go to show that he wasn't all bad but committed to country, his father, his legacy, his cause. Then you see a flash of his former self before he goes when he was perhaps not all bad or may have been redeemable. There was a definite budget, time, and effects issue. It was probably a little too poetic, too heavy. That ending probably would be very much embraced if that movie were made today. Villains were more black and white back then. I was trying to show that he was lost. There was too much theater, too many shades of grey.

I also thought that maybe it's easier to bring him back in a future movie if he falls into the mist than if he is vaporized, although I suppose he could just be transported to some other location or dimension.

What do you think of the final draft?

I was not the happiest I've ever been with a final draft, but I was happy with it.

Chris Gore
On-Set Journalist for *Film Threat*

You visited the set, put the cast members of the Fantastic Four on the cover of *Film Threat*, and made the film the center of the October 1993 issue. How significant did you think this movie was at the time?

At the time, I thought this *Fantastic Four* movie was very significant. The fact that it was even going to be attempted blew my mind. And there was a palpable enthusiasm among the cast and crew. Every person there was a Marvel Comics fan, a Fantastic Four fan, and we all loved and worshipped Stan Lee. Among the crew, hanging out we just told stories about our love of comics and how Stan Lee and the FF changed our lives. It wasn't my first time hanging out on a film set, but it was the first time I was on a set where I witnessed something I thought could be special. Now, of course, all of this was due to the fact that the *Fantastic Four* was my gateway comic book and I grew up reading it from the time I was a single-digit-aged nerd. I thought this could be really good, but there were little signs that stood out.

Roger Corman productions were always notoriously cheap. And I was recently on the same lot during the filming of a movie called *Carnosaur*. I had a bit part in the movie and we covered this film which was timed to the release of *Jurassic Park*. They had built a full-size T-Rex which was really cool and had this elaborate laboratory set. But I remember hearing a rumor from someone on the crew that the previous craft services person was fired for buying name brand soda. Corman sets always had the cheapest snacks and off brand sodas, so that was unusual. When I showed up to the *Fantastic Four* set, I noticed that they had redressed the laboratory from *Carnosaur* as Doctor Doom's lair. Those

Inside of Doom's castle. PHOTO COURTESY OF MICK STRAWN.

clues stood out that though this might be special, that other things were afoot.

How many days did you spend there and how many hours were you there each day?

I was there on and off during most of the shooting. I was at the *Film Threat* office during the day and then late afternoon would drive to the Westside to hang out. I was there often enough that the crew got used to me being around, which led to chatting with each department head. In particular, I was friends with the special effects team from Optic Nerve — John Vulich and Everett Burrell. As for actual number of days, I'm not quite sure, but I recall being disappointed that it was such a short shoot. It was over in just a few weeks.

Did you observe any tension on the set or behind the scenes?

There was no tension that seemed out of place or unusual. There was only the typical kind of tension one would observe on a film set where the budget is low and the time is tight.

You said that someone joked that the film should be renamed *The Average Four* because there wasn't enough money to make it fantastic. Can you tell us who that person was?

I cannot tell you exactly who that person was.

In the article there is a picture of Scott Billups' effects rig that wouldn't look out of place at NASA. The article mentions that his hardware was worth a million dollars. Was this an estimate or did he say this?

Scott Billups told me his equipment was worth $1 million. I had no reason to doubt him at all. Although the production looked cheap up close, it was Billups' confidence that gave me hope that the FF could turn out to be something really special.

While *The Fantastic Four* set looked cheap up close, there was no telling how it would look on film. I had set up a photo shoot for our cover with photographer Ilona Lieberman and we set it up after hours on Doom's laboratory set. With the lighting, this really was the best these costumes were going to look. Up close, the costumes looked so cheap. They even had frayed threads. I visited the set of *Evil Dead III: Army of Darkness*, and I recall that the tombstones and rocks were made of Styrofoam and you had to be careful not to damage the set, but on film it looked great. So my impression was that this could turn out the same.

Scott Billups has received a lot of criticism for the special effects. Is this criticism fair or unfair?

Although Scott Billups' effects were criticized, I think you have to look at where digital effects were at the time. I mean, this was the early days of inexpensive digital effects and it was all in Billups' hands. He is just one guy. So that criticism is unfair. There are not very many effects shots to begin with and what was completed looked fine considering the era and the fact that it was basically a one-man team.

The article from the October 1993 issue of *Film Threat* ends with the report that as the issue went to press, you learned that Steven Spielberg's Amblin Entertainment was interested in making a big-budget *Fantastic Four* with Chris Columbus and the film might be shelved, but the company backed out. When did you learn this information? Was this the first time that you had heard about something like this?

When the issue of the magazine first came out, through Corman's company, we set up a signing with all four cast members at the *Film Threat* booth at San Diego Comic-Con. We sold 2,000 copies that weekend, including to people who already had the issue, but they wanted a signed copy. We had a VHS tape with the trailer on a two hour loop that played all day, every day that year at SDCC. And to this day, I can quote that trailer from beginning to end: "The diamond is not for sale at any price!" says the Jeweler. In any case, the actors were so genuine. There was a giant line that clogged the aisles near our booth. The question that the people in line asked over and over was, "Is the film going to be any good?" There clearly was a lot of skepticism among fans at Comic-Con. Michael Bailey Smith who played Ben Grimm would look each fan in the eye and tell them, "It's going to be great." All of them were so enthusiastic and kind to each person who waited in line.

After Comic-Con, months later in fact, I recall speaking to the publicist at Corman's company and I just asked if this movie was ever going to come out. While the publicist was reassuring, I never really got a straight answer.

What did you think of *Doomed!: The Untold Story of Roger Corman's The Fantastic Four*?

I thought *Doomed* did a great job of telling the story of this "lost and unreleased" film. However, I don't feel we ever got a straight answer from the business people behind the scenes about why the film was shelved. I think it's easy to read between the lines and figure out that it was done to hold onto the rights and nothing more, but a straight answer would have been nice. But I guess it would only be a short film then.

Mark Sikes told me that was one of the pieces of feedback he had received about *Doomed*, and he advised me to put together some sort of a wrap up or conclusion that tries to put everything together. I think that one of the challenges is that it's tough to take multiple narratives and make a single, consistent narrative out of them. Complicating that, people have gaps in memory, different memories, and the people who do know for sure why the movie didn't come out either don't want to talk at all or may be holding back information. *Doomed* doesn't really gives us a final version — which may be impossible — of what happened, but it gives us a lot of objectivity, primary sources, and room to make our own interpretation of events instead of ultimate closure. I feel like it doesn't try to make my mind up for me. Another of the strengths of *Doomed* is it really lets the story be told by the people centrally involved, and they tell it in their own words. Contacting all of those people, getting them together, filming and editing all of that — I can't imagine the work that took and it's just Mark and Marty Langford doing it all. I think it's a great film.

What's your opinion of the 1994 movie?

The 1994 *Fantastic Four* film was cheap and low-budget and frustrating because it had so much potential. But the one thing they got right that no version of the FF has been able to do yet is be true to the original characters created by Jack Kirby and Stan Lee. The characters felt very genuine and true to those first 100 issues that Kirby and Lee did.

What's your opinion of the 2005 version?

I was not a fan of the 2005 version of the *Fantastic Four*. Including Victor Von Doom in the origin of the Fantastic Four was just lazy writing to me and an unnecessary change. So the story and tone just felt off. The only thing that seemed to work was the dynamic between Johnny Storm and Ben. And this film also seemed cheap, even though it had a much bigger budget. It was as if lawyers and countless producers got the bulk of the money and whatever was left over was onscreen and that wasn't much. I did not care for it. As for the 2015 version, it's even worse. I am not a fan of the so-called "Ultimates" incarnation of the Fantastic Four. It just doesn't resonate in a classic way that the 1961 comic does. That original run of Kirby and Lee is pure imagination and the birth of the Marvel Universe as we know it today. I am hoping that Phase Four of the Marvel Cinematic Universe (MCU) includes a version of the Fantastic Four that finally captures the adventures of this superpowered, scientific-exploring, lovable and dysfunctional family.

The *Fantastic Four* films have not been as successful as some of Marvel's other movies. What is the difficulty with successfully transferring *The Fantastic Four* from the page to the screen?

The chemistry of the actors is key and that was actually done best in the 1994 version, oddly. Even though the MCU films are big-budget productions, much of the approach is like that of an indie film — character over spectacle. But with the Marvel films produced under Kevin Feige at Disney, you get the best of both worlds, character-driven stories that include spectacle. The reason that did not work in the 2005 and 2015 versions is that mandate was not upheld. Instead we have lackluster characters that were not true to their comic book counterparts and unremarkable special effects that were distracting in their cheapness. But let's be honest, the Fantastic Four have some of the most challenging superpowers to bring from the comic book page into reality. With *Avengers: Infinity War*, Marvel has proven that innovative effects are possible, including rendering a giant purple titan that looks photorealistic. I believe that with today's digital effects, it may be possible to finally bring a faithful *Fantastic Four* to the silver screen — hopefully with the Silver Surfer at some point.

What are the unexplained mysteries surrounding this film?

I think the biggest mystery is who made the decision to shelve the film and what business dealings behind the scenes led to that choice. It would just be nice to finally put that question to rest. And it would also be nice to see this film in commercial release — at least for the historical value.

Mick Strawn
Production Design, Miniatures Creator, Director: Miniature Unit

Let me ask you a question. You've seen the film. What did you think of it?

I don't think it's a bad film, though it has some limitations. I think it's dated in some ways as a lot films are that came out during the early and middle of the 1990s. Everyone that I've talked to found out about the film quickly, got the job quickly, and worked on it quickly without much notice and without much of a budget. Especially given the fact that there was so very little time and money relative to that size of film available to make and work on it, I think it's good. The only movie based on Marvel characters with a smaller budget is the 1944 *Captain America* serial film. I don't know the budgets of some of those Incredible Hulk movies connected to *The Incredible Hulk* show and Bill Bixby, but those were made-for-television.

I definitely think it's the best of the pre-X-Men Marvel movies and it's my favorite film featuring the Fantastic Four. One of the things I really like is how faithful it is to the comic — unlike the ones that have come after, which have taken some liberties with the source material. Not all of those liberties have been well-received by the fans.

What do you think of the look of the film?

I feel that the look of it is unique and hasn't been done since. Most of the Marvel stuff that's being done right now doesn't look like the comic book or look like a comic book. We did try to make it look like a comic book. It's a very simple look.

What was working in the Corman studio like?

I was coming from much higher budgets down to a level of budget that I had never even done before. To work on a Corman film was bizarre. The guy had an old lumberyard

Doom's throne. Somebody probably paid with their life for taking this picture. PHOTO COURTESY OF MICK STRAWN.

that he had converted into a stage. The floors and everything in there were old plywood and they would put new plywood down over the old plywood. You could literally — this happened to me a couple of times — put your foot through the floor. The environment itself screamed below cheap. He had people that worked in this lumberyard that did things like tear old flats apart and then pull all the nails out.

Please talk about how you came to work on the film.

I came into the environment after working at New Line Cinema. I worked in fantasy and horror, and in Hollywood at that time if you worked in horror or fantasy you were just above working in porn and below lawyers. These are the people that were making this film. I get the call to come and work in this environment. It was a little odd to me. It was a really firm gig and it was between two other gigs. I was told from the get-go *exactly* what this project was, that we had to do 50% of this project before the end of the year. Whether it would actually ever be done was left open. The idea is that you needed half of it done before the end of the year to retain the rights for Constantin, which they wound up doing. Later on they went on to do other really bad versions of *The Fantastic Four*. It's not like we were the only one *(laughs)*.

I knew the challenges that are involved in this kind of a film. At the time you didn't have a film that had four stars in it. Stuff like that was reserved for thing like *Magnolia* or that kind of crap. Certainly, you didn't have four superheroes in one film in which you were trying to follow all of their stories at once. It just didn't happen. It was interesting that we could make an agreement to do that film at all in the first place. I get called in November, I think, and we had to have 50% of it done before the end of the year. This is all anybody ever told me.

And who told you that?

I don't know. I'm trying to remember who hired me. Who hired me? I haven't got the slightest idea *(laughs)*. It was a long time ago. It happened really fast. I don't remember knowing anybody on the film. I think my agent might have gotten it for me or heard about. I think somebody might have called and literally said, "Do you have anybody that's got experience with this sort of thing?" Obviously, I did. "And isn't working right now?" I think that my major qualification for the job may have been that I wasn't working anywhere else right that minute.

That may have been the major qualification.

It very well could have been the major qualification for everybody who was involved in it. I came in and I got used to this terrifying brave new world. I'm going to put this in context for you. If you would look at someone's resume and in a six month period they did twenty films, then you knew that they were from Corman. I think it was called New Horizons, right?

After New World Pictures, there were various companies that he created, merged, split off again, and renamed. If you play around with the words New, Concorde, Horizons, Pictures, Home, **and** Entertainment, **you can make them all. At the time of** The Fantastic Four, **I think it was Concorde-New Horizons.**

You knew that they came from that world. So then you had to give them credit for one film out of the twenty *(laughs)*.

Can you talk some about the budget, such as it was?

At the best of times it was the blind leading the hard of hearing around here. They didn't really give us a budget at all. That wasn't what they were used to. Their thinking was you do it for the cheapest possible amount that you could. We didn't go hugely over budget, but we did spend a little money. What they were used to was somebody coming in and painting a piece of plywood again. It was just barely a step above using toilet paper and trying to paint it. They said they were doing it with a million dollars, but Corman would have taken the million dollars and tried to do it for $75 because that's exactly what he did. I'm going to be completely candid; we just hacked their accounting system.

How did you do that?

It was super-easy because nobody worked there for more than two or three weeks anyway. We listened around for the names of some of the twenty films that were coming up in the future and started to apply all of those numbers to our accounting. For example, some plywood would come in and we would give them the number for *American Ninja VII* or something like that. We would give them their production number and we would liberally sprinkle that around and we got at least enough money to do as bad of a job as we actually did *(laughs)*. That gives you an idea of how low the budget was in this. Nobody's going to tell you about the actual production line end of this but me, I'm quite sure.

If you look at the film, you notice that it looks really dark. It's because we literally didn't have enough power to put up more than a couple of old-fashioned Mole lights at a time. You certainly didn't have a generator. You only had enough money to put up a couple of lights, so everything is very dimly lit.

How did you compensate for the lack of lighting?

We worked with that as best we could. We would light certain pools of things as the filming went on, which gave it its own look all by itself — a sort of poor man's filming at night. I directed the second model unit. An awful lot of what we had to do was reverse back. We shot in reverse, like the models of the antennas coming up through the ship that's in space. All that was shot in reverse and we just used a bunch of bottle jacks to release them and use the spring to give us that smooth look.

We're in the middle of a meeting and I say, "One of the things that we're going to have to do is the paper spinnets. We're going to do it in the old-fashioned style." We're going to use a reverse mag and start in the final position. Then we spin them. Then the reverse mag makes it so that it spins in to that last position. You can follow why you would do that, right? It's kind of natural. Otherwise, you're going to have to do it a thousand times to try and get it to land so that it's in the perfect final position.

You start off where you want it and then...

Exactly. I'm not that patient of a person, so I want it in the final position. And that will be a reverse mag. The cameraman who is doing camera work for the second unit said, "Well, we don't have a reverse mag. We're only allowed to use the equipment that's here in the building." I said, "That's not a problem. We'll just turn the camera upside down."

There seems to have been some tension between the camera department and the art department.

Well the camera department were always thinking they're better than the art department — although I had at least eight years in the business on these boys in the art department — they're like, "Here's the thing. That doesn't work. That's not a thing." I go, "Well, yeah it is totally a thing, and it totally makes sense." He says, "No, no, no, no. We'll just find another way to do it." I say, "We don't have time, and we're going to be shooting this tomorrow, so that's what we're going to do." After the meeting he's still arguing with me, and I went over to editing.

They were in the same horrible position that we were. Corman had built a little editing bay right there in one of the offices. I went in and said, "Hey, give me about thirty inches of exposed film, like a thrown away scene or something like that." The editor who handed it to me asked, "Well, what are you going to do with that?" I said, "I'm going to go out and not prove somebody wrong." He said, "What?" I said, "Don't worry about it." I went out and I held the film up. I went to the cameraman and got him to look at it. I held the film up in the air and then I waved it. I said, "See, this is normal, right? That's going forward. We are going to reverse it." I turned the film around. I said, "We're going to go like this. See? Then it looks right." Then, I handed him the film.

What I was pulling was the old the emperor's new clothes game because that doesn't work. There's no way that anybody has got the persistence of vision that is required to actually wave a piece of film in front of them and be able to see the action in it, right? But he didn't know that. He waves the film in front of himself and then turned around and he goes, "*Oh, I see exactly what you mean now.*" *(laughs).* Then I walked away.

The day went on and probably it was late afternoon. Our art director walks up to and me goes, "Let me ask you something. What is this stupid thing that people have been doing around here all day? I wanted to ask because it just kind of reeks of you. Did you tell somebody that they could hold a piece of film up in front of themselves and tell anything about it at all?" I said, "I mentioned something about that this morning." He says, "Everybody around here is taking this same three foot piece of film and waving it in front of their eyes and then nodding at each other and saying, 'Oh yeah. Yeah. I see it.'" I said, "That might have been me" *(laughs).*

Do you think that there might be people to this day who are still using that technique and passing it on to others?

People are incredibly gullible. Especially in Hollywood, you didn't want to admit that you didn't know what I was talking about. I have to say that I was complicit in leading them down the path to hang themselves. *Nobody* came up to me that day and said, "Hey, this doesn't work." In my defense, what I did convinced them to do what we needed to do. In the end, they would turn the cameras upside down and, of course, it worked exactly like it was supposed to because gravity is what it is. Right? Right! I kind of felt like a lot of times that at that time I was the senior in that situation because everybody was at the beginning of their career. There was a guy that was doing optical effects.

Scott Billups?

Oh, God. Scott. That's his name. What a fuckwad. I'm not an optical effects guy, but boy I gotta tell you. Look at my resume. I've done a lot of effects, and I've done a lot of preparatory effects for a lot of optical effects. From the very moment he came on set, the only thing I would ever say about him or to him is "Dude, you have *no idea* what you're talking about." He wouldn't set a shot up with any reactive lighting. Let's say Johnny Storm was going to have flames coming out of his hands. I just happened to be walking by and they were setting up for that shot. I asked, "So, where's your reactive light?" Oley and him turn to me and said, "What reactive light?" I said, "You're going to need reactive light for the flame. The flame is going to throw out an orange light." All of a sudden Scott goes, "Yeah, that would be a good idea." I was like, "A good idea? What the fuck are you talking about?" The guy was such an idiot.

I think it said on his resume that he worked on *Independence Day*, but I'm guaranteeing you he was craft service, if anything. There's the possibility that he was cutting fruit up, but that's the only thing. He wasn't cutting film; he was cutting fruit. And he was obnoxious. He was very arrogant about it. We had arguments, so towards the end of the film, I started to collect little pieces and stuff.

In my garage I had kind of a little shop, and I made all the miniatures. I made the top of the laboratory, and I made that little opening optics for the beam to come out. I made some of the pieces and even made the diopter for it. I built the rocket in space with the device that comes up and goes around. I built the ceiling with the lamp things that burned out on top of them. I did it in my spare time knowing that I was gonna get a call from them saying, "Oh, my God. Where are the models? This guy doesn't know what he's talking about." Sure enough that phone call came and I had all the miniatures that we needed. If I hadn't made all those miniatures, then the film would not have been completed. I made the miniatures that they were going to need because I knew Scott was lying.

I've tried to get in touch with Scott. I'm sure he's aware...

...That nobody likes him?

Basically. Nobody I've come across so far has anything good to say about him. It seems that any job you take on that film is going to be tough because of the lack of money and time. I just wanted to get his perspective on the film and let him make his case for himself if he has one and wanted to present it. I didn't hear from him.

(Laughs) I've never even looked him up. Did he go on to do anything?

He did go on to do some other projects. He has his own company, which I tried to contact him through. His listing on IMDb shows fifty-three credits for visual effects. I love this one from 1997: director of digital productions for *Pterodactyl Woman from Beverly Hills*. **I haven't seen it. Maybe it's great. But a lot of the credits are along those lines. He was visual effects supervisor for** *Mulholland Drive*.

You can never tell. Maybe he did go on to become a visual effects guy, but at that time he didn't know what he was doing and he was conning everybody. Either that or he just took a lot of stuff on and didn't know how to do it and crawled under a rock for a short period of time. I don't know what happened, but in this case he didn't know what he was doing. It was a simple as that. He didn't know what he could do. He didn't even have the required experience for us to give him what he could work with. You understand what I mean?

The basic story I have is that he came in and said he could do all this stuff, but he wasn't able to do it. I've done some other interviews besides *The Fantastic Four* **ones for a separate project with some friends about Roger Corman and**

New World Pictures. Those interviews and these indicate that there seems to be a place for someone who comes to Corman without maybe a lot of experience but has the energy, has the talent, and is willing to learn, so they're teachable and trainable. I've haven't heard from anyone so far who seems to think that Scott was that kind of person when he came to *The Fantastic Four.*

That's what I'm saying. I'm saying that right there. Maybe this was his big learning moment when he thought, "I better not fucking do that again," and maybe he went on and actually learned something. In *this* case, he was doing something he was not qualified to do. The only reason this film actually got done is because Oley did it. I can say that on my part at least I had all the miniature work done for him that he could never have afforded because I always used to do miniatures. That was one of my fallbacks from production design because you did production design six months out of the year and then the rest of it you find other stuff to do. That was the name of the game back then.

So the film was filled with trials and tribulation. Any good memories?

There was one fun experience that I did have. We determined that we were halfway though four days before the end of the year, which was a couple of days after Christmas. I'm closing up the building. I was the last one off of the stages. I was putting up the hot set signs and stuff. I was making sure everything was closed up, clean, and wasn't going to burn down while we were gone. I was over in the Mole Man's lair, which I was pretty proud of designing. The other miniature I made was the extension down to the Mole Man's lair. I was there because I knew there was this one sneaky door that always got open all the way back in the far corner that opened up to the alley. I went in, got back there, and made sure the chain was on that door.

I walking back through and I just see an older man who looked like he was in his late fifties or early sixties. He had pulled a chair up on the middle of the stage. He was sitting with a legal pad on his knee. I saw him, wondered what he was doing there, went back to the stage, and said, "Hey, look man, I'm closing up in here. Are you supposed to be here?" He goes, "Yeah. Yeah. I can be here." I said, "Do you know how to clean up?" He says, "Yeah. I think I can handle it. I can take care of the door down there. You got the one in back." I said, "Yeah. I'm good. Uh, who are you?" He introduced himself. He was Roger Corman. I started to leave and I asked, "Just out of curiosity, what are you doing just sitting here on this set?" He says, "Oh. I really like this set. I'm gonna write a movie around it." I went, "Okay."

I went out the door, went home, and we wound up staying off of the stage for six days. We came back down to finish the film and when we did everything had been completely moved around and was painted a different color *(laughs)*. It was the first time that I was incensed. I had this absurd thought that if you put a hot set sign up in an area in Los Angeles, nobody would cross that line. To me, that would be the way to stop the freeway. I was blown away. We had to go to work and put everything back together.

Given that it was six days, it's entirely possible that Corman shot an entire movie.

I absolutely know that he did. I'm pretty sure it wasn't just one.

Somewhere there's a whole series of something like *Attack of the Mole Men I-VII* including *The Mole Man's Lair*, *The Mole Man Returns*, *Revenge of the Mole Man*, *Bride of the Mole Man*, *Son of Mole Man*, and so on.

Let me tell you another story illustrating how little we had to work with. One day they were getting ready to go to a location. We were out there with them. The key grip and the gaffer are walking away from their truck laughing and holding something in their hands. I asked, "What's so funny?" They said, "We asked for a generator, and this is what they gave us." What they had was these two heavily insulated clips, and underneath it was an electrician's busbar connection to hit into the distribution system for their electric. Somebody had taken it and put a tie on the side of it that said, "generator." They were saying that they had gone into the office to get the generator and the secretary at the front desk reached underneath the desk and pulled this out and said, "There's the generator right there." So that gives you an idea of how low the expectations were.

That's a great story. It's good stuff, too, because the story of the movie in some ways is kind of sad, even tragic. It's a good balance to have some of these other tales to give some comic relief.

I gotta tell you something. It's not sad at all. For one thing, the whole story of the film is absolutely hilarious. It actually got made and finished despite everything. People don't understand today how all these problems could come together to do that, right? The distribution and everything, it's nothing like that today. That world is *gone*. It's now kind of quaint. Let's face it; it's not a great film. Certainly nowhere near as many people would have ever seen it, if it hadn't been for this odd way of it getting it distributed.

That's one way to put it.

It's just a certain amount of things that came together to create what's left of that film. I'm sure that this kind of thing happens more often than you hear about, but this is the first one that actually got finished because Oley went in and grabbed the footage that he needed.

The funny thing is that it's kind of charming in its own way. I wish that we had had an actual version of the film itself that we could have edited and that somebody would really go in there someday and spend the time and money to really finish it. The thing is the way technology is going in probably another five years you could take what they did of that film and actually make it into a pretty decent film.

So many people bring that up about my resume. The biggest points that people talk about in my resume are usually the *A Nightmare on Elm Street* movies and *The Fantastic Four*. I got to meet Oley and Oley is an amazing human being.

I think that some of the things we did on *The Fantastic Four* were amazing. I think that it did better than expected, especially considering that nobody expected it to do anything at all.

And considering that resources seemed to be next to nothing.

We did all right. The Mole Man's lair was pretty cool looking.

I thought the lasers were pretty cool, too.

I've got a story about lasers. There was a point where we used a green laser. This was the early 1990s. I said "If you're

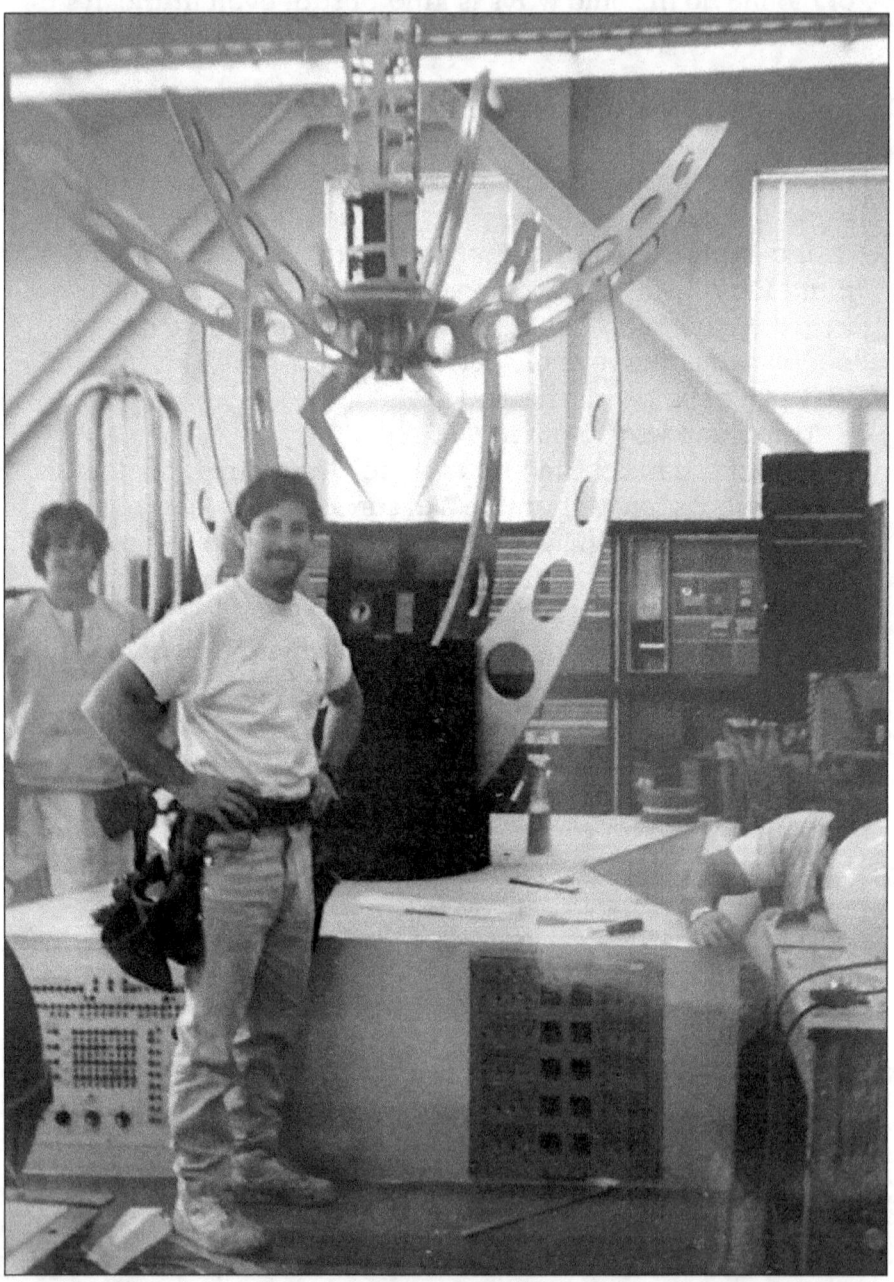

Carpenters installing the machine Reed and Victor built to attempt to harness the cosmic power of Colossus. PHOTO COURTESY OF MICK STRAWN.

going to use a laser to define the space, the only thing that I ask is that you don't use a red laser." Everybody asks, "Why?" I said, "Because a red laser is so overplayed." They had just started coming out with laser pens and shit like that. You don't want something that's supposed to be a cool, otherworldly effect that is going to be on people's keychains in another five years. Get a green laser. Get something that's different. So they got a very powerful green laser. These guys were professionals that were just starting to work with lightshows and stuff like that. That was a powerful laser.

The way that they did that effect is they ran the laser though a splitter. The idea was they hit a diamond with it and the diamond refracted the laser out into a whole bunch of different beams. Then, they went around the inside of a stage and they had these little light stands with mirrors on them. They mirrored them up to a big mirror on the ceiling and then where it hit that mirror, they immediately came straight down. They were bouncing light all over the inside of this dark stage in order to get it to come down like that and make those cages lit. What they didn't really take into account was they hadn't really done it this way many times and there were a couple of stray defractions. I'm in there just as an observer standing there watching this. About five feet from where I'm standing a stray beam had come and was resting on the wall, right?

I wouldn't have thought anything about it. Then, it starts to smoke and all of a sudden it burst into flames. It was like, "Holy shit! That's a real laser" *(laughs)*. I walk over and put

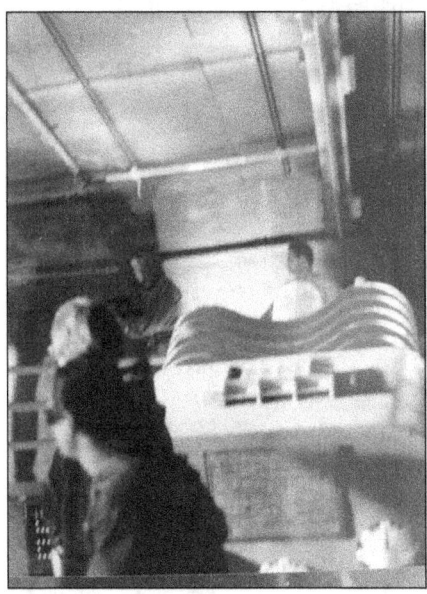

Mick Strawn identified this as part of "the big ray gun in Doom's castle." PHOTO COURTESY OF MICK STRAWN.

that out. I found one other place that the laser went off in a direction that they hadn't figured, so I found another little spot that was burning.

You may have saved the whole thing from burning. Roger might still have figured out a way to use it as a set, maybe a post-apocalyptic setting.

That building would have gone up really fast. You know those fire zones: yellow, orange, red? Walking around through that whole stage area, it would be red all the time.

I think the movie looks good in a lot of ways.

My personal favorite is the observatory at the very beginning. The inside of it looks so cool and then we go to the outside. The ray is such a rotoscope kind of effect, like somebody put a scratch on the negative to make it look like that.

There are some moments here and there where there are some deficiencies and sometimes people pay more attention to that than the whole of the film, unfortunately.

Actually, the acting is pretty interesting. I love the guy that played the Mole Man.

Ian Trigger.

Yeah, he was really good. Rebecca looked gorgeous. Everybody did a better job than you normally get out of a small cast like that. You have to admit that they hardly did it any better when they had money.

I don't know if there is something about the Fantastic Four that doesn't work fundamentally as a franchise or not, but the later movies demonstrate that even if you do have the budget and you do have the time, it's still not guaranteed.

It's not necessarily in the bag. If you're trying to spread your lead out amongst four people, it's difficult. What was the most recent *Avengers* movie?

The one with Thanos. *Infinity War*.

To me that suffers from the same problem. Too many leads. You don't care anymore. Considering that they had as much money to do as many effects as they possibly could — and they obviously did — it's missing something.

Speaking of missing, any suggestions for someone else I should talk to?

There's *absolutely* somebody you should talk to.

Who is that?

Have you talked to Peter Von Sholly?
No.
Peter Von Sholly did the storyboards. You know how important the storyboard artist is because the storyboard artist takes things apart with the director and visualizes it so that we can turn around and do our jobs. Having his point of view in here will definitely help round things out because he's the connection between me and the director and between the special effects people and the director. All of us are channeling to Oley through the storyboards. That's how films work. Your storyboard artist is such a critical role.

It's hard to know who is good to talk to sometimes. You look on an IMDb page and you can see the position, but...

...it doesn't mean shit. My IMDb page is a pile of smoking shit *(laughs)*. It doesn't mean anything. It's missing a third of my credits and there's probably three or four in there, at least, that don't mean anything at all. I've got a credit for *Buffy the Vampire Slayer*. I was in there originally with the original director, but we were all fired three weeks in before we actually did anything other than the initial drawings, but that still hangs on my resume. People just go nuts over that credit. I was one of the team of art directors for *Sid and Nancy*, which is an ultimate rave cult film.

Yeah, the Sex Pistols.

I built the Chelsea Hotel. It was a great job. You couldn't tell that was all a set. We were all really tired, so there were some snafus. We couldn't get back on the stage for three days at the very end just before they left for Britain. Because of that I had sent a guy down there with a crew of laborers to clean up the set. The British PA came in while we were all off because we'd been up for thirty-two hours straight filming. While we were asleep she came in to look for a crew sheet. The guy there didn't know. When she asked who he was, he told her the construction coordinator and director. He was pulling her leg, but he got the credit because she was serious. I didn't get any credit for doing that. Am I going to try to correct that now? I don't think so. So it's like you say: It's really hard to tell what people did just from IMDb.

People have different relationships what they have done. Some people you mention a role to them that they did and

it is near and dear to their hearts and they have lots to say. Other people it's like reminding them that the cat's litterbox needs attention.

It's 60 to 150 people that are in different places in their lives and they all intersect at one time. Back then it was hard work, super-physical, and super-stressful. Then, you went on. People just remember it differently. Life is that way.

You gotta talk to Peter Von Sholly. He is the most interesting being to talk to. Peter is an old friend of mine and I sucked him into this horrible situation. He rides that line between storyboards and working in the comic book world. He brings those two things together.

I'm looking at him on IMDb and, wow, he's got a million credits. Gee whiz.

He is the best storyboard artist that's ever existed.

Pete Von Sholly
Storyboard Artist

Please begin with an explanation of what a storyboard is.
You start with a script, and you end up with a movie. Somewhere in the middle is the storyboard. The storyboard is the point where the script becomes visible. You get the director's vision down on paper, and then everybody knows what the director wants. The storyboard artist can have a lot of creative input and a lot of influence on things, or very little depending on the director's receptivity.

Please talk about your involvement and what you did with *The Fantastic Four*.
I did all the storyboards for the special effects, the stunts, and things like that. I didn't work one-on-one with the director. Different directors work different ways. Oley basically just trusted me with most of it, so I went with it. Sometimes they want your ideas and input; sometimes they want to tell you exactly what to do. He was pretty easy to work with that way.

I brought in Kirby comics and Kirby artwork to him. He liked it. He knew he didn't have an unlimited budget and could only get so much on the screen, but he liked and respected the material. He wanted to honor the comics and what was good about the comics as best he could.

How many storyboards did you make?
I have no idea exactly. Many pages worth. All the effects sequences where somebody would stretch or transform, flame on, and things like that.

What kind of feedback did you get?
They seemed pleased with what I did. There was not a lot of nitpicking. I felt that once we'd seen Ben Grimm turn into the Thing, seeing it again was kind of needlessly expensive. I knew the budget was tight, so I did one shot where you're

looking at his shadow and the shadow transforms, which I thought was a way to show variety in how the transformation happens and to make it more interesting visually. Oley was fine with all that kind of stuff.

So for that scene you show it in full once, and then there were other ways to suggest or represent it a little less expensively.

Yeah. I just thought also it would be more visually interesting. They didn't have CG effects to play with very freely. What year was the movie?

They were shooting it at the very end of 1992. Post-production would have been 1993.

Right. That was when *Jurassic Park* came out. So CG was sort of new and expensive, so it wasn't an option for them, I don't think, except maybe the Human Torch. They might have had some crude CG available for the Torch.

What was the process for making the storyboards? Did you look at the screenplay and then adapt images from it, or how did this work?

You go through the script and look for sequences and scenes that require storyboarding. Storyboards are useful for the production people because you can imagine a thing many different ways. Not everything is explained just because it says on a page that somebody walks into a room and fires a gun. Okay, well, how does that work?

You could shoot that a hundred different ways. Once there's a storyboard of it then everybody involved can look at that and go, "Oh, okay. I see what the director wants. I see what we need to do." So that's kind of the purpose of it. A lot of times they don't have the time or the budget to storyboard the whole movie, and so I would say to directors, "Well what are your priority sequences? Maybe pick the shots that absolutely need storyboarding and make that your A-list. If we finish that and have time, do you have a B-list?" Some directors don't use much storyboarding, some don't use it at all, and some like to use it a lot. It depends on how much time and budget there is as to whether a film can have somebody like me on staff.

When you make that storyboard, that common visual reference for everyone, is that what everybody including the special effects team and the director refers to?

Yeah. I storyboarded a lot of movies in those years and in the 1980s a lot of *A Nightmare on Elm Street* movies, *Darkman* for Sam Raimi, and stuff like that. Once the storyboards are drawn, everybody starts referring to them. Storyboards can even help with designing the sets. If you're storyboarding a scene that takes place in a room but the camera is only looking in one direction, maybe you don't need to build the whole room, or maybe you don't need to dress the whole room. If Reed needs to stretch, then what, exactly, does he have to do? Does he have to reach out to pick something up? Is it just him stretching? What is required? A storyboard lets everybody down the line know what their responsibilities are. Things change a lot from the storyboard stage. Sometimes things come out just like you storyboarded them, and sometimes they come out really, really different for a variety of reasons.

Are there examples of that that you can remember from *The Fantastic Four*?

No, I'm not that familiar with the finished film. Some directors like to sit together with you and go through a sequence shot-by-shot and say, "Okay, I want to open with a wide shot, or a medium two shot of these two people. Then I want a high wide angle of them. Then I want to boom down and push in on them." So you sort of figure it out beat-by-beat that way. Other times they turn you loose because they're busy or they want your input, so you get to kind of play director for a minute. In this case, I just remember having a lot of freedom and Oley liking what I did. I wish I had more specific memories and could tell you more. I know you're going to hear this a lot, but it was a long time ago.

I storyboarded a lot of films. You're interested just in this Roger Corman film, I assume?

Yes sir, primarily.

Okay. I ask because I worked on another version of it that didn't get made years later. Raja Gosnell was going to direct it. He directed the *Scooby-Doo* movie and some other things. This was another version of *The Fantastic Four* that we did a lot of work on, but it didn't happen for some reason.

So what happened with that version? This would have been after the unreleased Corman version but before the 2005 one that came out.

Yeah. It might have been Fox that was going to do it. I could tell that they didn't really understand the characters. They talked about the Thing like he was the Rock Guy, like he's actually made out of rock. I understand that you could look at him and think he kind of looks like that, but he's not made out of rocks. Jack Kirby actually told me once that the Thing is like a gorilla covered in dinosaur hide, so it's a scaly texture. It's organic. It's not rocks. In some of the concept designs people were putting crystals on the Thing and stuff like that trying to play with the idea that it was rocks. I was just shaking my head thinking, "That's not right" *(laughs)*. They were redesigning everything. It was just stupid stuff going on. I don't know why they ended up not making the movie, but I think it's just as well. They still haven't made a good *Fantastic Four* movie.

You actually met Jack Kirby, then?

A few times over the years. I was and am a big fan of Jack Kirby. To me that's the Fantastic Four.

Tell me about him. What was he like? What else did he tell you about the Fantastic Four?

Nothing about the Fantastic Four. He was a wonderful, polite, welcoming, gentle man. I went to his house a few times. His wife Roz would always welcome you and maybe give you a tuna fish sandwich and a cup of coffee or something. You were always treated like guests even if you were someone that had only met them at conventions and things. I bought a couple of pieces of original art from him over the years, so I went over and visited them. I was not what I would call a close friend of the family or anything like that. Roz usually handled the invitations and all of that. Jack was Jack sitting there doing comics. You'll never hear a bad thing about Jack from all the people who knew him, met him, and worked with him. He was always encouraging. What he always encouraged you to do was find you own style. Don't copy his style. Find your own style. Be yourself. He always had a good thing to say and was just the nicest man you'd ever want to know.

Did you ever meet Stan Lee?

I did. I worked at Marvel Animation for a while. Stan had an office there. I grew up reading *Fantastic Four*, so Stan and Jack were important to me. I didn't know the ins and outs. You know it's controversial about who did what, the credit and compensation, and all that. I didn't know anything about that. I just knew that when I grew up, I wanted to be Stan Lee and Jack Kirby because I wanted to write and draw comics. For me, those guy were big inspirations for that kind of comic. You could go into Stan's office and say hello to him. He knew who I was and I would visit. I was doing paintings and he would critique them if I asked. He was very lively and friendly. He would jump around and strike poses. He would say, "Well, look, in this drawing here, you should do this or try that." He seemed like he appreciated the fact that there were people who knew who he, Kirby, Ditko, and all of the Marvel comics makers were. They were important to people. He was not aloof or unfriendly at all…to me, anyway. It was just a special thing, to meet both of those guys. I was like, "Wow! These are the guys I grew up with, and here they are." Your heroes are real human beings. You can meet them and talk to them. It's very cool.

You mentioned Steve Ditko. He passed away recently. Did you have any interaction with him?

No, I didn't. I called him up once. When I was a kid, I was in New York at my Grandma's house on Flushing, Long Island. She had a phonebook that I was looking at, and there's his name, Steve Ditko. I called him up and he answered. What are going to say? "First of all, I didn't think you'd answer the phone. Is it really you?" He goes, "Oh, yeah. Yeah." He was still doing *Spider-Man* at that time. I just said some stupid stuff like, "Gee, you're great. I love your work" *(laughs)*. He was very friendly. He didn't say, "Don't bother me." I didn't get an unfriendly vibe. He seemed to just take it in stride because his phone number is listed, so people are going to call him up. That was it. I just got the impression of him as a friendly guy.

Marvel had offices on Madison Avenue in those days in the 1960s. My older brother took me there one day. He said, "Let's go see if we can meet Stan Lee." We went up and saw Flo Steinberg — who was this wonderful lady — who was Stan's secretary for many years. You might have heard of her.

"Fabulous" Flo. She did a lot things at Marvel. Left Marvel, came back, and in between published *Big Apple Comix*. Her name doesn't come up in comics as much as some others, but she has a very interesting story in her own right.

Yes, she does. She came out into the reception room. She said, "Hi. Stan is busy. I'm sorry you can't meet him. What can I do for you?" I had this little shitty comic book that I had drawn, and I thought, "Gee, I bet Stan will like this." As a kid you don't have a clue as to whether what you did is actually any good or not, or else you're in denial about the fact that it's just amateur work. That's a blessing because it allows you to keep going and not get discouraged. She said, "We can't take things from outside sources. Good for you. Keep working." She was very sweet, but I didn't get in the office. I had the feeling from reading Stan's letters page that there was the bullpen and Steve Ditko, Jack Kirby, and everybody else all in there working together, talking, and it was this big gang having fun! It wasn't like that really, but that's the way Stan made it sound.

Did you save that little comic book that you had made up?

Somewhere, somewhere I think I have it. It's just awful, though.

What was it about?

It was a superhero named Nerve Master. I guess I was the one with a lot of nerve *(laughs)*. The character could control your nervous system, so he could make you think that you heard things and saw things that you didn't. I tried. It was just a few pages. When you're a kid, in those days at least, you didn't know that comic artists drew the pages bigger. You just saw the printed page and assumed that you had to draw it that size. My stuff was drawn on eight and a half inch by eleven inch paper. Just tiny. You think, "How do they do this? This is really small." Then later on you find out that's not how they do it.

But I always loved *Fantastic Four*. Growing up that was one of my favorite comics, so getting to work on a couple of movie versions of it was great fun. Anytime you're drawing *Spider-Man*, *Superman*, or *Fantastic Four* professionally, you stop to think, "*Damn*. This is cool."

What is about the Fantastic Four? Why do you like them so much?

Because of Jack Kirby, really. You know when I read those now, sometimes the dialogue is kind of ridiculous. They don't hold up that well for me, but the artwork does. Kirby's creativity is on another level. It looked to me like Kirby always wanted to entertain himself, and he wanted to have a good time. He would always start an issue off with this really strong visual to get you interested and get you excited and get you into the story. He has a really good sense of "What would I want to see? What would I think is cool?" and that came across.

Then, there was that period when he was creating the Silver Surfer, Black Panther, and Inhumans. This was the mid to late 1960s, which was just amazing. And Thor. At that same time, the *Thor* comic book was introducing all these incredible, new characters and they were in outer space and all sorts of places. Jack was really on a roll, creatively. It was exciting because this was all brand new stuff. Now, there's thousands of issue of all these books. There's so much history, but in those days it was all pretty new. Every time the new Marvel comics came out — especially during the heyday of Ditko and Kirby — it was fresh and exciting.

How did you get involved with the film?

I don't remember who referred me, but a lot of storyboard jobs get referred. You work on a movie and maybe somebody there likes what you did, so they get another movie and they say, "Hey, I met a guy that was a good storyboard guy. If you're looking for a guy, here's his information." The phone would ring and they'd say, "We're looking for a storyboard artist. Are you interested?" You say, "yes," and they send you a script, usually. You read the script and you're supposed to tell them if you're interested or not.

I got one script that I thought was awful. I thought, "Jeez, what am I gonna say about this?" The producer called me up and asked, "Did you get the script?" I said, "Yeah." She said, "Well, what'd you think? People either love it or they hate it. Which were *you*?" I said, "I hated it, actually." She said, "Does that mean you don't want to work on it?" I said, "*No*, it doesn't mean I don't want to work on it. I'll do my best to do what I'm supposed to do." They hired me and I worked on it, so they didn't hold it against me because I was honest.

What film was that?

Heathers. Winona Ryder. Christian Slater. The movie was actually a lot better than I thought it would be from reading the script. The script just didn't appeal to me for some reason.

I read the script for the first *Buffy the Vampire Slayer* movie, and I did not get that job, but the script was great.

To get back to your question, it was usually word of mouth and referrals that got me jobs. I liked the *Evil Dead* movies, and I read in *Fangoria* or some place that Sam Raimi was making something called *Darkman*, and I thought, "Man, I'd like to work on that," so I called Tony Gardner, the effects guy. I had known him and worked with him. He was working on *Darkman* and he told me to call Universal and ask for Sam Raimi. I called and they just put me though! I told his secretary I wanted to work on the film, she arranged a meeting, and I got hired. Sometimes you can aggressively go after something like that. Other times, you work for a director and they like what you did, so they hire you again.

Did you ever meet Roger Corman?

Only once, just to say hello. I think I had a meeting with him. I don't remember why. I think I was trying to pitch him a project. He was nice. He was friendly.

I understand you also worked with the Marvel characters for Disney.

I worked at Disney Imagineering for eight years, and I did a lot of stuff for them involving the Marvel characters for theme parks and things like that. That was another case of getting to draw Spider-Man, Captain America, Iron Man, and everybody as ideas for park attractions, things that you could do and play in parks. There was going to be a Doctor Strange ride and stuff like that. It was so much fun to storyboard Doctor Strange and what the ride would be like. That was another time when I couldn't believe I was getting paid to draw Doctor Strange and these characters I grew up with *(laughs)*. I don't think most of those things got made. You develop things and illustrate them and go through the process. Some things come out the other end and some things don't. I don't know what become of any of that stuff. It's all kind of secret. It was such a treat for a guy like me.

It's always fun to talk to people who love this kind of stuff because it's been a real fantastic career to be involved in making movies particularly when they're good movies.

It was really fun to do *The Fantastic Four* and draw those characters professionally.

Chris Walker III

Effects Technician: Spectral Motion, and
Special Effects Makeup for *Fantastic Four* (2005)
and Effects Technician with Spectral Motion for
Fantastic Four: Rise of the Silver Surfer (2007)

Please tell us about your involvement with the 1994 *The Fantastic Four*.

You may have found it listed on IMDb but I did not add that credit and despite a number of requests they have not removed it. I met the cast of the Corman *Fantastic Four* movie at a convention back then, but that is about it. I know Optic Nerve made the practical effects and suits for the film. I did work there, but it was just after they had done that movie. I'm not sure if you have spoken with Everett Burrell. He was the former owner during that project along with John Vulich who has since passed away. If you get in touch with Everett he might at least have some stories from set that John Vulich can no longer provide.

Let's see if we can set some of the history and credits straight. I'll start with my understanding and then you can correct it. Scott Billups did not provide satisfactory visual effects. Mr. Film did the effects and finished the movie. You essentially were Mr. Film. IMDb indicates you are the only person to have worked on both the 1994 version and the later big-budget versions.

So why does everyone connect you with the movie, then? What's your connection to Mr. Film?

I did work on the practical effects stuff for the later *Fantastic Four* movies, but not the Corman one. I am not connected to Mr. Film and haven't heard of them. I assume there was an animation director named Chris Walker on that film, but it was not me. The first professional work I did was on the *Friends* television pilot, and the *Fantastic Four* movie was already made by then. If anyone mentions Chris Walker while referring to that unreleased film, there must have been another person with the same name that maybe left the business. It's a common name and it may belong to one of the other Chris Walkers on IMDb (I am Chris Walker III). Sometimes productions submit the lists of credits to the wrong profile — I have three or four credits from that time that I cannot get removed. IMDb itself has jumbled some of my credits to other people as well. Believe me, I wish I could straighten IMDb out better. It seems automated and until recently, I didn't even bother with IMDb.

Got it. So you are Chris Walker but not the Chris Walker of Mr. Film. That Chris Walker helped found Mr. Film. A lot of the purpose of this project is to set the record straight or at least let people tell their story in their own words. If you are open to it, could you answer just a few more questions for me?

Sure thing.

What are some examples or details of the practical effects that you did for the *Fantastic Four* movies?

My involvement was not significant for the new movies. I'm definitely not an authority on the films. As I said, I did not work on the Corman film, but I was part of a crew at Spectral Motion for films made in the 2000s. I was not in charge of anything and, as I recall, I left both productions for a different gig both times. I was simply a peon doing finishing work on the Thing suit and cowl for the first film and wasn't on it that long. Other people did most of the work. I don't remember why I left the second production or what I did on it or even how long I was on it.

I remember I left the first film because I wanted to meet Michael Jackson — he was considering having a life-size silver back gorilla statue made at that time and I wanted to see Neverland Ranch. Unfortunately, this all fell through when he was accused of child molestation.

Can you tell us more about the work you did on the Thing suit?

I dug out some pictures I had from my days at Optic Nerve studios. I thought I had a picture of the Thing suit on display along with Doctor Doom, but couldn't find them.

If you spend a lot of time looking, you may be able to find some of the promo stills they did for the 2005 *Fantastic Four* movie where you can see that the Thing's gloves aren't glued down and are sort of flaring out around the wrists. On the 2005 movie I remember we needed to have some of the sculpted rocks on the Thing cowl be removable while Michael Chiklis wasn't shooting so that he didn't feel claustrophobic. We also had to thin the rocks that covered his ears so he could hear more clearly. This was some of the work I did on the movie but the majority of it was done by others since I left before the production was finished. I don't feel comfortable taking credit having only worked on those films for a short period.

Did anyone connected to those later movies ever talk about or make reference to the 1994 unreleased version?

As far as I can remember, nobody connected the new films to the old one in any way. Everyone was just trying to do their best work. I don't think many people knew about it except a few extreme nerds like myself. I believe the Corman movie's existence was buried by the studio when they bought the rights, but I'm not sure about that.

Do you have any opinions/comparisons regarding the 1994 version and/or the later versions you worked on?

I loved the Fantastic Four as a kid. I even had the Thing Underoos! But as far as the movies I worked on I just saw them as a job. I thought the Corman film was funny, and I don't really remember the newer movies very well. I do remember the guy that is now playing Captain America was playing the Human Torch.

Chris Evans. He was also in a great movie called *Snowpiercer*, by the way.

Any other thoughts?

I really didn't work on the movies for very long and my contribution was minimal.

If you know of any way to get that credit removed from my IMDb page, I'd love to know. Looking at it again, I see a credit for *Sleepstalker* and one for *Terror T.R.A.X.: Track of the Vampire*, both of which I DID NOT work on. Also, I should not have any credits for visual effects, producer, or miscellaneous crew on IMDb. The same credit for *Sleepstalker* is under visual effects so I assume that's the Chris Walker you're looking for.

    Unfortunately, I don't know much about how IMDb works. If it is automated as you suggested, then good luck! Other people I have talked with have said they have inconsistencies in their own records as well. I wonder if it's your connection to Optic Nerve that has "helped" IMDb get their wires crossed.

Chris Walker

Director of Animation for *The Fantastic Four* (1994), Co-Founder of Mr. Film

My understanding is you were contacted to work on, redo, and/or finish the special effects for *The Fantastic Four*. Please tell us what you were initially told.
It was kind of a problem. I got contacted by Scott Billups and he later was persona non grata there. Obviously, that was a problem, an issue we had to deal with.

Quite frankly, what happened was Scott came to me and he had *The Fantastic Four* effects project. He was quite upfront. He said, "Listen, this whole project is being done just to make sure the rights were established." The rights were going to run out and they had some option on the Fantastic Four and they had to produce something by a certain time. I understood that.

I was excited about *The Fantastic Four*. It's my all-time favorite comic book. I was *totally* in love with the Fantastic Four. "Oh, man, I want to work on that!"

Scott had come up with this idea of digitizing everything through a video format. Essentially, he took all the film and transferred it to digital video resolution, which I think is something like 720 by 480 — pretty low-resolution. Scott asked us to do a few scenes that he couldn't do, specifically the ending which had not been boarded yet. I think originally we were going to do three shots. I don't remember what the shots were exactly.

Then Oley got some of the shots back and they were low-resolution. I was actually doing all the film output for Scott, too. Our company was Mr. Film, so we had a way of digitizing and film recording. We had a 1K and a 2K format. When they saw the upresed digital video projected on film, Oley immediately just said, "Hey, man. This is not good. It's fuzzy." I imagine there was some discussion whether it was even going to be produced for film or not because for video it was okay, but for film it was pretty low-resolution. Scott Billups was thinking that he was going to do the whole thing that way. I think we were doing our shots in high-res.

Oley came back to us and said, "Hey, can you redo everything? I've got $30,000" or something like that. I said, "You're kidding me. That's all you have?" He says, "Well, yeah." I said, "Well, okay. I'll see what I can do." We wound up doing all the effects, a lot of inserts with Johnny Storm's hand catching fire and all that sort of stuff.

So you met Scott Billups and interacted with him, correct?
Oh, of course.

The impression I had was that he came in, he created some stuff, it didn't work, and then they brought you in, so there wasn't an overlap between the two of you. But you're telling me he was creating effects, and you were brought in while he was still actively working on the film.
He was doing the whole thing. He had his girlfriend working in his house doing all this rotoscope work on video frames. It was digital video, which was new at that time. We were upresing it with a little bit of a sharpness filter and then putting it out to a 1K film recorder. He was coming to us to record all his shots. It was kind of weird for me because Scott was the one who brought me into the project. Then, the director and editor were saying, "Well, you know, we all like your shots. Is there any possibility you could do them?" I'm going "Well, what about Scott?" *(laughs).*

Unfortunately, Scott just tried to cut too many corners. I think the way he looked at it was "This was going to be garbage anyway. Let's just get this out the door and call it a day." Oley came back and said, "No, man. We can't do this. This is not good." I know Oley was really burned by it because it was his reputation on the line, too. And I got caught in between trying to finish it with no money. That's a gory story, and it's not that great. I don't know what happened to Scott. It was a tough situation.

What kind of person did Scott Billups seems like? Did he seem like a nice guy who had talent, but saw the handwriting

on the wall and just didn't take the movie seriously enough? Was he arrogant, cutting corners, and trying to hide his lack of ability? Was he somewhere in between?

He was a nice guy. Like so many people in Hollywood, he was a smooth talker trying to impress you in some way. To a degree he might have been on to something. His whole idea of trying to digitize video as a format for doing effects work didn't pan out, of course, but it was an interesting idea. Back then nothing was set in stone. This was all new.

He was the kind of guy who would really try to get on your good side and then not really care about what happened. He wasn't able to follow through and perform. He'd get people like me to get the work done. But that's how Hollywood runs.

Scott gained a bad reputation. Some people would call me and they would say, "What do you think about Scott Billups?" There was a point that I remember really distinctly in my career where I thought, "You know what? I have to be responsible to someone else who doesn't know Scott Billups, and I have to tell them what has happened on his projects." Basically, they've always been sort of a crash and burn. I got a call from his agent wanting to know why I was saying this about Scott. I told him I was asked pointblank about Scott, and I had to tell the truth. The agent accepted that. It's weird because the Hollywood community is obviously kind of protective. We don't want people to get burned. We want projects to be successful.

How are you going to handle Scott Billups?

I tried to contact him early on. I found a company that he's with, PixelMonger, and there was a "contact me" feature, so I used that and told him what I was doing. I didn't get any response, so I can't include him. In terms of what other people say, their comments are their comments. I'm not fishing for negative comments, but I'm not going to ignore them either. No one I've talked to has had anything very good to say about him, and that is indicative of something.

That's one of the reasons I wanted to talk to him. I'm not the President of the Scott Billups fan club, but by the same token, he's done nothing to me. I don't know him. I don't have a stake in it. But I thought maybe he has a side. Maybe his side is something like "I had personal problems," or "The stuff

they wanted me to do relative to the budget, timeline, and available technology was absolutely impossible." Maybe he just wants to look forward and thinks it's beneath him or unnecessary to get into all of this. Maybe he has no defense or explanation. I don't know.

Everybody has a perspective, a side to their story even if it's not the truth or the same truth everyone else would agree on. I didn't hear from him, so okay. If he reads people's opinions in this book, then all I can say is he had his chance to share his thoughts but declined to get involved with the project.

I think the bottom line with that situation is maybe Scott isn't as bad as everyone likes to make him out to be. He creates a mess. People bumble things. I think he was just much shrewder with his approach to the project than anybody else was. I think he read between the lines and realized, "Hey, this film is just a commercial being made to keep the rights, and it's not going to go anywhere."

What are the qualifications for doing special effects?

At that time — zip. We had built the studio up, were really birddogging all the technology, and just trying to keep moving forward. But it's not like you went to college to do special effects. There's no place you can go to become a producer, except to hang out in Hollywood and maybe know somebody who can get you in. The fact is people get into powerful positions who are completely unqualified. It happens all the time.

Do you recall or can you offer an estimate of what you were paid?

(*Laughs*) It was pretty small. It was $14,000 for three shots.

What's your opinion of the film as a whole?

I think it holds together for a low-budget film. There are some cheesy moments. The people who were doing it really gave it some authenticity. They were really feeling the characters. I think Doctor Doom had a tough time with that mask on his face. I think the movie was done really well. Kudos to Oley and the actors for that. I think the actors wanted it to be real and heartfelt. I was disappointed when I saw the newer ones. There was something about the characters that wasn't authentic to me. I can't pinpoint it.

When we were doing this, it was so exciting because the only thing that had been done to that date was *Terminator 2* with the cop who turned silver. We thought we were opening up all of these characters to being done in film. Of course, it didn't get released, and that was a letdown. We did our best. Those were the days when we were young and fearless and trying to do something for not a whole lot of money. We had some really good talent, so that helped a lot.

Who else from Mr. Film worked on the movie? Was there a division of labor in terms of who worked on what scenes, or was it more of a collective effort as Mr. Film?

Geoff Fennell, Doug Smith, and Juliet Bashore were part of Mr. Film. Habib Zargarpour he did a lot of the fire effects. He mapped fire onto a 3-D object that was rotoscoped on Johnny Storm's hand. Pietro Bonomi was the master sculptor. Macky Beheshti was our IT guy. Glen Grillo did the explosion, and I had two programmers at the time, Larry Luthor and Frank Little. That was Mr. Film.

What's your opinion of Mr. Film's work on the movie?

It's okay for our first shot at it. It looks really cool. We could have spent more time on the animation. We had really crude tools back then. We didn't even have deformable bodies. That was really new technology at that time. We didn't have skeletons on anything like that. We were animating body parts, interpenetrating. We were developing motion-capture, but we never wound up using motion-capture for *The Fantastic Four*. We definitely had talking heads at that point. We were doing face tracking at the time. It was very new, wide open territory. No one really knew how to approach it. We felt like we were inventing everything. I think we used ALIAS' particle system. They had just released it two months before we needed it. Nothing really worked that well. We did with what we had. We got something out there, and it was a real rush to do it. I would consider it more like Saturday morning animation. We were sort of going for an aesthetic like that. We were definitely trying to get a graphic look. As far as holding up as a motion picture, I don't think all the shots really held up that well. The technology has come way far forward and become fairly seamless. I think there's still room for a hybrid look and feel.

What do you think about what films have done with animation since then?

As soon as Pixar started coming out with its films, I started getting a little bit disappointed because it seemed like that was setting the mold for what animation was going to look like. Everything was going to look like marshmallows and soft lighting. Certainly it is a far cry from classic anime with hardline edges and clean graphics. I feel like we missed something along the way. There's a hybrid in between going for total realism with balloony characters and trying to maintain a sense of the graphic, a sense of visual excitement that isn't totally fastened down to the god of realism. It's gotten less interesting for me. I used to go and see every single effects film. I saw it from the beginning, from the 1980s all the way forward.

I have that feeling with some of the superhero movies. Sometimes there are too many effects, and they're too big. You have to have something else to balance that out like character development and plot. Otherwise, it's like repeatedly biting in to something that's too sweet.

Yeah, exactly. Well, a couple of things happened to me. One is I would look at these films and I would just get tired (*laughs*) because I know what it takes to make them, the amount of human labor that goes into these things. Occasionally, you get one that sticks out like *Life of Pi*. That's one of the most beautiful effects films ever done. The ones where everything's exploding and there's robots and all that crap, it just kind of wears me out. I think, "What the hell is this all for?" If you don't have a good story, you don't have much to build on. A lot of films depend on the effects more than the story.

I've heard some people speculate that if *The Fantastic Four* had been made two or three years later, it would have looked better because of the state of the technology available at the time. Either there were things that weren't available yet, or, as you talked about, you had some of these things, but they were so new no one fully understood how to use them yet.

Absolutely. Three years would have made a *huge* difference just from the standpoint of having storage space. We were just running around trying to figure out how to move film files from one place to another. A 2,000 pixel image was gargantuan for us. We were storing things on Bernoullis, which were only twenty megabytes. It was absurd what we were trying to do. Our server was only a couple of hundred megabytes. We were pushing compositing through Photoshop. Certainly the face tracking got way better even in just two or three years. We were doing deformable characters in three years.

The budget was absurdly small. We needed more time. Having more manpower to be able to perfect things would have helped. Get it out as soon as possible was the expectation.

The only things computer graphics were used for in those days were flying logos or explosions and gunfire. No one had thought about doing full character work. We were pioneers, and we knew that we were onto something. I pushed it pretty hard. We later developed a series called *Jay Jay the Jet Plane*, which was the first full motion capture television series. It has its own suite of technologies. That was about three years later.

Our main thing was performance animation. We did a lot of live television work with full characters interacting with live action. Oddly enough, we didn't do any film work.

When did the first Marvel film come out?

It depends. The first Marvel Cinematic Universe film was *Iron Man* in 2008. *X-Men* came out in 2000 and was sort of the first modern Marvel movie. The 1977 *Spider-Man* was a made-for-television film.

So it took six years — and a lot of money — to get from *The Fantastic Four* to that first *X-Men*.

Please discuss the ending of *The Fantastic Four* a little bit.

And then there was the big ending. I can't believe you forced me to look at that again *(laughs)*. I'm a little bit embarrassed. The ending was actually inspired by Max Fleischer because he made a Superman cartoon that was similar to that where Superman was fighting a laser beam, so it was really a tribute to him. It was such a beautiful cartoon.

I'll tell you another little anecdote. I was reshooting the very last shot, the last explosion sequence. Back then we would work around the clock, so I was waiting for the film recorder to finish. Around four in the morning, there was an earthquake. I woke up and looked at the film recorder. It was dead and the power was out. I remember thinking that the shot might have finished recording because I had timed it. It was literally the last shot, and I desperately wanted *The Fantastic Four* to be done. I rolled up the film and put it in a film canister and decided to take it out to the lab because I figured I could still make tomorrow morning's lab. I should have turned on a radio to find out what was going on.

The nightly lab run was a familiar routine, but this time as I shot up the 405 with no street lights in the dead of night, I hit a bunch of concrete and blew out a tire. I hobbled off the freeway around Sherman Oaks. I changed my tire and decided to see if I could still make it to Burbank. Then I realized I didn't have enough gas and since the power was out, I wouldn't have a way to get any. I decided to turn around. I went through this neighborhood and everybody was sitting in the middle of the streets with blankets on. They were afraid to go back inside of their houses. The whole place looked like it had been bombed out. I thought, "God, what an idiot I am trying to get out to the lab" *(laughs)*. I *really* wanted to get it done and this was the last shot. What a weird night that was.

Are you going to include some images?

I think so. I have folks who have offered to give me images. I don't have anything in mind yet for the cover, so one of the images I get could become the cover.

I think I've got a few things. I'll look around. I've got one in particular that you might be interested in. It is a special poster image I made for self-promotion. I made the poster on my own time after the effects delivery to New Horizon. It is not 1:33 aspect. The final image was designed apart from the actual movie footage and was never part of the delivery to New Horizon.

Thank you.

When you came to the project did anyone give you the impression that this movie wasn't going to come out and you just had to make it or make part of it to hold onto the rights, or was it presented as a "real" project that was going to come out for sure?

According to Scott, his whole thing was he was holding out to get the video rights and the point was to just get this thing done so that they could hold onto the rights. I think he was shrewder. As far as Glenn and Oley, I don't think they really knew. I think they were hoping that there was gonna be a release. I remember when we delivered everything, all of a sudden everything went silent. No one really knew what was gonna happen. Then, I remember Glenn coming to me and saying that it looked like Marvel bought the film and they're going to shelve it.

Do you recall when he told you that?

It was probably a couple of months after. We delivered in January, so it would have been March maybe.

Did you ever meet Stan Lee?

I remember after we did *The Fantastic Four* I had a chance to meet Stan Lee. I was telling him, "Hey, this is gonna be really great. We can make films with your characters." He was talking about it but didn't really think it was going to happen. He was a really jovial character.

When you were trying to pitch Stan on all this, what was his response to you?

He was treating me like a fan. I don't think he really understood that I knew *some* of what I was talking about. In 1991 at SIGGRAPH, we presented the first real time performance character, Silver Suzy, who was a female Silver Surfer in the Tomorrow's Realities gallery. It was a simple interaction; you could pick up a small surfboard with a magnet attached to it in the center of a performance arena, and "fly" a real time rendered chrome Silver Suzy banking and turning through space on a 10' projection screen. It was really impressive.

I remember specifically saying to Stan, "You could do Silver Surfer. It would be completely chrome and everything would be reflective. It would be so amazing to see this character in real life." I think that he didn't take me seriously *(laughs)*. I was really young.

I think part of it was how Hollywood is. If you don't have the money, if you're not representing some distribution company or something like that, people just take your ideas as small talk. That's what it comes down to. If you make a film, you've got to have some financing. Then people start to listen and start to move.

How tough is the business?

It's a tough business, a really tough business. I got out based on unfortunate circumstances. The most tragic story I have that sums it up is Rhythm & Hues winning an Academy Award for Best Visual Effects and then going out of business because of *Life of Pi*. That's a crime. That just shouldn't happen. There's something wrong.

Trying to keep up with all the graphic machines and software is difficult. I went through that whole thing with buying all the equipment and the software. You just wouldn't believe how much stuff costs. We spent hundreds of thousands of dollars on software. I had two fulltime people continuously writing software with me. The producing in Hollywood is really difficult. You're often looking at a project that you're not exactly sure how you're gonna finish. You're held to a bid unless you can get a cost plus. You can estimate the costs of shots, but you're not totally sure what it's actually going to end up costing. It's extremely competitive. We were just scraping around doing effects shots for New Horizons, so there wasn't much risk there. Just think of what it's like when you get into the millions of dollars, and you've got armies of people doing it. And then you go out of business once you get the Academy Award. It drives me nuts thinking about it.

Everybody who's been in the business knows exactly what I'm talking about. It always felt like I was risking the whole company with each project, and yet it was so fricking exciting that I just kept going. Everybody who worked on it felt the same way. That excitement was definitely there for *The Fantastic Four*. People were willing to work and get it done. We all knew no one had ever done this stuff before. That was part of the rush.

One of the disappointments was that nothing ever really came of it in terms of working with New Horizons. I think that was mainly because they were working with such low budgets. They started farming the stuff out to a studio they had in Eastern Europe. I kept having the problem of studios farming the work out to really inexpensive labor areas in the world. I was sort of hoping that something else would happen as a result, and it didn't. As it turned out, the big boys really control everything. Sony brought everything in-house. I started really focusing on television because we couldn't quite get over the hump of doing film work. We did a lot of television.

How did Mr. Film get started?

I started out in a shoebox on the 3rd Street mall in Santa Monica in 1987. It was two rooms. The area now is super-gentrified, but back then there were homeless people sleeping on the benches. We started out with two PCs, an IMI flight simulator, and eventually we built our first film recorder, using a 1280 x 768 black and white medical flat screen. John Allen and I started the studio and shortly thereafter Pietro Bonomi joined us as master 3D sculptor. We knew we could do flying logos, but in the back of our minds I think we knew that animation would be taken over by computer graphics, but the tools still needed to be invented. People just kept coming with projects. And we just kept going. We moved and opened up more space. At one point, we were renting four or five spaces in this one industrial building down in Venice near the Rose Cafe.

What became of Mr. Film? Did it morph and grow into Modern Cartoons, or are they two entirely separate things?

We had created a real-time character named Basil the Bingo Basset, who became the host of a twenty-four hour bingo channel operating out of New York. The parent company that owned the show, Kinnevik, a Swedish media conglomerate, bought Mr. Film and started a partnership called Modern Cartoons, Ltd. I had fifty people working with me and a full technical department. It just kept going. It was like a miracle. We were creating characters, and television pilots, designing bodysuits, face trackers, and gloves, and along the way we were awarded four patents in the field of performance animation. We were still way out on the bleeding edge. We were doing live television work, cutting live cameras with integrated real time characters, 3D sets, and green screened live action. We invented a pipeline for post-production called "Storyboard" that effectively managed twenty minutes of finished animation a week. We were just kicking ass on so many different levels. There were only a couple of moments in a seventeen-year flood where we had no work. It was like riding a wave. Then it got to the point where all I was doing was looking at spreadsheets and contracts. It just wasn't fun.

I think part of that was after seventeen years, there was a little less invention. A point came when the business was not forgiving.

What are you doing these days?

I'm working with my dad who's a fairly well-known landscape architect, Peter Walker. I do all his computer graphics, and pre-visualization. I moved back to the bay area, which is where I'm from. I guess I'm cured *(laughs)*.

(Laughs) You're over it now?

I don't need to produce motion pictures anymore. I'd love to do it, but it's an all-consuming thing. You have to be in really good shape *(laughs)*. It's very intense and exciting. And fulfilling.

Everett Burrell
Special Effects Makeup, Co-Founder of Optic Nerve Studios

Have you seen the documentary *Doomed*?
Yes. Have you?
I've not seen it.
It's good. You'll enjoy it whether you're into comic books, *The Fantastic Four* movie, or movies and Hollywood in general.
I'll definitely check it out. So how can I help you?
I'm curious to talk some about the special effects because Scott Billups is always associated with them and I don't think he's got a particularly...
(Laughs)
Yeah, that's kind of the reaction people have when I mention his name.
I have not heard that name in twenty years.
I've tried to contact him but that hasn't worked out, so I've taken some other avenues to try to talk to some people about some of the effects and I saw your name. When I contacted you and said that you were willing to talk and wanted to set the record straight, I thought this sounds really good. Sounds like you have a few things to talk about.
Just to be clear, Scott was visual effects. John Vulich and I were makeup effects, so we were totally different worlds.
Please tell me about some of the makeup effects that you did.
John and I had been doing stuff as Optic Nerve for Roger's Company on a few shows. There's a producer named Mike Elliott. Mike's a really good guy and he really liked us a lot. He was very invested in making sure we were taken care of whether it was $100 or $100,000. My first job was with Roger

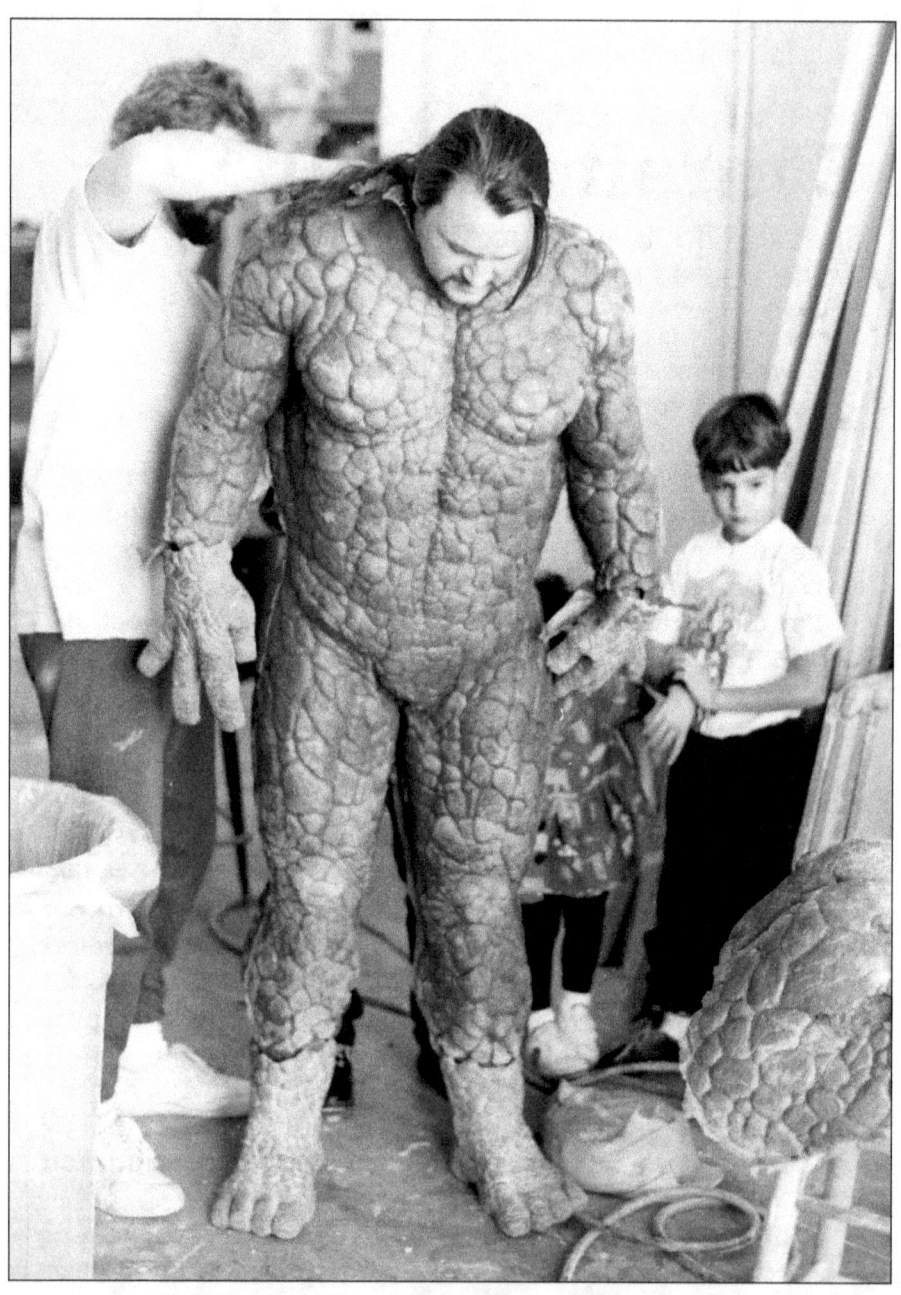

Everett Burrell trying on the Thing suit. PHOTO COURTESY OF EVERETT BURRELL

working at the Hammond Lumberyard and that studio was a big part of my growing up, so it was actually a big honor to help out on the show. We never knew that the show was just a diversion to keep the rights; we always thought it was a real movie, so we worked our asses off. We built the Thing and Doctor Doom. We tried to approach it with a high level of quality and treat it as a feature film. We had a lot of fun. It was a blast. The director was great. The team was great. We had a really good time on the show. We knew it was low-budget, but the fact that it never saw the light of day is really funny after all these years. I get a lot of calls about that movie. People say they love our Thing suit better than the one that was in the 2005 film.

I know you couldn't go the CGI route because the technology wasn't available, but were there other options that you and John considered for rendering the Thing?

No. It was always going to be a man in a suit. I'm a big comic book fan. It was sort of based on the John Byrne *Fantastic Four*. If you know comics, John Byrne is a very famous artist in the 1980s.

I know he worked on the *Fantastic Four* from 1981 to 1986 and that run is well-regarded.

He was one of my idols, so when I got the job we started looking at that set of issues. Then, we had talks about how to make it organic, how to make it look like rock. We made a bunch of test sculptures. Roger and Oley approved. He said, "Go for it."

Roger has a really good eye. He's really smart, and he's very decisive. One of the things about moviemaking nowadays is people don't want to make any decisions before they're afraid they'll lose their job, but Roger just makes a decision. It may be the right one. It may be the wrong one. But at least he makes decisions. So he was great.

I think one of the most disappointing things was the costumes. They looked a little cheap. Again, it was low-budget. What are you going to do?

So how did you approach Doctor Doom's costume, armor, and so forth?

Again, went to the John Byrne run of *Fantastic Four* issues. We sculpted the face and molded it in silicone. Then, we cast the plaster and sanded that down and made a new mold to get it nice and smooth. Then, we made a fiberglass copy and sanded that down even smoother with bondo, really buffed it, and then made a final mold, so the face is pretty pristine. Then, we vacuformed the other parts of the armor around Joseph Culp.

Pieces of Doctor Doom's armor. PHOTO COURTESY OF EVERETT BURRELL

Then, we had the costumes. That's sort of the lackluster part. The material was really thin and it didn't fit the costume so well. It is what it is.

Did you design those knives or blades that extend from the end of his fingertips towards the end of the movie?

I think so. I think we built that hand that had retractable knives on it. I remember the Mole Man makeup was fun.

So you did the Thing costume and Doctor Doom's costume...

...and Mole Man. We tried to do a lot of the gags of Mister Fantastic through practical methods, but they didn't work very well. They're like pneumatic arms. We built a big cable arm that waves out of the limo when Reed and Sue get married. Just stupid shit, but it was fun.

So you guys were responsible for his stretching effects?

Yeah.

So what were some thoughts about how to accomplish those?

CG just didn't exist back then. We had to try to do it practically the best we could with a lot of tricks. Now that Marvel films are so big and the visual effects have caught up with the storytelling, that's the perfect character to use the CG for because there's no other real way to do it.

Are there other effects that you and John are responsible for creating in the film?

Let's see...Doctor Doom, the Thing, the Mole Man, some of Mister Fantastic's gags. I think that was about it.

Do you have memories or thoughts about specific people?

Carl Ciarfalio who played the Thing was just amazing, so much fun. It was the first time I ever used the astronaut cool suit, which is sort of a skintight leotard that has hosing sewn through it that you pump cool water through and that's hooked to an ice chest. Astronauts used to use it to keep cool when they would walk from the tarmac to the space capsule. Carl was really into being the Thing. Carl sold me my first cellphone. In 1992 he had one in his car and I thought it was the most coolest thing in the world. I think I paid 750 bucks for it, which is not cheap in the big scheme of things.

Working for Roger was always a lot of fun because I don't think he had super-high expectations. We always tried to really go the extra mile because he wasn't a jerk. He would come visit occasionally on set to make sure we were doing good and we were on time. He had fun with the material and he let us all have fun with it, too. Again, I can't speak highly enough about Mike Elliott and Roger and the team.

Have you seen the movie?

A couple of times on bootleg DVD. I was pretty impressed with the fire effects. The Human Torch stuff was pretty neat. It

The Thing sneering and posing. PHOTO COURTESY OF EVERETT BURRELL

was really neat how they kind of mimicked the Max Fleischer kind of look from the old *Superman* serials. It was the really early days of CG.

I'm curious about something you mentioned. You were talking about the cool suit in Carl's Thing costume. My understanding is that there wasn't a cool suit.

No, no, no! We had a cool suit on him every day.

Really?

Yeah. One-hundred percent. Maybe he doesn't remember. In fact, Roger George, the great effects man from the 1980s, lent us the suit for Carl. He wore it every day with a little ice chest attached, and a little hose kind of coming out of his ass.

Let me ask this question because he talked about having to dump the boots a couple of times a day to get to the sweat out. I've seen video of somebody holding a fan up to his mouth trying to cool him down. Are those things consistent with having a cool suit?

Absolutely. The cool suit was only a shirt, so he still would sweat. You could only plug it in when he wasn't on camera. So when he's on set doing his thing in between takes, we'd plug it in. I think we shot January and February, so it wasn't too hot, but still he sweated a lot.

So the cool suit wouldn't exactly have kept him comfortable, but it would make him less hot than he would have been otherwise.

Yeah. We could only turn it on when the camera wasn't rolling. There was an ice chest with a little motor. You plug it in through a tube in his back and it would circulate the cold water on his chest through the tubing, but you could only do it when he wasn't shooting. Of course he's sweating. Yeah, absolutely.

And you said that cool suit was loaned to you?

Roger George let us borrow it. I think he's passed now. The history of Roger George is fascinating. He was one of the old time physical effects guys in L.A. He did everything, big-budget, low-budget. You always knew him because half his face was burned. He suffered an accident when one of the pyro devices blew up in his face. Half his face was red. His company still exists. I think they rent equipment to all the major companies. He was a really, really sweet guy. Always a pleasure to work with.

If you had to buy that cool suit how much would it have cost?

I'm going to say back in the day maybe a couple of grand.

I have another questions about the cool suit. You said that it was loaned to you, so it was separate, then, from the Thing suit?

Yeah. We built the Thing suit and Roger George offered us the suit. He might have rented it to production. I don't know because we didn't make it. It came from Roger George. He showed us how to use it.

I don't know why you would want to, but you could wear the Thing suit without the cool suit, correct?

You could. Absolutely. There might have been times when Carl didn't wear it. I just can't recall. I'm not trying to call Carl a liar, but I specifically remember him wearing the cool suit.

One other question: When did you have to return the suit to Roger George?

At the end of production. It was his, so he took it.

The reason I ask is that later on, at the end of production, Mark Sikes did some pick-up shots in the Thing suit, so he wouldn't have had the cool suit available to him.

That's weird. I don't remember that. Did we do pick-ups later on?

After formal production and main shooting had closed, a lot of people left to do other projects. Carl was already on another job. Mark spent about five hours in the suit. He and Oley went down and shot some of those shots at the end when the Thing walks down Hollywood Boulevard.

Oh, that sounds really familiar. Now, that makes sense. I do recall that.

So Mark wouldn't have had the cool suit?

I have no idea. I just don't know.

Okay, I'm going to ask Mark but if he says he didn't have it, it doesn't mean Carl didn't because if you had to give the cool suit back after production was finished, that would have been before Mark would have been in the suit. In other words, the cool suit wouldn't have been available to Mark. I'll see if Oley remembers anything about it.

Roger George had it as sort of part of his kit rental. Stunt guys wear it a lot when they're wearing fireproof suits. So he saw Carl sweating and said, "Hey, I've got this thing on my truck. Want to try it out?" I think he gave Roger a really good deal. I think we definitely used it on stage. I can't remember if we used it on location or not, but we definitely used it at the Hammond Lumberyard.

Did Joseph Culp ever give you feedback about the comfort level of the Doctor Doom costume?

We had many fittings where we had to sand things down or grind rivets or put padding against his skin in certain areas to help him. He was great.

I knew Alex Hyde-White from another movie that we had done. I knew Carl. We had done a couple of movies before

Doctor Doom. PHOTO COURTESY OF EVERETT BURRELL

with him as a stunt coordinator. There's a couple of people we knew on set. Plus, a lot of the crew we knew.

Tell me some about the approach to the Jeweler's (AKA the Mole Man's) costume and outfit.

We just did the prosthetic. He had like a fedora and a trench coat which was the costume. The wardrobe people took care of that. One of the things I learned on the *Fantastic Four* is how much you need to communicate with the costume department because makeup and hair and costumes go together. They need to really be in sync. We were working so much in a bubble by ourselves that we had no idea what was going on elsewhere. Even on the day of shooting we didn't know until we showed up. John Vulich sculpted the makeup himself for the Mole Man. He thought it was a fun character. I sculpted the Thing. Mike Measmer supervised Doctor Doom.

Anything else you can tell me about making the movie or anything related to it?

It was made in a hurry. I think it was only a four-week shoot or something like that, right?

If that.

We just *banged* it out. Oley Sassone directed it, right?

Yes.

Always a great guy. It was a labor of love. We're all big fans. I'm a comic nerd. We had a great time. Good people. Worked hard. I'm happy to work hard for somebody who appreciates it. When you work hard for somebody who's a jerk, it doesn't make you want to get up in the morning. You want to be inspired. You want to be happy to go to the set in the morning.

I try to instill that in my team to this very day. Let's have fun. I work for Netflix a lot. I just did a show called *The Umbrella Academy*. We're working long hours. I said, "It's a 5 p.m. call. We're working to 7 a.m. Just have fun tonight. I'll make jokes. I'll tell you stories in between takes. Let's just have fun."

That's what the professor in the classroom scene during the first minutes of the film says, too: "And above all, have fun."

I just really try to keep the crew upbeat and have a good time. Because we're lucky. We're very lucky to do what we get to do. A lot of people have horrible jobs. They're digging ditches or doing something bad they don't like doing for a

The Thing and the Jeweler in the Jeweler's lair. PHOTO COURTESY OF EVERETT BURRELL

living. We're very lucky. I get to do something for a living that I grew up loving as a child. I'm happy.

Do you ever recall there ever being any talk about a sequel?

No. Never. It was so quick. I remember the movie kind of being in trouble and trying to finish it. I remember Oley calling me and asking about places to put CG stuff in and if I could help. I said, "Look, the technology isn't there yet." Now, they could do it lickety-split. Then, I realized, "Oh, this movie is never coming out" *(laughs)*. That's the whole point.

When did you realize that?

I think a couple years after it never came out. Then we started seeing mumblings about *X-Men* and *Spider-Man* movies. Our movie was just about keeping the rights.

So you're while you're making it and doing your work, there was no indication the movie wasn't going to come out?

No. Never. Not to me. We never knew that the film was a fraud. We were just hoping to have a fun time and do something cool. I was a fan. We really tried to honor the comic book the best way we could.

The work you did on the film was through Optic Nerve?

Yeah. John Vulich and I start started Optic Nerve in my garage in Granada Hills, California in 1989. We did a bunch of George Romero films. We worked for Savini a lot. We got back after *The Dark Half* and we set up a little building in Sylmar, California. That's where we built *The Fantastic Four*.

So you didn't have to use any of Roger's equipment or space?

No. We had our own company, building, corporation. We had a great crew, Mike Measmer, Ron Pipes, some really fun guys whom I'm still friends with to this very day.

That's probably good you had your own resources. From what I've heard about the studio resources, things could be a bit on the lean side.

(*Laughs*) Yeah. Roger's the cheapest man on the planet. It was so fun being on that lot. There'd be a crashed spaceship in the corner or a blown up car. It was just all this shit in the Hammond Lumberyard. He was so cheap he never changed the sign. It was a fun studio. It was definitely a college dorm. I could literally sit in Roger's chair and read copies of *Fangoria* every day. No one cared. You had free reign of everything as long as you didn't steal anything. If you stole something, that was it. That broke Roger's trust. He definitely said this, "Never steal from me. You have complete free reign to use props or chairs or crash spaceships. Use whatever you want. Just never steal from me." I never did in a million years.

Regarding the Hammond Lumberyard sign, I heard that since he didn't take it down, there were still carpenters showing up to buy supplies since they didn't know it was a studio. Corman was in need of people, so he was hiring some of them on the spot *(laughs)*.

(Laughs) Exactly. He hired surfer dudes off the street as day laborers. Venice was pretty rough back then. Venice was a seedy area. It's kind of gentrified now, but back in the late 1980s, early 1990s it was bad. Bad, bad, bad. It was like heroin city down there. Crystal meth was bad. You couldn't park your car on the street.

Anything else to add? Final thoughts? Stuff that stands out?

My final thought would be about the late, great John Vulich who was my partner and my friend for many years. He was so supportive. We did a movie called *The Skateboard Kid*. Mike Elliott just said, "Hey, you guys wanna do *The Fantastic Four*?" We said, "Yeah." I told John it would be a fun gig even though there's not a lot of money in it. John's like, "Oh, my God. This is the most fun we can ever have and get paid." We were getting paid $350 a week or something like that. That's what we paid ourselves. We were paying our crew more than we were making just so we could keep the shop open. It was a good bonding experience for John and I as brothers and as teammates. We had more fun than we did on *Babylon 5*. I think it was the last best time that we had together because after that it went to shit. Our relationship just went downhill after that.

What happened?

We won the Emmy for *Babylon 5* and John got a big head and felt that he didn't need me anymore. We had a big fight, a huge fight. I left the company and forced him to buy me out under California law. He had to pay me a lot of fucking money. He didn't like that, so we didn't talk for five years. But in the end before John died, we spent a lot of time together. We had some good talks. He explained to me what his problem was with me, and I explained to him what my problem was with him. We definitely buried the hatchet before he died, so I'm very satisfied that we didn't leave on bad terms and that his respect for me was immense. He was my older brother in a lot of ways and I really looked up to him and I wanted him

Everett Burrell, the Thing, and John Vulich. PHOTO COURTESY OF EVERETT BURRELL

to respect me. He one day said, "Listen, dude. I'm so proud of you. You have no idea."

Now that I'm older and wiser I want history corrected. There's a lot of things out there about me, about Vulich, and about Optic Nerve that I don't like and that are completely incorrect.

That's good you had an opportunity to work things out with John. There's some unseen footage from the *Doomed* documentary that Mark Sikes and Marty Langford are letting me use to make an interview with John, so we'll hear from him once more and I'm curious what he will talk about.

I miss those days. I wish I could have a *Fantastic Four* experience every show.

John Vulich

Special Effects Makeup, Co-Founder of Optic Nerve Studios. *Courtesy of footage generously provided by Mark Sikes and Marty Langford*

I have this image of you guys sculpting and finishing some of these costumes with pictures of the comic book. Maybe tell me about the studio and the era of the comics you may have been referring to.

(*Laughs*) Here's the big, deep, dark confession that I really hate to make because comics are so prevalent in the industry as a source of inspiration: I really don't like comics books. The majority of the knowledge in that area would have been Everett, my business partner at that time. He knew comic books. He was a big fan. I couldn't tell Ditko from who and who. I've really no concept whatsoever.

Maybe you could just talk about the fact that you had comic references.

We did, but I'm trying to think of who it was. Who were the main guys drawing it at that point?

The really early stuff was Jack Kirby.

I think it was all Jack Kirby that we were following. I just don't know that world.

You're, like, an asshole nowadays if you don't know. Comics just kind of rule. Even before things like Comic Con and that whole push and Marvel and DC really, really getting their shit together. Instead of just niche product that a small group of geeks want to see, they're making films the whole world wants to see and being tremendously successful at it. Comics still influence the style of filmmaking and the tone and if it just isn't a comic book adaptation, I think a lot of writers and directors have been inspired by the aesthetic of comics and it finds its way into films one way or another. I kind of feel at a loss that it's not something that I really liked when I was a kid. I think I like stuff more like Boris Karloff's *Thriller* or those kinds of creepy, eerie things.

The main driving aesthetic and period we're looking at for *The Fantastic Four* is basically the Jack Kirby era where we try to copy as closely as possible that look because we felt that was the definitive, classic period of that franchise. With the Thing we definitely had different drawings we had blown up and had around as inspiration. We tried to modernize it and make it a little bit more realistic and natural. The comics always tend to vary a little bit from panel to panel, so there's some room for interpretation. But with the Thing and Doctor Doom, Kirby was the era that we were really striving for and was our major source of inspiration.

Did you have any kind of rules or guidelines that were handed to you by Concorde or Oley or by any other people who said, "You have to do this. You can't do this. Make sure you do this?"

Mostly that you can't spend too much money *(laughs)*. There really wasn't any mandate that I can recall from the director or from anybody at Concorde as far as what we could and couldn't do or how we were to approach the work. There were probably some conversations that we thought Kirby was the way to go as far as the aesthetic. I think everybody pretty much was in agreement with that. The Jeweler was done outright from our own inspiration. There were some elements of the script that had a few details and told you what the character was like. We just generated a few sketches of what we were thinking the Jeweler could be like, went through a process, went back and forth, made a couple of changes, and got that settled. There was no real "you have to follow this." It was a little bit more of an organic process.

The early versions of the script called the character the Mole Man.

That sounds vaguely familiar. In the early drafts of the script — maybe even before we were hired — the original bad guy was going to be the Mole Man, but I think there was a rights issue that they couldn't resolve at that point, so that's why they decided to go the safe route and just create their own bad guy. I'm kind of surprised that Marvel didn't have any input on what kind of bad guy we would use. I think the way the rights and stipulations were dealt with was probably a little bit more lenient back then than now. We've worked on some projects recently with Marvel where they want to sign off on every little step of the way. Now they have a vast universe that they have to double-check everything against to make sure it's consistent. With the advent of the Internet you now have all these geeks really dissecting what belongs in what storyline and how you're deviating from the universe you've created, so I think Marvel is much more particular about how properties are deal with now than back when we were doing it.

You were in the early stages of your company and your career when you worked on *The Fantastic Four*, **but since you've moved on can you place** *The Fantastic Four* **and Roger Corman's way of making movies as compared to the rest of the industry now that you've seen other ways of making movies? Is there a Corman way to do things?**

This is one of the early experiences for our company so we were still kind of learning. We obviously worked for a lot of other people like Rick Baker, Greg Cannom, and Tom Savini. Everett and I worked for all of these other people throughout our career. We'd been exposed to a lot of different ways to do things. We'd worked on Charlie Band movies where you just did it quick and dirty. We worked on some bigger films like *The Lost Boys*, *Fat Man and Little Boy*, and *Hook* when I was at Greg Cannom's. You learn the big-budget way to do it and the low-budget way to do it. So when we first started our own company, obviously we're not jumping right into doing big films. We still have to earn our street cred with the executives. So you're typically doing small films for people like Fred Olen Ray and Roger Corman. We'd already been exposed to those kinds of workflows working for people like John Buechler who worked for Roger Corman at some point before we did. It wasn't really anything we didn't expect. I think we'd already had a good basis in reality for what to expect and how to manage this workflow on that kind of budget and make it work. It wasn't anything unusual for us.

We'd kind of shifted back forth between the low-budget studio world and the big-budget studio world. There's something to be said for both. Even when you're working on the best-funded and best-planned big-budget movie, at some point in the process something's going to come out of leftfield and you're going to have to do something overnight that normally would take a week to do just to make the schedule. So it's always good to have those tricks where you can cut the corners and do something quick and dirty even when you're doing something on a more established big-budget project. So this was all quick and dirty, basically. We had no problem shifting gears and doing it in that manner. I think the training we'd had working for a diverse group of shops prior to that really set that up and got us acclimated to the process pretty easily.

That's terrific. Do you remember any kind of fires you had to put out or emergencies that would come up during production where they're about to roll and, for example, Doom can't get the mask off or something is so bad you have to glue it together?

I'm sure it happened. I can't remember. Did any of the other people you interviewed mention an instance?

No. No. Not at all, really. No.

I'm hard-pressed to think of instances, but I'm sure there were. There's always something. What I may consider a tragedy someone else might be like, "Oh, so the elastic ripped on one of his fingers." There are always things that go wrong like servos not working properly. Let's say we're working the Thing and all of a sudden the eyebrow servo is not working because a cable snapped or the gears in a servo are stripped or a little wire popped out because the actor turned his head a certain way. You try to bulletproof that stuff the best you can, but there's just no way you can fix everything because we're ultimately making prototypes. It's not like a car you buy off the assembly line where the prototypes have been built and everything is set in stone. What we are making are things that are only meant to last a month or two at the most. They're not finished products. No matter how nicely you try to put it together, it's never going to be perfect. I'm sure there's instances where the eyebrow wasn't working on the Thing.

Our general strategy on set is just don't even draw attention to it. Don't let anybody know. Don't let the director know. Just work around it and try to hide it. Work everything else until you have the chance to go in there and fix it and play with it. That's pretty par for the course on any kind of film where you're doing mechanical effects. That's the area with the most issues.

We'd worked at Corman before on another film called *The Skateboard Kid* with remote-controlled skateboards that we had to work, and the skateboards were constantly being over-ridden by some other radio system that was in their vicinity. There was a Greyhound dispatch station across the street. I think the radio frequencies would take over the skateboard sometimes and crash it into a car. Hopefully, I wasn't crashing buses with my radio, but I don't know *(laughs)*. But those were all the difficulties working in Corman's place.

I don't remember any major difficulties. The suit tore a lot. The guy doing the suits figured all this stuff out before everybody else did. His thing was to go ahead and let the suit tear ahead of time. Like when you're in the shop, start tearing it up and then re-patch where it's going to tear because it's naturally going to tear there anyway.

What's it like working with Carl? Talk about Carl, his temperament, the work he put into sitting there, the frustration that actors sometimes have — I'm not saying he had any.

He didn't, actually. Carl comes from this background of being what the industry refers to as a "stunt grunt," which sounds kind of like a demeaning term, but it's not meant to be. It's a stuntman who also acts. I think as a stuntman, he's used to being in uncomfortable situations and even dangerous situations. We were just putting him in one of those two — uncomfortable. He was fine with it. I never once remember him complaining or saying anything about the suit, which could not possibly have been comfortable whatsoever. Normally, those kinds of suits are done in a foam latex, which is like a soft pliable material, kind of what you would encounter with makeup sponges. Because of the time constraints and budget and also that we weren't set up to do it, we had made it in a urethane foam like what mattresses are made out of. It's not as flexible or comfortable or as pliable as latex, so the suit was pretty stiff and probably not fun to be in and hot and sweaty and icky after a while.

He'd just kind of plod along and did what he was supposed to do and focused on his performance. It kind of seemed to me that he was having fun with it, actually. I think you can't not have fun playing the Thing. Even if it's a pain and uncomfortable, it's such an archetypal, fun kind of bad boy character. It's like the Hulk, these big creatures that can do whatever they want and destroy whatever they want. You can't not have the kid in you come out when you're inside that suit and have fun with it. I think whatever discomfort he may have experienced was kind of evened out by just having a chance to have fun with it and do all those crazy things.

Did you control the mouth servos in terms of mouthing the words from the script?

Us a crew or me individually?

As a crew.

The performance aspect of the Thing is really something that comes down to a combination of the actor and us, the makeup effects crew, because a lot of it is articulated by servos that are built inside of the head. Even the lips, the eye expression — all that is controlled by us. The actor has some part of the control. He's basically moving the jaw and opening the mouth and we're doing all the rest of the work. He's emoting with his eyes. Really, the eyes become a lot of what it's about when you're in that kind of a makeup. It's one of the few human parts that shows through on something that elaborate, so, if anything, more attention should be paid to the eyes in order to express what the characters has to express.

So in respect to how we would go about synching the performance up with the dialogue from the script, we generally don't spend a whole lot of time studying the script the way the actor would to get the performance down. A lot of that happens during the rehearsals. The actors are more in touch with the script than we are. He's actually speaking the line on set. They just get dubbed in later or modified sometimes with sound processing like pitch shifting or something like that to give it more resonance, but the actor is actually talking through the mask, so we'll just watch him, run the rehearsal two or three times, see what he's saying, what he's doing, and then that's when we start learning the parts and articulating them.

There's a certain benefit. On the one hand, it might seem lazy that we're not studying the parts ahead of time and trying

The face of the Thing. PHOTO COURTESY OF EVERETT BURRELL

to remember it and go through that, but also there's usually three or four of us working the character's face. For all of us to interpret the performance the same way is a little difficult to do in advance. There's something to be said for making it be organic and spontaneous. We'll just watch the actor run through it two or three times, and then we'll all figure out what to do. You're moving the lips to match the words as best you can. If someone's doing the eyes, maybe the eyes are going to be sympathetic or angry. That usually comes through in the rehearsal. You realize what emotion the character should be showing and adjust the eyebrows that way. It's more of an organic process. It's not as thought out. In some respects it might be even more difficult to think it through too much ahead of time.

In general, I think even without makeup effects the real hallmark of a good acting performance is for it to be spontaneous and in the moment anyway. It shouldn't look rehearsed. If you magnify that times four or five people, it's going to get that much more complicated, so it's not as thought out as you would probably think it was, at least for us. I don't how other companies would do it, but for us it was just all on the set and in the moment.

What were your hopes for the movie? I'm sure you wanted a theatrical release.

This was very early on in our career with our company, so we were very excited to be part of a film like this. Of course, we were hoping it would be a theatrical film or something elaborate that would promote our work.

Very early on we became aware that the film was never really intended to be a film per se. It had a lot more to do with retaining the rights to the movie. He had a certain deadline by the end of that year that if he hadn't produced the film, that the rights revert back to Marvel. But if he had shot something, he would continue to hold onto the rights for another window after that.

There was a German company called Constantin Film. They were Neue Constantin at the time. They're Constantin Film now. They had the rights. They hired Roger to make the movie and either there was a clause in the contract that they could buy him out at any point or someone — Constantin,

Fox, Marvel — made an offer to Roger to buy the film from him and he agreed. They needed to go into production by December 31.

So he was just fulfilling services for them more than anything.

Exactly.

We were very excited to be a part of this film, obviously. We had this fledgling company that was just starting off, so we were hoping *The Fantastic Four* would be this great, big theatrical film that everybody would see. It would help promote our company and we would be proud to be a part of it. It became very apparent early on that something else was going on with this movie. We weren't just there making a film. We had started to hear little rumors and get word that the company that owned the rights, Constantin, was more interested in retaining the rights to the property than they were in making a film, so they contracted Roger to make this movie at that last minute.

I don't think they cared so much about the film or the quality of it as long as they were able to produce something by a certain deadline that extended their rights on the project. I think they were more interested in selling it to a bigger studio who at that time were starting to indicate that they were interested in making the film. The money that the studio would have paid for the rights was probably a more lucrative deal than even producing a small film like this and distributing it could have generated for him. We started hearing this at some point, maybe halfway through the film. That made us a little disappointed that there was something else going on than just trying to make a neat movie. It kind of explained a lot of the strange things that seemed like they were going on or why our budgets were getting cut here and there, why people didn't care about certain things. I think it was kind of obvious that the movie may not ever be released, ultimately. Somewhere through there we started getting that feel. We didn't to be a part or something that was nothing more than someone's contractual obligation, which is not what we're there for. We're there to do cool work that we want the fans to see, that we want to resonate with the fan community, and that we are proud of.

We're building a timeline and there are critical things we are hitting. Was it during principal photography that you started to hear these rumors swirling?

Yeah, I don't know. Somebody knew at some point.

Exactly. It depends on who we're talking to.

When are other people saying they were aware of it?

Some have said toward the end of production and some are saying months and months after.

I think towards the end of production. We were trying to get a friend of ours, Kevin Kutchaver, involved in the digital effects but they decide to hire Scott Billups. It was around that point... Actually, it was probably more towards the post-production end when we started hearing little rumors. If I remember correctly, Scott had done some work that wasn't quite finished work. It was more like animatics, like a morph that might just be done off a still to show you a demo of what the morph might look like. To me, that's more like temporary work. He's trying to get the director and producer to sign off. "Yeah, that's the right way to do it. Let's go do a full-motion morph." I think Scott wasn't budgeted or set up to do the stuff to that level of quality they were expecting.

It's almost like they wanted to give the *illusion* that we're doing a movie, not that they really wanted to do a film.

That actually does back up something that's been talked about in terms of Billups.

Did you get to talk to Scott?

Not Scott. We talked to Oley and he was talking about post-production.

It gets presented in different ways. Some people were saying that Scott pulled a fast one on Corman and never told him that he was just doing temporary work, that it was going to be demos, and he would have to be paid more. There is also the perception that he never warned them that he was just doing temporary stuff. Did you try to get Scott?

I did reach out to him a number of times.

He didn't want to be a part of it?

No.

I think there's some controversy as to what he was...Is that the way Oley presented it?

Yes.

That Scott may have pulled a fast one on them?
Yeah.

Yeah. Like, "Oh, you didn't pay me to do full shots. You just paid me to do animatics." Something like that?
Yeah.

And they're saying, "No, no. We paid you to do the full shots." "Well, I don't have the budget to do it. Sorry. This is all you get."

There's an ulterior motive to making the film as far as holding onto or extending the rights, but at the same time it still would have been nice to do a film that stands up and is finished. At this point, the film kind of comes off as a rough cut. It feels like it's two-thirds finished. It's not the greatest film in the world, but we all tried our best to do what we could with the resources we had. We didn't have a $100 million to do it. It's not fair to judge that film against a $100 or $150 million version of it like the ones that came later. I'm not always the proudest of everything we did in it, but I'm proud that we did it. I'm sure that everyone else that was involved in it feels that way. It's disappointing that it wasn't finished the way it could have been finished. With just a little bit more effort, a little bit more money, I think we could have had something like a cute TV movie. Unless some fan gets in there and tries to spruce it up a little bit, this is the only form it's going to be seen in.

At some point you saw the movie. Was it as a fan? From a bootleg? Or was it...

(*Laughs*) This is horrible. I've seen the film, but probably not all of it. I've scanned through it. I don't know that I had the heart to really sit there and watch it. I'm sure that I will someday. It's freely available on the Internet or as a fan bootleg at a convention. It's really the only way you're going to get it. I don't know if it's piracy if it's not available. I saw it through the usual methods like that. I was wincing a little bit. Again, I was disappointed. For better or worse, we all knew we weren't doing a huge studio movie. Oley was really trying to do the best he could do and we were trying to support him and take it seriously. It was an uphill battle to try to make it as good as we wanted it to be, so we really put our heart into it. Whether it's a little $100,000 film or a $100 million film, we still put all out heart into it because we have a passion for what we do. It's heartbreaking when you know that with just a little bit of effort it's not going to be a great film but at least it'd be a finished movie. It was apparent that it was a rough cut, and that's all it was ever gonna be.

Mark Parry
Director of Photography

Please tell us what you did as cinematographer for the film.

My job as cinematographer was to conceive and realize the photographic look for the film. The first steps were reading the script and talking with the director about the ideas he had about how the film should look. Then, I supervised the camera and lighting work on the set, as well as operating the camera. Once the film was shot, I was involved in color grading the film to refine the look and make all the shots match seamlessly for the final print. And yes, this is before digital, so all of the work was done on film.

How did you start working for Roger Corman?

For the first movie that I ever worked on at Corman, I was a grip. A friend of mine called me. "Hey, I'm working over at Corman (Concorde/New Horizons). They need a grip. Wanna come on?" I said, "Absolutely!" I was so excited to be working on a "real" movie. I think I worked sixteen or eighteen hours that day. I had to buy my own lunch, and buy my own dinner. I think my rate for the day was a flat rate of $40 or $45. After buying my meals, I just about ended up owing money because I did that job. Where else can you work eighteen hours in one day and have to pay for your own lunch?

In those days Corman typically would release a movie into the theaters or just one theater for a week or so to give it theatrical legitimacy, and then it went straight to video. But *The Fantastic Four* was different. It was getting more resources. There was a lot of buzz at Corman about it at that time. By the time *The Fantastic Four* came around, I had shot three or four features for Concorde.

Please talk about working with Oley Sassone.

I hadn't worked with Oley before *The Fantastic Four* and I don't really remember how I got the film, but I met with him and we got along. I liked Oley's style and his personality. He had a bigger than life presence. We had a very similar sense of what the movie should look like. We talked about the comic books, the graphic style, and how we would translate that sensibility into a live-action picture. There were some elements that we borrowed from comic books and other elements that we did not. Working with Oley was great.

What was the feeling around the set during filming?

Everybody was pretty excited because of this crazy Marvel thing. We all knew it was a big deal. Nobody knew anything about the fact that it just being made as kind of a way to hold onto the production rights, so everybody was sinking their heart and soul into this project. That's what made it so heartbreaking a year and a half later when we found out that it was being shelved. I think everybody thought that this might be the thing that would put us on the map. There were a lot of high hopes.

When did you start shooting? How long did you have?

We went into production around December 28. It was incredibly late in the year. Usually, there's nothing that happens around that time. Hollywood shuts down. Getting a movie that starts on one of the last days of the year was odd, but we went with it. For a Corman movie, it was a long schedule. I think we had something like twenty-two or twenty-four days. When you come from making movies in the fifteen to eighteen-day range, twenty-four days seems like "Wow! What will we do with all this time?" We were able to have bigger setups and we went on location whereas most of the Corman movies were shot at the studio.

What do you remember about locations?

We shot quite a few scenes on the campus of Loyola Marymount University. We were there for several days. We took over a science lab for Doctor Doom and Reed's laboratory. We also shot some exteriors there. That whole scene where people are looking up at the sky at the Colossus effect was done out on the big lawn there. There was an old house in the Los Angeles Crenshaw district that we shot in as well as the old Stock Exchange building downtown.

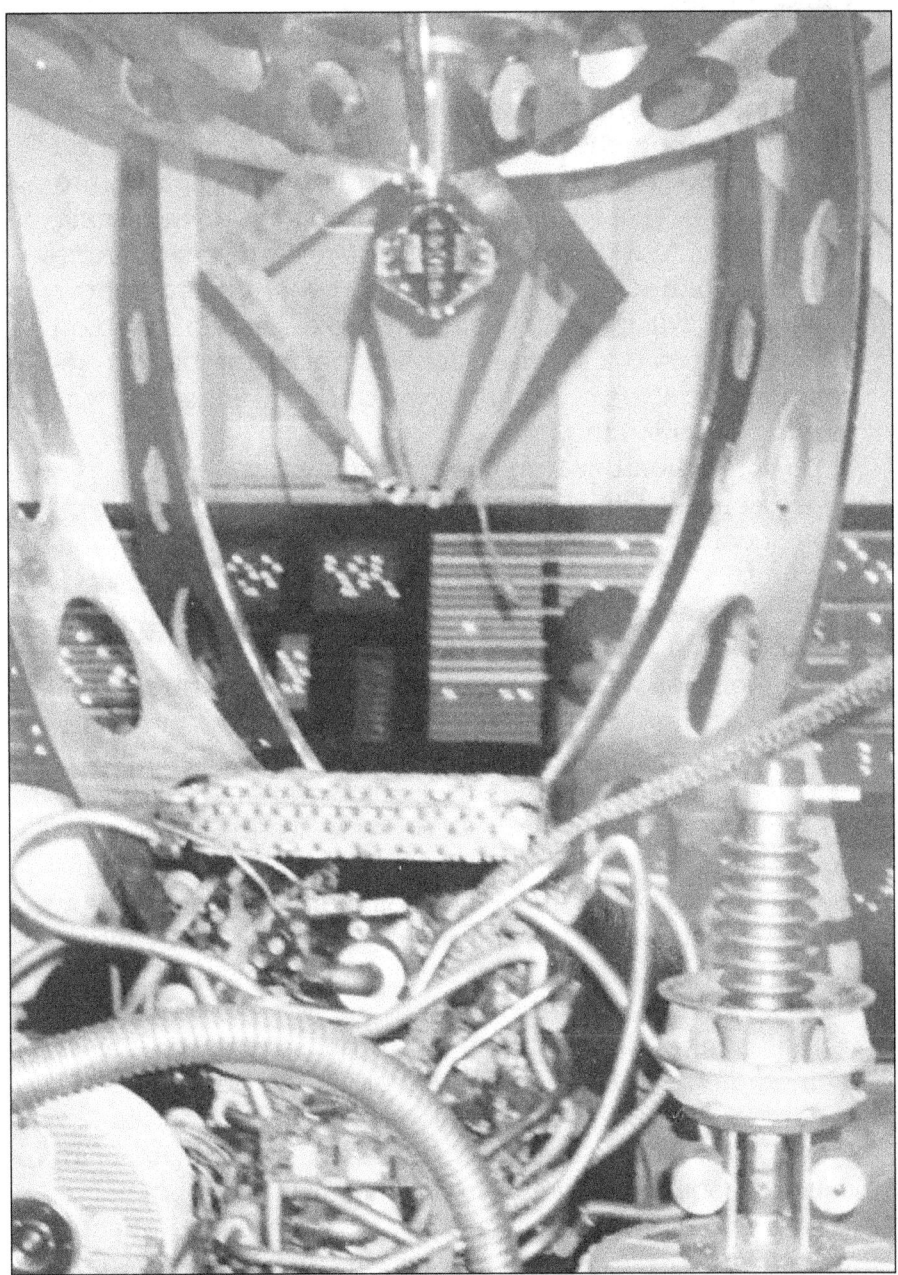

Another angle of the machine Reed and Victor build to channel Colossus' energy. PHOTO COURTESY OF MICK STRAWN

And, of course, there were several scenes shot on Corman's Venice stages.

How were things in terms of equipment and physical resources?

We made the most of what we had, which wasn't a lot, but we had more than the usual Corman package. We had some older Arriflex cameras and a lighting truck from a rental house. There were various numbers thrown around in terms of actual budget, but it was more than your average Concorde film. That said, it was still a very limited-budget movie. Regardless, I was excited to make a movie based on a known piece of material. This was before the big Marvel comic book movie era, but there was a sense that this was the start of something.

Do you remember Stan Lee visiting the set?

I remember when Stan Lee came on the set. That was pretty cool. That was another thing that made us think this film must be real: Stan Lee is on the set to visit us!

Do you recall if there were any opinions of the film footage?

I remember we were on the set and I had one of the representatives from FotoKem — we were sending our negative to be processed and printed there — and the rep was like, "Mark, everybody at the lab is looking at your footage and they're loving the way it looks. It looks great!" We went through the whole production and editing process, then I did the timing of the film. Timing is the process where you make adjustments to the color and brightness of the image before a film is printed. I was really pleased with the result. The expectation was always that this was the movie that would springboard me into the next phase of my career as a cinematographer and push me up into larger budgets.

Very few people ever saw the finished movie on film, or even a decent video transfer. Yes, there's a video on the Web, but it's a bootleg transfer from a print, not the original negative, so the image quality is pretty awful. Anytime anyone ever says, "Oh yeah, I *saw* that on YouTube. You worked on that?" I cringe. Photographically, it looks very different from what the actual movie looked like. Like I said, we finished on film in those days. It was a good-looking movie. Certainly, for me at that time, it was the best work I had done, so I was excited. Then, I had heard Corman was going to do a premiere out in...

The Mall of America.

I have a copy of The Hollywood Reporter from February 22, 1993, that says on the cover "The Fantastic Four" and has Constantin Film down at the bottom. All of the signs were pointing to this movie coming out in theaters. It was a week before the premiere was scheduled that I got the word from Oley that they had pulled the plug and the film would be shelved. That's when we learned that the whole thing was really a sham.

I think The Fantastic Four became this bit of Hollywood lore. I mention it to students now and they say, "What? You shot that? Ah man, that's awesome!" Anybody who watches it now is going to think, "God, this looks pretty hokey. It doesn't look anything like what a Marvel movie should look like." By today's standard, they are absolutely right. By 1992's standard we were still a very low-budget movie without a lot of money for physical effects, visual effects, or production equipment, so I think what we were able to accomplish was notable.

Did anyone tell you how much of the film needed to be completed, or was the assumption that all of it needed to be shot all the way through?

No. There was no inkling at all, at least in my mind. We went through the entire process of making the film. The final step was doing the color timing of the picture. Oley and I worked together on that, so, at least as far as I could see, there wasn't any indication that there was something else needed.

Do you think that he had high hopes for the movie also and that maybe he thought this was a way to get back to theatrical releases?

It's one of those things where I didn't any kind of sense from anyone on the production team that there was some kind of alternate intention with this movie. I don't think that Oley knew. I just expected that it was going to come out in theaters. With Corman you never knew. You made a movie and then... it went where it went. I didn't have any idea who made that decision. I figured it was Roger Corman himself.

I've wondered if the "premiere" was a way for Roger Corman to build a bit of leverage. He made the movie and jumped through all the hoops of making it look like he was taking it out to make something of it. Perhaps that way he could make more money.

Did Corman expect to take this out into theaters or was it a work for hire?

I think the impression most people had is that it was a big deal, a big opportunity for everyone, and that it was going to be released. Corman was preparing for the movie's release. He had some stills made. There was a poster. A couple of the actors were doing promotional work on their own time and out of their own pockets.

A film set is like a little family. Most of the people that you know you've worked with before. Certainly, many of my crew were people that I had worked with before. Anybody gets some kind of hint of something and everybody knows pretty darn quickly. Now, that doesn't necessarily hold true for people that are on the producer end of things. They may have been holding some cards that we never knew about. I never had *any* kind of sense that this was going to eventually get shelved. We started the end of 1992. By early 1993 we had shot the whole movie. There never talk of stopping it at any point.

Oley is passionate about his work, so I would be surprised if he knew while we were shooting that there were plans to shelve the film. He was excited about making the movie. I was too. We made a good team.

I think there was the feeling that resources were being pulled away at the very end, but people weren't sure why.

In terms of the editing of the picture, I went on to that next film with Oley. I didn't really keep track of what was happening with *The Fantastic Four*. Glenn Garland, the editor, was a friend of mine from film school, but I was on to my next project, so I didn't know how it was coming. After all of that time I remember getting the call from Oley telling me they pulled it and he didn't think anybody was going to see the movie, ever.

It's funny now because there have been calls to see the movie, but I have some mixed feelings about that. In 1993, when it should have come out, I was extremely excited because it kinda worked. Now, it really shows its age. It would be great to actually see it in the form it was intended to be viewed in, but in terms of a movie experience I fear that there would probably be some laughs.

So you think too much time has gone by?

Well…for the budget level we shot on some decent sets and good locations, but there are some things where you can see the lack of resources. It certainly doesn't have anywhere near the same kind of production value of any other Marvel movie. It wasn't possible for us to do that with our resources. For that time, for that budget, we did a great job.

Do you have memories of Roger Corman?

Yes, I was on the set the first week of my first movie for Roger Corman. A friend of mine that I went to film school with was the director. When we were in film school, we did a lot of work with the dolly and moving the camera to make engaging shots. We had every intention going into this movie — which was a space-alien-monster-kills-everyone kind of movie — of moving the camera a lot. In one of the first production meetings, the production manager says, "Okay, now, I just gotta tell you. I know you guys like using the dolly, but you can't have dolly track. Roger doesn't want to pay to rent it." We said, "Well, okay, so what do we do? We can't have moving shots?" He says, "No, no, no. Dolly shots are fine. What we do is put down some plywood and that makes a smooth surface for the dolly." It seemed odd, but we went with it. This was our first feature, so who were we to question it?

Then, during the first week of production, we heard that Roger was coming to the set. This was maybe day number three of the shoot. So we're doing this shot and using the dolly to move the camera in on Marc Singer's face when he learns there's something really wrong at the space outpost he's at. We didn't have the dolly track, just some sheets of plywood on the floor. The floors of the warehouses at the studio were really rough, so you couldn't run the dolly over them. We're doing the shot without the dolly track and thinking Roger is going to be really happy. He comes in, watches us do the shot, and leaves within a few minutes. Later in the day, word comes back that Roger's one comment was "You know, they were doing that dolly shot and they really don't need to take time to use the plywood. Just put the dolly straight on the floor."

That was my initial interaction with Roger, which made it pretty obvious that some of the technical quality that most of us were concerned with were not what was important to him. He had a way of churning out movies very quickly; his studio was kind of a machine. I did several movies that were eighteen day schedules. You're shooting five, six pages a day very quickly. I was able to make the camera and lighting look interesting in a way that maybe some other people couldn't, so the movies ended up having compelling visuals. But in terms of some of those other things it wasn't a big deal to him if they were right or not.

So perhaps he felt that the best film was a finished film, not necessarily a perfect film?

Exactly. Get through production. Get the movie done. It was a manufacturing process. He was manufacturing movies and he had figured out that if he could makes these movies for X amount of dollars, he makes this much profit because he has a market for them. If they cost any more than X amount, that's money just wasted. I came from an aesthetic and artistic background, so I was most concerned with how things looked. It was hard for me when I had to come to terms with Corman's unabashed sense of capitalism *(laughs)*. We're making a movie? Let's just get it done.

Instead of three weeks for *The Fantastic Four*, we had four weeks. That was something that convinced me that it was different. It ended up different, all right.

No release was certainly different.

Right *(laughs)*. We were all looking for that next thing, that next level. My hope was that *The Fantastic Four* was going be that project. It wasn't. It was disheartening.

It was, at the time, a really thrilling experience. I really enjoyed working with Oley and the entire crew.

David Wurst
Music, Orchestrator

Eric Wurst
Music, Conductor/Orchestrator

What instructions were you given for developing the soundtrack?

We spotted all the places for music with the director, Oley Sassone. Oley was very specific about where he wanted the score and the kind of music it should be. After a lot of discussion with Oley we decided that we would create themes for all the various characters, basically a *Star Wars* approach.

The story is you pitched in $6,000 of your own money to hire a forty-eight-piece orchestra. Why? Please discuss that experience.

Well, the music budget was quite low. However, the film cried out for a big adventure score. Oley certainly hoped for something epic, but we all realized the limitations of the money available. So, the two of us put our heads together and tried to map out the requirements of the score, along with what we thought the scale of each music cue ought to be. We decided to use orchestra for the bigger moments and to write that music in a way so that it could be used in multiple scenes within the film. The remainder of the score we created in our home studio.

In those days we were just starting out and really needed the money, but keeping the money would have meant an all-synth score, which we knew wasn't going to give us the sound we wanted. Also, we were hoping the film would turn into a calling card for us, so we decided to bite the bullet by putting all of our composer's fee and more into recording an orchestra. Eventually we recorded about eighteen to twenty minutes of score with about forty musicians at Capitol Records Studio A in Hollywood.

People have made comparisons between your soundtrack and the work of James Horner. Do you see that connection? Was he a reference?

The Fantastic Four had been temped with — among other things — some of James Horner's music from *Battle Beyond the Stars*, which was an earlier Roger Corman film. In fact, if you find the trailer for *The Fantastic Four* you can hear Horner's music. Anyway, it's obviously flattering to be compared with Horner. He had a great gift for capturing emotion, but we weren't specifically trying to emulate him.

Did you have any specific references or models in mind?

We all wanted *The Fantastic Four* music to be heroic. The only well-known superhero music at the time was Williams' *Superman* and Elfman's *Batman*, but *The Fantastic Four* characters aren't dark like Batman, so the models were more John Williams and Jerry Goldsmith. We loved Goldsmith's and Horner's *Star Trek* music. The opening titles in *The Fantastic Four* were set over space images, so there's some of that space-adventure sound in there.

Please tell us about the process of making the soundtrack.

Well, the two of us each set out creating various themes and motives for the characters and situations in the film. That took some time, and we eventually ended up with many different ideas. We then chose the ones we thought were working the best and sat down with Oley and went through what we had come up with. Right from the start he was a big fan of the main fanfare theme we presented, so we knew we were on the right track.

What challenges did you encounter while creating the soundtrack?

Time and money are always factors. On *The Fantastic Four* we had an abundance of neither. Since there was no budget for support, we had to do all the jobs ourselves. We had to write the score, orchestrate it, copy all the individual parts for the recording session, perform the remaining 60% of the score that wasn't played by the orchestra, book the studio and the musicians, and create all the final hybrid mixes. We didn't get a lot of sleep.

Did you fulfill your vision for the soundtrack? If not, what would you liked to have added and/or edited?

We always wish we had more time and money to perfect things. Because of the limited time we had in the recording studio, every take had spots with performance problems. We were able to edit and mix the various takes together with MIDI to create a hybrid that turned out pretty well considering.

How is scoring a film different now than it was twenty-five years ago? If you had to make that same soundtrack now, how different would the process be?

The technology has changed tremendously. The digital audio workstations we use today along with sampling technology allow us much more flexibility in terms of creating orchestral emulations and editing hybrid scores. We still have to come up with the music though. That hasn't gotten any easier.

Steve Cohn, Paul Di Franco, Marlena Morton, and Odette Springer were all members of the music department. Any recollections of them?

Steve Cohn was a great music engineer we worked with on several of our early scores. He was responsible for the final music mix used in the film. Paul DiFranco was the music supervisor for Roger Corman's production companies. He's a real music guy and was always a kick to work with. We were pushing pretty hard to get on board *The Fantastic Four* and Paul connected us with Oley early in the process. We remember meeting Oley for the first time in Paul's office. We mentioned we had been listening to composer Carl Stalling's music for *Looney Tunes* in the car on the way to the meeting. Oley burst out with "I was just listening to that myself!" That kind of helped seal the deal.

What's the division of work between the two of you? Do you each have your separate area, is everything done collaboratively, or is it a mixture?

We generally come up with musical ideas separately, and then we bounce them off of each other. Once we decide on the best approach, we divide up the various musical cues and create them individually. We always play the things we've written for each other as we go along to make sure we're both on the same track.

We can see examples of musical brothers that cannot get along such as Oasis and the Black Crowes. How have you two managed to hold it together for all of this time? How do you resolve conflicts or differences of opinion?

We've been working together in music since we were kids and have a lot of mutual respect for each other. We've also learned over the years that no musical idea is so important that we need to fight over it. Actually, being able to rely upon one another when things get crazy is often a big relief.

Looking back at the movie, what do you think of it and your work on it?

All things considered, we're happy with our contribution to the film. Everyone involved faced a myriad of challenges. We feel we held up our end the best we could. The film has had an interesting afterlife and we've gotten a lot of positive feedback on it over the years, which has been gratifying.

If you had known that the movie was not going to be released, would you have still taken the job? Why or why not?

The answer is YES. We would have taken the job for two reasons. First, we were just getting started. Second, we wanted to write something great that people might find inspiring. We got that chance because we said yes instead of no. Scoring *The Fantastic Four* gave us so much. We got to work with some great people on a truly exciting and challenging project. We learned early in our careers that we could handle a lot of pressure and come out OK. And we're certainly glad to have written the music we did. Without the film, that music wouldn't exist.

That last point is probably the most important thing we can share. When you're just starting out as a film composer, COMPOSE. Try not to obsess about money or scoring the perfect film so much that you miss out on an opportunity. Compose all you can, whenever you can, with whomever you can.

The Fantastic Four was your first superhero movie, but certainly not your last. How did all of these other Marvel and DC projects come about?

We had the good fortune to write the score for Marvel Super Heroes 4D which is a great attraction that has been playing at Madame Tussauds locations around the world for nearly ten years. That led to many more Marvel and DC films for both TV and theme parks. We've been able to work on great projects featuring *The Avengers, Justice League, Guardians of the Galaxy, Batman, LEGO Hero Factory, Black Panther,* and more.

Right now we're about halfway through what may be our busiest year of scoring ever with six films in the can and five films in various stages of production.

Oley Sassone
Director

How did you find your way to *The Fantastic Four*?
I had already directed two good films for Roger Corman on time and on budget, so I was in the stable, so to speak. He trusted me.
Tell us about those films.
One film was *Bloodfist III: Forced to Fight* with Richard Roundtree AKA "Shaft," who really elevated everyone around him with his presence and professionalism and Don "The Dragon" Wilson. It was written by an ex-con who had spent eight years in prison. It was a really good script. The good thing about that film was when you're shooting a movie with no money, you have a limited location so you're not spending a lot of money moving the circus to various locations. You just kind of get a better product because you can use the money and time for other things. We had a shot at making the film really good because we didn't have to break anything down. We could just leave everything at the Lincoln Heights Jail, walk in the next day, and go right to work. All the time was spent shooting the film. It got a good write up at *Variety*. Getting a good review on a Roger Corman movie at *Variety* was kind of unheard of. The other film was *Final Embrace*, a fun film. Dick Van Patten was a street guy from Brooklyn. He played a grizzly detective, a Columbo-type. He was another real professional. I loved working with that guy.
Then what happened?
After that Roger Corman just called me out of the blue and said, "Oley, we're going to do a movie about the Fantastic Four, and I'd like for you to direct the film. Are you interested?" "Hell yes." I was a big Marvel comic book fan. Spider-Man was my favorite character as a kid, but I loved the Fantastic Four. I

knew there was no money for this film, but it didn't matter. It was the Fantastic Four and I was a hell of a lot younger at the time.

What recollections do you have about making The Fantastic Four**?**

I knew it was a challenge. The script was really faithful to the characters and the backstory of how the Fantastic Four became the Fantastic Four. Most people like the Marvel Universe because the characters are ordinary people; they didn't come from another planet. That's why I identified with Marvel characters more than DC comic book characters. They get bit by a spider or exposed to cosmic rays and now they are regular people with extraordinary powers, but in their heart and soul they are still a normal person. They're still that guy or that woman.

The first thing I did was go to Golden Apple Comics, bought a dozen of the reproductions of Fantastic Four #1, handed them out to everybody, and said, "This is what we need to do. We need to look at this like we're working on a film based in the 1960s." They had all the Fantastic Four comics hardbound like an encyclopedia, so I bought every one of those for research. I read every single one and marked pages with sticky notes.

Although we had a really difficult time with the schedule, the actors, the crew, the production designer — all the people I worked with — were totally into doing this film and trying to make the best film we possibly could. That's one of my best recollections about it.

Looking back I'm glad I got the call to do the movie.

Was anyone a problem?

The one bad apple was the guy we hired to do our special effects, Scott Billups. That guy was full of shit. He claimed he could do all this great CGI, and, of course, he couldn't deliver anything; he didn't know what he was doing. We had something like $15,000 to do all the visual effects and he took all of it. Today, they spend a million plus, sometimes more like three to five million. I had to scramble after we had finished the film and I saw the visual effects he was turning in, which were really bad. I went to a company called Mr. Film that we found in Santa Monica to try to save the movie as best we could. I don't think they charged anybody. They may have gotten a few hundred bucks. They just got into it. Everybody got into this movie because it was the Fantastic Four. They wanted to do something really great. It's the first time I really had that experience in Los Angeles and the last time, really.

Tell me a little bit about the soundtrack.

The Wurst brothers, David and Eric, did a fabulous job with the music. They spent money out of their own pocket. We rented the studio where Frank Sinatra recorded at Capitol Records on Vine Street. They hired a forty-eight-piece orchestra. The soundtrack is very James Horner-esque. They did a brilliant job with it.

What was co-executive producer Roger Corman's role?

We shot at his studio in Venice with his equipment, his old cameras, his stage. It was his production company, his production services. It's a one-stop shop, real quick, down and dirty, get it done. Roger cranked out all of his movies like that for years. He would shoot his films in ten days, fifteen days, twenty days, whatever. He was known for doing those kinds of films. His studio was an obvious choice. It's where we built the sets, though we did some location work. For example, we shot somewhere in some hills outside of Los Angeles.

Any encounters with Roger Corman or memories related to him?

You'd shoot for a couple of days and Roger would look at the dailies. Roger was a filmmaker; he'd look at the footage and know immediately if you knew what you were doing or if you needed some guidance. Once you passed the dailies test, he'd leave you alone. Every now and again he'd walk by the set and just take a look. As long as you got everything shot according to the schedule, made your day, and had the film cut together, you were okay. He's a good guy. I really loved working for Roger and I really like him as a person. He not only helped so many people in this business, but he also had the right attitude about the whole creative process. When he trusted you to make a film for him, you made the film. He was really good.

He was hired by Constantin Film to make this movie. They went to the king of the B-movies. He had a reputation for getting films done on a shoestring, and that's exactly what Constantin Film wanted to do. They knew he could get it done.

They just wanted to get something shot out so that they could satisfy the contractual obligation to Marvel. Unfortunately, nobody told us that.

What challenges or limitations did you experience while making the film?

We didn't have a pot to piss in. We were shooting with old Arri 35 mm BL cameras.

Roger never bought a new roll of film that I can remember. Every piece of film was shortends and recans, so none of the emulsion numbers matched. It was a nightmare for the guys at the lab to do all the color correction. They did beautifully at the end of the day considering that within one scene we'd cut from one shot to the next, and one was green, and one was blue, and one was yellow. They did a fabulous job of pulling it all together.

We didn't have a budget to do something like Tim Burton's *Batman* with these incredible sets and the big, wide set of Gotham. It was a gothic sort of Gotham, dark and scary at night. He left a lot to your imagination with the way it was angular and German expressionistic. Your imagination filled in the spaces of the shadows. We knew we were not going to have the money, the budget to do anything that spectacular. Instead, we built sets suggestive of larger and deeper things. The sets were designed and built by Mick Strawn. All original and very imaginative for the space we were shooting in. The costumes were designed and made by Reve Richards and the Doom costume and the Thing were accurate replicas from the comic books and meticulously made by John Vulich who went on to *The X-Files* and *Buffy the Vampire Slayer* and Everett Burrell worked on projects like *Pan's Labyrinth* and *Altered Carbon*.

We had a difficult time with the schedule and trying to get everything done. Some of these days were eighteen hours. Every shooting day was an average of thirteen/fourteen hours over six-day weeks. We only had around eighteen days to finish the film.

We worked really hard on this one. As difficult as it was making the film, it was a lot of fun.

Do you remember what date you started shooting? Different sources say different things.

I don't. Somewhere I saw a call sheet. It might be in the *Doomed* documentary. The schedule got so screwed up. All of a sudden we pushed the call because we had gone over and we had to have turnaround for the actors because there was SAG. When we started shooting the movie, the call time was seven in the morning. By the time we finished, the call times were two in the afternoon. We'd be shooting all night.

There is a report that Carl and you had a conversation during filming in which you told him you thought that the film might not come out. Do you recall this?

I cannot recall saying the film may not come out during the actual shooting. My focus and that of the cast and crew was on just making the days. It was frantic, to say the least.

At what point did you know or have reason to suspect that the movie wasn't coming out?

My first recollection of feeling something was awry, was during post-production when we couldn't get all of the elements we needed out of the lab to finish editing the picture. It had become even more evident when I wanted to shoot another scene with the Thing running through the streets of Los Angeles like the Elephant Man. We had to beg for a couple rolls of film and the Arri 2C camera. We were well out of production at this time, so Mark Sikes volunteered to put on the heavy rubber Thing costume for us. I picked Vine Street near the Capitol Records Building because it was brightly lit by street lights. We had no lights or crew. I got set up with the camera on the street. We put Mark in a van that pulled up to a red light at an intersection with a lot of additional headlights from cars. He jumped out and took off across the intersection and I got the shot. We then did a shot of the Thing approaching two girls on the street, no sound, so it was dubbed later. Of course, what I had envisioned could not match the powerful scene I was trying to replicate in *The Elephant Man*, but we accomplished my intention and the scene is in the film. In spite of our frustration, we were not going to be deterred from finishing this movie.

Why was the film never released?

They didn't want to damage the franchise. Marvel and Constantin had high hopes for creating this massive franchise, and they thought this little film would have damaged that opportunity. They're probably right. You can't go out half-assed with a low-budget version and expect people to come see another one. They wanted to come out big and they came out big with the 2005 version, but it wasn't that good. The 1994 film was never intended to be released. Constantin's intention was always to maintain the rights. They had a deal with Marvel that they had to finish the film before a certain date or they lost the film rights. It had nothing to do with us.

Do you think Roger Corman planned to release it?

Once Roger saw a finished film, he saw an opportunity. Roger's a smart dude. He realized this film is pretty good and he had a plan for releasing it because there was nothing in the contract that said he couldn't — I guess they all had a handshake deal, a verbal understanding, that they would just knock the film out and then get rid of it. He had a trailer cut that was running in theaters. Roger had every intention of releasing the film. Constantin Film paid him, the rumor is, another million or a million and a half dollars not to release the movie and to hand over the negative. Hey, I don't blame him. He called me directly on my old Motorola flip phone while I was driving on San Vicente Boulevard in Los Angeles to tell me they weren't going to release the film that he just made a deal and got paid a lot of money not to release the movie, and he thanked me for making a good film. I waited to see if he was going to offer anything, but that was it; no check for me, the actors, or the crew. Nothing. Zip. After that, Bernd Eichinger had me up to his house in Beverly Hills to explain the whole situation and he put in a good word for a project I did in Prague that was a really great experience.

How big did you think the film was going to be?

You make a low-budget movie, it breaks out, and makes a lot of money, then it's a boost to your career. Who knows where we would have ended up had the film been released. It may have flopped. At the same time, this thing was getting a buzz. Michael and Alex Hyde-White spent money out of their own pockets promoting it. They were going to comic book conventions and doing promotional touring to build up the release. We cut a five minute trailer. The line at the convention to see it was around the block. They had to run it as a loop because, literally, thousands of people were streaming into the screening room.

They made the movie for $2 million or under. If it had been released, most likely it would have made about ten million bucks. Then, we're heroes. Hollywood recognizes you if you make a good movie, but they really recognize you if your movie makes a lot of money. That's how you get a job. From an executive point of view, you made this movie for nothing, it appealed to a lot of people, and it made multiple times what it cost to produce it, so come make a movie for us.

Because the movie was never released, that opportunity wasn't a possibility. My understanding is people got paid, but it was modest. However, there would be none of the possibilities a film — especially a comic book film — might generate: no residuals, no merchandising, no exposure, no next job because of what someone saw you did with this film, no possibility of a sequel with a bigger budget or more money for everyone.

It's a shame. We thought maybe we could get a shot at doing something bigger and better, but it never happened. We were all just kind of thrown away with the film.

What did you learn from working on The Fantastic Four?

I learned not to trust executives *(laughs)*.

If you can get everybody on the same page from the get-go, then you've got a better shot at coming out with a good product. In all the other shows I've done where I've had actors, lead actors, badmouthing the script in front of everybody, I would ask them to step off the set. I'd ask, "Why are you doing that?" They'd say, "Well, I think the script sucks." I'd look them right in the eye and explain, "You're the lead actor. Guess what? Every day player and every other actor here looks up to you. You start badmouthing this material then everybody else is gonna think the script sucks. And then we've got nothing. And then the whole thing goes to shit." I'd say, "Let's figure it out. If you've got a problem with the script, let's wait and get the executive producers down here at lunchtime. You guys can go off and have a script session. As a director I have a contract that says I deliver what's on the script as written. Period. I can't change a word."

You can't hesitate when you make a decision on a set. You have to know what you want. Everybody looks up to you — you're the director. Also, I learned to listen. Listen to people. Listen to everybody. The best idea wins. You never know where the best idea is going to come from. You have to trust the people around you. It's a collaborative effort; one person can't do it all. You have your vision, but you have to be open in the moment. I try to get everything done in prep and pre-production, but there are always logistical things that come up later. Some things just happen in the moment and you can't figure them out until then.

I learned that everything you make in a film is incremental. Everything is precise. A camera moves an inch or two to the right or the left. An actor moves from this side of the room to that side of the room and gives a look in a close-up to the right or the left. It's not all big, wide shots and crazy shit going on. We would do some of that, too, but I would never really shoot master shots because masters don't completely tell your story. You gotta dig.

I learned patience, how to keep a cool head, and juggle a lot of different things. Have fun while you're doing it, or don't go to work.

It's not just one thing I learned.

Does the movie have a message?

It's basic good versus evil. Because of Ben Grimm the message on one level is acceptance. That guy was damaged goods and he's the one that turned out to be the real freak. I tried to express that in the film in various places. For example, when Ben Grimm is out there alone and feels like he's such an outcast that he can't even be around the people that he loves because he's in such emotional distress, he goes below the ground and is accepted where he thinks he can be accepted which is by a group of outcasts, beggars, and tramps. Another time is when you see him in the back of the restaurant, covered up in a blanket, and a guy comes out and says, "Hey man, you can't be here," and he walks up to these girls on the street and he's like, "Wait a minute. Don't be afraid of who I am. You have to know who I really am. Don't judge me by what I look like." The comparisons I made at the time were to *The Elephant Man*.

I'm thinking of the connections and direct contrasts with Doctor Doom. They are both monstrous in a way and

disfigured, but the fundamental difference is that there is something really good inside of Ben. He does have a surrogate family with the Fantastic Four, but Doom is alone. Doom is a monster inside and out. He wants people to fear him whereas the Thing doesn't.

Most people are raised to have compassion, to have understanding, to love their fellow people, and then there's people who have a regimented upbringing and a strict, authoritarian environment. They have to be over-achievers. They cannot fail. That's what I have in the film with Doom. He's like the Phantom of the Opera.

How finished is the film? What else needs to be done to it? My understanding is you had to finish it on your own time and in secret.

We never really got great special effects. We realized after we finished shooting the film that nobody was in a hurry to get it done, to get a print. Nobody was truthful or forthcoming about what was going on. We just said, "They don't want to finish this movie for some reason." We kept working on it. I had gotten another job making another movie. I hired the same editor, Glenn Garland. We'd finish cutting the film I was working on, then we'd take the film reels off and put *The Fantastic Four* reels up after everybody left the office and we'd work on *that* until we got it finished. The post-production supervisor at Concorde-New Horizons, Jan Kikumoto, who was also an associate producer for our *Fantastic Four*, smuggled our film into the lab with some of Roger's other movies to get us workprints and to get things done until we finally finished the movie. Nobody expected the film to get done; we did it anyway.

People look at the copy of the film online and they think, "God, this looks like shit." And you know what? They're right because we never got a decent print or a good transfer from the negative with color correction so that we could make a pristine copy of the film. We never got that opportunity.

The trailer looks pretty damn good. Those were the only scenes that were transferred from the negative. I saw the screening of one finished answer print at FotoKem when it just came out of the lab. That film looked good. For the time and what we had to work with, the lighting, and the production design, it looked great.

What can you tell us about the copies that are floating around?

Mike Elliott, Roger Corman's in-house producer, felt bad for us and said, "It's a horrible situation. You deserve to have a copy of your own work." He handed me a ¾ inch copy under the table and said, "You can get a copy made and then you have to give the ¾ inch back." I think what happened was this film was bootlegged somehow from Lightning Dubs or one of those dubbing houses where I had the copy made. Thank God some video transfer person in the middle of the night bumped a copy off so something is available. There was no digital then, so the copy comes from a grainy VHS of a VHS of a VHS. That's why it looks so bad. That's not what we all worked hard to do; we worked hard to make a good film and a good-looking film. My biggest disappointment is we never got a good copy. At least they could have given us that.

Glenn Garland and I went snooping around in the Roger Corman film vault, which is basically a big empty room where they stored lumber, looking for the negative. We were going to risk jail time and steal it. I was going to get a film transfer, a decent telecine, from the negative and then bring the negative back. By the time we got into the film vault, the negative was already confiscated.

Marvel's Avi Arad claims that he "burned" the film. Do you think there is a print, negative, or other high-quality copy hidden or forgotten somewhere? Do you think it will ever be released? What would it take to release it?

That's the one thing that I'm angry about: not that they buried the film, but the fact that they did not give us a decent copy of the film to recognize our work and so that we can see what we did. I don't care how ruthless people are in the business, I cannot imagine anybody taking film negative and throwing it in the trash or destroying it. That's total blasphemy. That's beyond comprehension. I feel like that negative is tagged and sitting somewhere.

I told Robert Kulzer at Constantin that they ought to take the film now that the franchise has burned itself out, clean it up, get a good transfer, and release it as it is. Spend a million or two million to redo all the visual effects and release it as a double set. The mystique and cult status would sell it. I'm sure they would make at least five million or so. Of course, that's my opinion; I made the film.

Things are released all the time with a few minutes of additional footage or a handful of deleted scenes, and people go crazy over those bits. This is an entire film with no official release, and it comes with a built-in audience of Fantastic Four fans, Marvel fans, and comic book fans. Whether someone put a little money into it, or releases it as is, it's already made and just waiting.

The *Fantastic Four* films have not been as successful as some of Marvel's other movies. What is the difficulty with successfully transferring the *Fantastic Four* from the page to the screen?

I don't like to knock anybody's work. It's tough enough to get a job out there. With that said, I don't think they ever really looked at the Fantastic Four as an ensemble piece. They didn't dig deep enough. The personality traits were superficial. They didn't respect the comic book fans and the audience. I was amazed by some of the questions the fans were asking us when we were at the first comic book convention after we cut the film. Not only do they know everything that's written, they've surmised a lot of different things about who these characters are, what they are, what they've become, and how they've struggled. The fans know this stuff inside and out.

Comic book fans are hardcore. They pay attention to details and identify personally with the characters. It's an intense connection. I learned to read because of comic books. A lot of the best comic book movies have depth, three-dimensional characters, and complexity.

I think the guys that handled the franchise at the studio glossed over all that. That's why they haven't been able to translate this franchise into something successful. They blew it. They took a really special franchise, great characters, and just fucked it up. I think they thought, "It's another superhero film; let's just cram it full of visual effects." I think the casting wasn't good. We screened the documentary at Aero Theatre in Santa Monica when it first came out. We had two screenings and the theater was packed. We did a Q&A and afterward people from the audience said, "You movie's way better. You got the characters right."

The 2005 version really deviates in some key ways from the comic series. For example, instead of Doctor Doom wearing his armor as an external suit like Iron Man does, it's an ability that he has like Colossus from the X-Men. There are a lot of changes alone those lines, and I don't know that they are necessary or enhance the movie.

They changed the look of the Thing. Why would they do that? He looks like a stealth-Thing. That's not how he looks in the comics or in our movie. I met with Robert from Constantin. He told me that when they came out of the screening at Fox studios for *Fantastic Four* (2005), Bernd said, "Oley's movie is *better*." I made a movie for $2 million. They spent $100 million and the main man said my movie is better.

The actors — Joseph Culp, particularly, and Alex Hyde-White — really did their homework about who these characters were, where they came from, what they were, what they wanted, and what they needed.

Since I can't interview Ian Trigger I'd like to ask you a couple of questions about him. What was it like to work with Ian Trigger?

Ian was the consummate professional actor. He seemed to relish playing a villain and embodied the heavy makeup and costume using them to his advantage. Ian attended the Royal Academy of Dramatic Arts in London and was known for his Shakespearean stage work. Admittedly, I did not know much about his resume when we were shooting *The Fantastic Four*. I did know in casting, however, that Ian was exceptional in his line delivery and his diminutive size was perfect for the role of the Jeweler, which was a sub for the Marvel character the Mole Man. The sidebar on this is that we could not use the Mole Man due to rights issues, so it was changed to a similar character by the writer, Craig Nevius.

What did you think of Ian's performance?

Ian's talent and performance elevated every scene he was in and made the character of the Jeweler believable, likable, and even sympathetic. The Jeweler gave comfort to society's outcasts in his underground lair and Ian played the maligned misfit and leader beautifully. He brought his Shakespearean mannerism and line delivery to his character that definitely made it unique and dare I say in a sense, classical.

Ian Trigger as the Jeweler. PHOTO COURTESY OF EVERETT BURRELL

Do you recall if Carl Ciarfalio had a cool suit or not?

I don't think there was any "cool suit." The budget was so low they would never have been any money for something that sophisticated.

Did you ever see him plugged into anything between takes?

I just remember him sweating buckets and unzipping the back of it and try to peel it off as best as possible between takes. I would say it was pretty much hell for him, and in spite of that he did a great job.

Oley, a legend circulates that your father is celebrity hairstylist Vidal Sassoon. Is this true?

Vidal Sassoon is not my father at all. No relation whatsoever.

Other than the similarity in surnames, how do you think this story got started?

His daughter Catya "Cat" Sassoon did some work at Roger Corman's on a couple of his films like *Angelfist* and two of the *Bloodfist* movies. Everybody just automatically assumed she was my sister.

That is a tragic story. She died from a drug overdose. She was young.

Please complete this sentence — referring to your movie — "The Fantastic Four is..."

...waiting to be released!

...sitting under Avi Arad's bed.

What have you been up to since making *The Fantastic Four*? Other than being in the documentary *Doomed!: The Untold Story of Roger Corman's The Fantastic Four* (2015), any more films or television programs related to comic books or Marvel?

Xena, Hercules, Mutant X, Martial Law, Viper, Adventure Inc., and *The Sentinel*. I wish I had done more stuff like that. There's a couple of shows I think I would have been good at like *Gotham*. It's a tough business. You're in it and then you're not. You just get older and then there are a lot of younger guys right behind you trying to make a name for themselves. Everybody wants somebody who's hot. What have you done lately? That's always the question.

You have to continue to reinvent yourself. I'm working on *Butterfly in the Typewriter*, a biopic about John Kennedy Toole who wrote *A Confederacy of Dunces*. It has a really amazing cast: Susan Sarandon, Diane Kruger, and Thomas Mann. That's inching forward.

What a story. His mother saved a copy of the manuscript after he killed himself, took it to multiple publishers who rejected it, and eventually got Walker Percy, the author, to read it. Eventually it was published and won the Pulitzer Prize for Fiction. He was unpublished in his lifetime. Great book.

I've also been working on trying to get a movie made about Louis Armstrong that may turn into a Netflix series. I'm working on three projects with a guy who was a record producer for David Bowie. It's not sci-fi, but they're good projects and good scripts. I'm still at it. I've got my hands in stuff. You just keep trying. You keep stirring the pot until something jumps out.

When we get off the phone, I'm gonna send another e-mail to Robert at Constantin Film, tell him we had an interview, and that people still want to see this film…

Carl Ciarfalio
The Thing

How did you find your way to *The Fantastic Four*?
I was the President of the Stuntmen's Association at the time. A call came to the office from a production company saying they were looking for a specific type: somebody that was about six feet tall, weighed about 230 pounds, and had blue eyes. I just happened to be that guy. They were looking for a stuntman who would play the Thing in the suit. So, I went down and interviewed, which was really "take a look at my body and see how things fit." They said, "You're the guy." I did have a bit of a tough time. I've got an Italian nose and the mask fit real snug. The nosepiece fit just above where my nostrils are, which meant my nose was flattened in that thing for the whole time we were shooting. But the suit was better because they built it for me. They made it over about seven to ten days. I remember going in for fittings every couple of days. I have a video of that. It's about twelve minutes of their work on me and me moving around in the suit.

They looked at a lot people, and, fortunately, I just seemed to embody the build of the suit. In my opinion, it's the most authentic Thing of the characters that have been made for all the movies.

What recollections do you have about making *The Fantastic Four*?
That suit was the heaviest thing I've ever worn. There was no air moving in or out of it.

There was no cool suit underneath it. A couple of times a day I would have to take the booties off and dump the water out. It was amazingly hot.

Every time I was in the suit, everybody — everyone who came to set and especially the ones who brought their kids — wanted

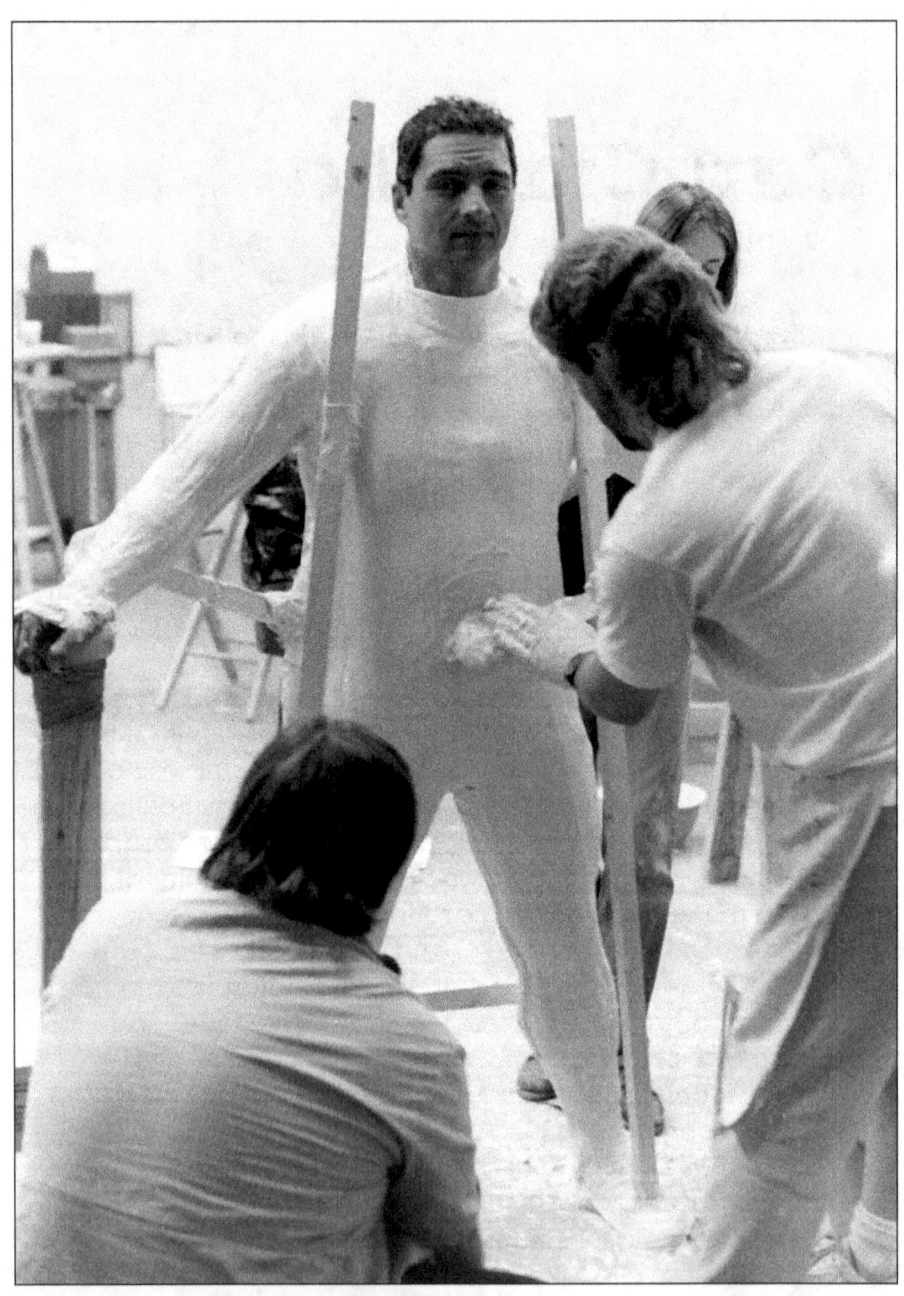

Carl Ciarfalio being very patient during the early stages of the construction of the Thing suit. PHOTO COURTESY OF EVERETT BURRELL

a picture with me. But as soon as I was out of the suit they were like "Who are you?"

I also have great memories of Oley being so competent as a director; what a wonderful man to work with and work for. He put his heart and soul into the project. He busted his ass for all of us, kept all of us together, and told the story the way it was supposed to be told. I made wonderful friends.

Of course, I realized this was a low-budget production. The studio, as Roger called it, was really just an old warehouse. It was one of those seedy old Hollywood places. The dressing rooms they gave us were very small and had couches you couldn't even sit on anymore because people had slept on them for forty or fifty years. And there were ants. That was fun.

I mostly remember working long days and being really hot. But in total, it was exciting and thrilling to be part of it even though the production was a challenge for all of us. Some of us handled that differently than others. Some rolled with the punches and others got miffed about the situation.

But for me, the uncomfortable part never stopped me from having a wonderful time. I knew going into the industry that being a stuntman means that the conditions usually won't be pleasant and you're almost never the highlight. I just love working. I love being on set. It's kind of my home away from home.

What was co-executive producer Roger Corman's role?

I really had nothing to do with Roger. I'm not even sure if I met him. Communicating with him was left up to Oley. Alex took the lead with expressing his thoughts to Roger as well. I wasn't into any of that.

My deal was go to work, put on the suit, and get into the action. I tried to help Michael Bailey Smith do the voice of the Thing and to help him get his character points across. I actually had to do all the dialogue and he voiced it. The Thing's head was RC — remote controlled — so that's how the mouth would move. I'd be doing dialogue, but all I'd hear were the animated pieces in the head moving the whole time. Even so, I tried to play it out so Michael could get the dialogue in.

I went to work, did my job, and stayed out of the politics — because you could tell something was happening, something wasn't a hundred percent. By that time, I'd already been around for fifteen years or so; I knew what was kosher

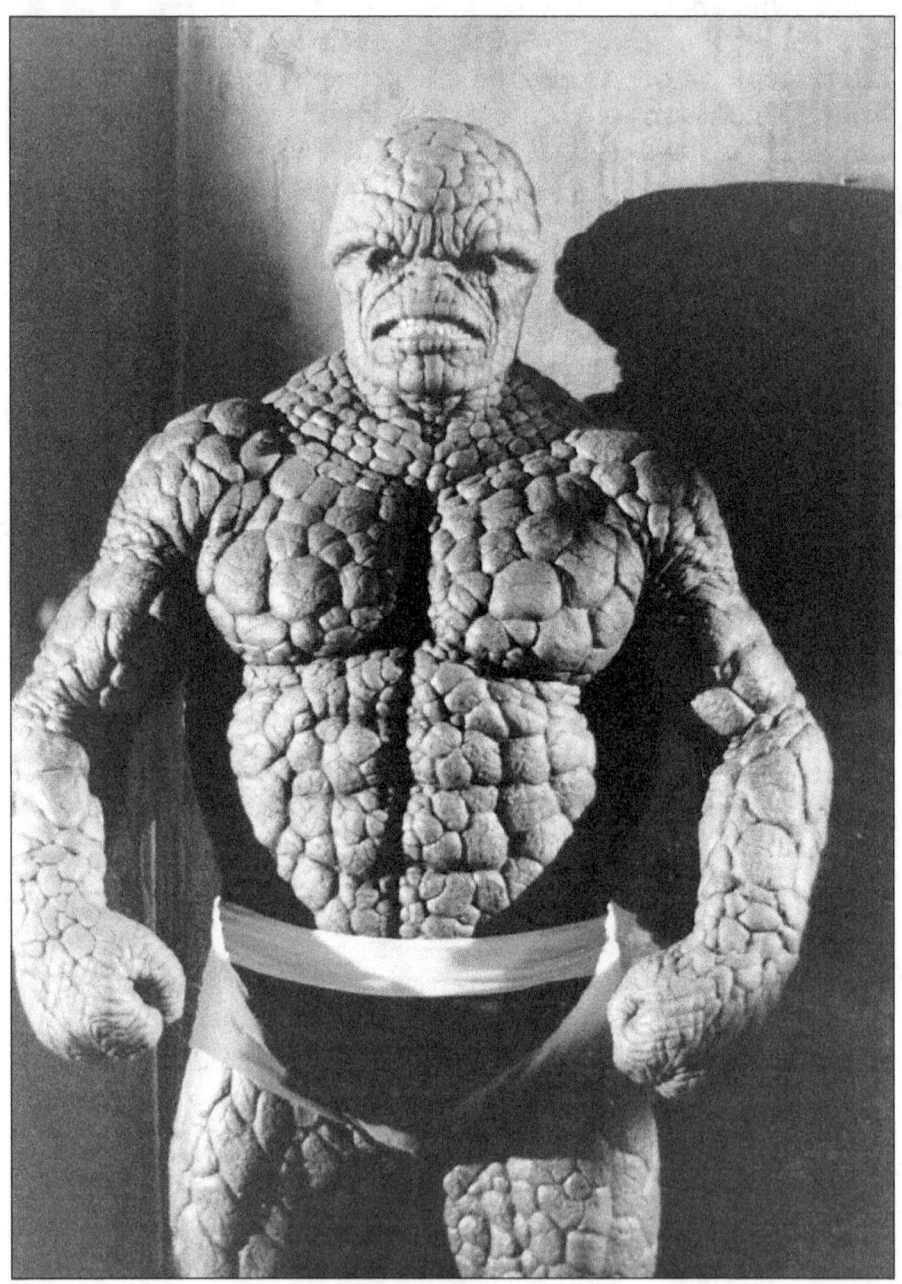

The Thing flexing his arms. PHOTO COURTESY OF EVERETT BURRELL

and what wasn't. The camaraderie we had for each other kept us together.

What challenges or limitations did you experience while making the film?

The day we started shooting, we were already over budget and behind schedule. Production limitations are always the result of budget. Lack of budget means we don't have the right lens for this, we don't have the right camera, or we need another camera or another day to set up.

Earlier in my career I had worked on the TV show *The Flash* — this was around 1990. On that series, both the actor and the stunt double had a cool suit that allowed them to be in their costume for hours at a time. It were basically a Lycra body suit with a network of tubes filled with a cooled liquid. A tech operated a handheld generator to keep the water flowing which kept the actor and stuntman cooled. With *The Fantastic Four*, they were like "No, there's no money for a cool suit. We spent it all on the costume." The right thing to do would have been to give me a suit, but I didn't want to complain. I wanted to be part of the team.

The spacecraft was created on the cheap, too. Basically, just cardboard, plastic, and plywood. They cut corners everywhere they could.

Oley made it work the best that he could with what we had. Not enough cameras. Not enough time. Not the best studio setup. We knew the money was short. As soon as you see a craft service table with nothing on it, you know the budget's pretty low. I got paid scale, and I was happy with that.

I think towards the end Oley became even more limited in terms of the support he was receiving. They wanted him to just finish and get out, but Oley wanted it to be good. He didn't want to just collect a paycheck.

Do you think $16,000 would have covered a cool suit?

I'd like to say yes, but I don't know for sure.

Oley said that's around what he had to spend on special effects. Instead, he says that they got nothing for it, and I thought, "Well that maybe could have been Carl's cool suit."

I think what happens with a Corman production is you put whatever money you have into your talent, your actors. Behind the camera, as far as crew and equipment go, that's where

Roger fell short. He hired people who gave him the right price but not the right job.

I read that you shared a recollection that during filming Oley mentioned the possibility that the film wasn't going to come out. Do you remember that?

I do. I remember being outside with the head of my costume off and talking to Oley. He wasn't happy. I asked him what was up. I believe he told that he heard that the film might not get released; it might not have enough money to get released — whatever that story was — but we can't confirm it. I haven't really talked to Oley about it either. People remember what they remember; that's what's in my head. I certainly don't want to put that memory onto anyone else. That's my truth; that's what I remember.

Why was the film never released?

In this industry when there's no answer for it, it's always about money. All the political dealings Roger was having with Eichinger — I can't even keep up with that. It's just such bullshit. I think that the movie was short on financing. If we had had another $250,000 to $500,000 it would have been releasable. But we're like ballplayers. We're a commodity. We're a property. No matter how great you think your painting is, it may never get in the gallery.

I can see Roger's business point of view. I think that the real pisser was when he wasn't honest with everybody. That's the side of Hollywood everyone talks about and hates because it fucks with you. They pay you what they can pay you. Then they take your work and make a lot of money and you don't. As one of my friends says, "If you want loyalty, get a dog."

It's a business. At the end of the day no matter how talented you are, it is still business and business is money. Everybody has made shit movies that never came out. For whatever reasons — whether it was finances, or the development, or the storyline — it just didn't come out. All you can do is move on. Some of us did and some of us didn't. Some of us got stuck there for a long time. I think this movie didn't come out because Roger wasn't being an honest businessman. I think Roger's honest with the people at the...let me do a comparison. Trump surrounds himself with yes-people. He gets the answers that he wants to get, and that's what I saw Corman doing. He got the answers that he wanted to get, and then he just moved on to the next thing. That's his prerogative. He's paying the money to do that. But in that model, the people who suffer are the cast and crew. We were good at what we did, and we wanted our best to show up onscreen. That doesn't always happen — and it's not always our fault. Listen, Roger was a great businessman — at his level. He's no Steven Spielberg, but there you go.

So you think Roger definitely knew more than what he claims he knew.

Yes. You never spend a million dollars to do a picture without knowing what's on the other end. He didn't have a release date. He didn't have any distribution. He obviously knew. He wasn't going to make a $1 million picture and then just put it away.

Do you think that it's possible Roger had it in mind for the home video market, which he had had success with?

I think that might have been a possible exit route. Still, if you're thinking about going to the home video market, then you throw enough money into the project to make it sellable to that market. You saw the movie. If you're over seven years old, the only thing you really appreciate is the story and the costumes. The action in the movie was far from what it could have been in regard to special effects. If I'm going to spend a million dollars on a picture, the intention is for it to come out onscreen. I've been around too long to tell people what they want to hear. This affected so many people.

Referring to the film's cancellation, Michael Bailey Smith said, "It's like knowing you had the winning lottery ticket and then lost it in the laundry." How big did you think the film was going to be?

It should have been a project that sent Oley over the top and it wasn't. I feel bad for him. I think Roger just fucked him in that. Sorry to say it like that. I just think he really got screwed.

If this film had been released, we would never be as famous as we are. I don't think we'll ever see the movie any place but the black market.

When we wrapped, I moved on to whatever my next project was, which was probably the following week. Some of the actors took their own money and did promotion for the film. I only came to know that much later. They were upset and wanted to show their wares and hard work. They thought their efforts to promote the film were worth it, but they obviously weren't. It's too bad they spent their time and money. But I get it. As an actor, you might think it's going to take you to the next level. I was never invited to be with any of them for any of that, any of those signings or shows. I started doing those types of things around 2010, 2012 when Scott Ray, a signing convention agent, thought it would be good to put me with the other Fantastic Four members at a convention signing. I get asked to participate now, but I didn't for the first ten or fifteen years.

As a stuntman I'm falling down again, getting beat up, catching on fire, and then next week I'm going to do it somewhere else. My attitude might have been different from theirs. A lot of the time, stunt people are outside of the circle. "He's a stunt guy. He's not really an actor. We don't really need the guy who was in the suit and did everything." If you get hurt, they bring somebody else in. Actors can't do that. They're "valuable." I think that's the reason I was never contacted to do any of those things. That's okay. I'm forty-something years into the industry, and I don't really put my money out for somebody else's project.

It sounds like what I imagine truck driving to be. You pick up you load. You drop it off. You go to the next job. If you can't deliver it for some reason, they find someone else who can. You are dispensable and treated that way.

Most definitely. That's a good way to put it. That's what we choose to do. Are you a football fan?

Yes.

We're the offensive linemen. The defense gets the big tackles. The quarterbacks, and running backs, and wide receivers are the stars. The folks in the middle don't get that same credit. When those guys get beat up, they just pull them out, put another guy in there, and the game goes on without it looking like anything has changed. That's kind of who we are. It's okay with me. I don't mind being that guy. I'm a great team player.

After the movie wrapped, I was hustling for my next job. I think what happened with the actors is they got their — ego is such a harsh word — core sense of themselves really involved. That wasn't my focus. They went after it because they believed in what they did. I think that's wonderful.

No matter how big the movie became would it have been huge for you because, as you said, you're just "the guy in the suit?"

The technology changed so much. These days they put a green suit with laser tags on you and then build the suit around you in post-production. I think the only chance I would have had for personal success was going on with them for a

Behind-the-scenes photo of the Thing being shot at or otherwise attacked. PHOTO COURTESY OF EVERETT BURRELL

sequel. Mostly if they had chosen to keep that suit because they made it for me. Maybe they would have built a suit for Michael because he's got a massive build. Or maybe the next installment would have been Jessica Alba and those people. Spider-Man changes. Superman changes.

Nothing's guaranteed.

When I first started in the industry, I worked for PM Entertainment. They did lots of movies with guys like Lorenzo Lamas. They did a lot of straight-to-video. Working on Corman's film, I saw that we were already at a lower budget than PM Entertainment had. I never had a great feeling about the movie coming out. I'm heartbroken for the actors and for Oley. I just didn't think that movie seemed like something that would come together for a blockbuster. I have to be honest: I thought we would be lucky to get it onto video.

What did you learn from working on The Fantastic Four?

Never trust Roger Corman (*laughs*). I learned how hot it can get for twelve hours a day in one of those fucking suits. I learned from Oley. I watched his passion, and his patience, and how he worked with the actors, his explanations of characters and situations. I was locked onto him as much as possible so I could learn from him.

I shouldn't say it like this because it was exciting to be that character, but in many ways, it was another day at work — throwing people around, getting beat up, and running through walls. It was fun to do. I always have fun at work no matter what I'm doing. It's a haven for me. With this experience, I learned to embrace the industry a little more and understand how the business side of it works. None of us got screwed; all of us got paid for what we did. There's no guarantee that a movie's going to come out. And it if comes out, there's no guarantee that it will ever play more than once. It's a life lesson in the industry.

I've been very lucky to not miss a step because of what happened with this movie. I've been lucky enough to be able to do interviews, and talk to people like you, and put a chapter in my book for people who want to dig into the production. Overall, I've learned how to communicate a little bit better in the industry.

Does the movie have a message?

The movie is about people who come together under the harshest of circumstances and overcome adversity in a way that is correct and not overly harsh or cruel. It's a story about people who think and act as one. More of that should be happening in the world. It's a universal story. We told a story about people coming together to help other people.

What have you been up to since making The Fantastic Four? Other than being in the documentary Doomed!: The Untold Story of Roger Corman's The Fantastic Four (2015), any more films or television programs related to comic books or Marvel?

I wrote a book titled *Stars, Stunts, and Stories*. I'm a working stuntman, actor, and stunt coordinator. Back in the early

1990s, I was in *The Incredible Hulk* television show with Bill Bixby and Lou Ferrigno, and *The Flash* with John Wesley Shipp. I was in Seth Rogen's *The Green Hornet*, *The Amazing Spider-Man*, *Daredevil*, and *Batman & Robin*. And *Mallrats*, which is not a superhero thing, but it's a Stan Lee thing. I did episodes of *24*, *Extant*, *CSI*, *Westworld*. I've been fortunate to do big films as well like *Natural Born Killers*, *Casino*, *Fight Club*, and *Far and Away*. I was also part of some franchises like *Mission: Impossible* and *The Fast and the Furious*. Each of them was different and amazing. I think all of that has informed my opinion of what a movie *can* be. What can be done with a million dollars and what should be done with a million dollars might be two different things.

You can't just roll over. Rebecca is in Canada doing a series right now. Joseph just did a film. Alex works now and again; I'm not so sure about him. Michael stepped away from the industry, but he still does signings and shows. He's such a good guy. Somebody is going to come after him to return and do a movie. He's such a strong presence on film. The one guy who really got hurt from this is Oley. He hasn't stopped doing what he's doing, and he's good at what he does, but I think if the movie had been bigger, it would have given him a bigger shot. He would have been doing much more. He's such a good director. He took a hunk of clay and made quite a statue. It would be nice for people to see that.

Please complete this sentence "The Fantastic Four is..."

...a long time ago. It's a great memory, a wonderful experience, and a learned experience. *The Fantastic Four* was a huge growth experience for me in the industry, personally and professionally.

Do you think there is a print, negative, or other high-quality copy hidden or forgotten somewhere?

Yes. But it may not come out in our lifetime. Who's going to take a $1 million picture and burn it whether it's good or bad? That's just not practical. It's sitting in somebody's vault somewhere.

The first time I saw it was several years after we finished it. I was walking around Dragonfest, which is a martial arts expo, and I saw it in one of the stands. I told the guy, "Hey, this is the original *Fantastic Four* movie." He says, "I know." I said,

"I was in that. I'm the Thing. I really want a copy of this." He says, "Great! Ten bucks." "But I was in the movie," I explained. He said, "I know. Ten bucks." I got a copy or two here at home. It's not bad. It tells the story. You can't compare that kind of quality to what they put out.

The *Fantastic Four* films have not been as successful as some of Marvel's other movies. What is the difficulty with successfully transferring the *Fantastic Four* from the page to the screen?

Buddy movies are okay, but group buddy movies are really tough to follow. The *Fantastic Four* comic was big in the 1960s, 1970s, and maybe into the 1980s. Even in current superhero movies, the story can get lost. I really love story. Too much of it is spectacle and green screens. I don't go to watch them because it's like watching a big frigging cartoon. I can't get into it at all.

Have you seen *Logan*?

No, I have not.

It speaks to some of what you are talking about. There's a lot of depth in terms of the characters. If I think about really good superhero movies like *Watchmen*, I put *Logan* in that class. It's depressing and it's brutal, but it has a really solid story.

It's the story and the human struggle that you follow. The Fantastic Four don't really have a human struggle. They're just in each other's way most of the time. I'll check out *Logan*. I liked *Thor*, *Iron Man*, and *Deadpool* because their stories allow you to get into the characters and really see who these people are. That takes time. You can't get that from a situation in which the producer says, "Look, you've got eight hours to shoot this scene. You get what you get and then move on." There's a big difference there.

Among the Fantastic Four is the Thing the deepest character because, as the outcast, he has the deepest struggle?

The Thing stands out. He can't hide who he is. He probably struggles the most and that is relatable to an enormous amount of people. The other characters can choose to be visible or invisible, on fire or not on fire, stretched out or not stretched out; they can control it, and they always come back around to being normal. The Thing is stuck. He can't turn his power on and off. He can't ever be normal.

Jay Underwood
Johnny Storm/The Human Torch

How did you find your way to *The Fantastic Four*?
My manager called me up one day excited that he got me an audition for *The Fantastic Four*. He expected that I would have the same enthusiasm. I'd heard of the Fantastic Four but knew virtually nothing about them. I just wasn't a comic guy. The comics I had read were things like *Mad* magazine and *Archie*, but I was happy to go in for the audition. I read a few comics real quick to figure out who Johnny Storm was before I went to the audition. I was in there with the producer and the director. I don't think Roger Corman was in my audition. Usually for a big movie you'll do multiple auditions in front of different people. I just did the one and I heard a week or two later, "Boom — you got it." It was quick. The next thing was "We need to get your hair dyed because Johnny's got blond hair and you've got brown hair."

I understand the dying process left you with blisters.
Yes, my scalp was blistered and burned, kind of like Spike Lee's character at the beginning of, I think, *Malcolm X*. It was the peroxide they used to bleach my hair. What a performer won't do for his art! It healed up fairly quickly but when it started burning, it wasn't done yet and my hair was kind of an orangey color. They had to complete the job by doing blond highlights.

What recollections do you have about making *The Fantastic Four*?
I don't remember how long after the audition and getting the part that we started production, but it was fast. There was no time to spare, it seemed. It was the end of the year. Right before we started shooting, Oley invited the main cast to his house to get together, to talk about things, and read through

the script. We all knew at this point that we had signed on for a lower-budget version of the Fantastic Four. I don't remember if we knew at that time exactly what the budget was or if it was in the million dollar range or not, but for the folks who knew who Roger Corman was — oh, my word — the expectation was not real high. It came up that there's a little bit more money than Roger's average budget for this one. We thought, "This must be kind of a big deal for Roger. He's taking it seriously." We all know to do a superhero comic book movie of this caliber takes millions and millions of dollars to do it right.

In the early 1990s, *Superman* had come out, *Batman* had started coming out, there was the original low-budget *Captain America*, and so forth, but in Hollywood's eyes Marvel and even DC were not proven, ongoing franchises. Some of the films had done well, but people weren't jumping on the bandwagon saying, "We've got to get the next Marvel project out; we've got to get the next DC project out." They just weren't seen yet in that light.

We knew that *The Fantastic Four* needed a bigger budget, but we knew that we didn't have it, so Oley gave us a pep talk like the coach to his underdog team who's probably going to get creamed. He said, "So here's the deal. We have to take control over that which we can control. What we can control is script, at this point, and character. Let's do our *best* to take this seriously and make the characters as authentic and as much like the comic as possible." We knew the special effects might not be there, but we could still do our best job.

If we made the characters the way they were in the comic, acted as well as we could, and kept the story and script as close to the comic as possible, we thought that even if critics attacked the special effects, we could have a strong movie. We took it seriously. There wasn't the feeling of "let's slap this thing together, get in, and get out as quick as we can." That's why I believe the movie has the heart that it does. We were all absolutely united, and Oley, the head coach and ringleader, kept us that way. He wasn't just some guy they hired to slap this thing together. He was a real director and a real leader.

The special effects are not going to be what we want them to be or what they really should be. In that sense, we'll make it a little more stylized. I don't know what Oley had in mind, but in my mind the way the movie came out was more along the lines of the *Batman* TV show from the 1960s. "POW! ZAP!"

A little campier maybe.

Campier, exactly. And that's okay. Let's have fun with that. Let's embrace that. I thought that was a great attitude from Oley. We all were gung-ho.

I've never had so much fun on a low-budget production of, say, a million dollars or less, and I've never felt so much camaraderie with any other cast, especially one that requires an ensemble cast like *The Fantastic Four*. I owe so much to Oley for setting the tone and bringing everybody in on the same page. We had a blast! We just had a blast. I stay in touch with the group from this film more than any other group I've worked with.

I had worked on lower budget projects. We had some experience on some bigger-budget things; we all had experienced low-budget filmmaking, so we knew some of what to expect. There were no prima donnas who couldn't stand or take it and said, "Get me out of here." We just laughed at some of it and kept going.

What challenges or limitations did you experience while making the film?

It was long hours and extreme conditions. The studio was a rat-infested shoebox in the industrial part of Venice Beach, California. This is a studio? The carpet needed to be changed fifteen to twenty years before. The reality of the budget sets in.

When they showed up with our spacesuits, we realized they were probably in ten other Corman films. It was anything but a high-tech spacesuit like you would have if you were shooting an episode of *Star Trek* or something like that. The suits had these cheeseball oxygen packs on the back with Velcro. I thought, "You gotta be kidding me." But you just do it; you just go with it. We tried to make the most of it. The Fantastic Four outfits don't match. Our costume designer made these blue spandex suits himself. Because of budget and time, they're not perfect. Some of our white belts go up and touch the round number and some don't. Rebecca Staab, who played my sister in the movie, made the point that it makes sense from the standpoint of the comic books because Sue Storm made the costumes. I was surprised they forked over a couple of hundred bucks to get my hair dyed instead of throwing some cheesy wig on me.

Still, it all came out pretty nice. The flipside of this coin is that there are some things that you look at and think, "*Wow.*" The Thing costume — even for 1993 and even for a low-budget film — is a pretty doggone cool costume. It was sophisticated and it photographed really well. Some of that is a testament to the costume's creators. Oley was able to round up talent — not just acting talent — because even when a special effects team realizes the project is low-budget and asks, "Oh man, that's the budget? How are we going to do this?" they still want to be a part of it because it's the first *Fantastic Four* movie that's ever been made. People were willing to work for less and put in more because of that. Some people kicked in extra bucks of their own to make sure their work looked good.

Referring to the film's cancellation Michael Bailey Smith said, "It's like knowing you had the winning lottery ticket and then lost it in the laundry." How big did you think the film was going to be?

We knew it had a built-in audience. Any fan of the Fantastic Four will come see this movie. We thought that even though it's low-budget, it has potential to help all of our careers and propel us to the next level, including Oley. The word got out to the comic community that this movie is being made. We started having sci-fi and comics magazines wanting to interview us. *Film Threat* came out to the set for a while doing photos and interviews and put us on their cover. Then, conventions started asking us to come out, so we started doing conventions before the movie was even out. We realized it's catching on. They had a premiere planned for the Mall of America. They had tie-ins with Ronald McDonald House.

I don't think we had a grandiose thought that this was going to be as big as *Batman* or *Superman*, but we knew if we could get the thumbs-up from that built-in audience, then the movie might have a bit more life and get into more theaters. I don't think we thought it was going to be a blockbuster, but it could be a stepping stone, a boost, that could help everyone's careers.

There's the $1 million lottery and the $250 million lottery.

Exactly. It was the four, five, maybe even $20 million lottery, not the $500 million. Still, there was a payoff. I can't tell you how many auditions I have sat in after that when people knew about *The Fantastic Four* and wanted to talk about it and ask about it. That's interesting to me because it tells me that people knew about it and it was and is still relevant. If it had come out and been received as mediocre, then it would have died and ended up in the history books as the first *Fantastic Four* movie and that would be it. Because the movie didn't come out, there's all this mystery and intrigue that's given it a life unto its own that continues even now.

Whenever you try to deny, hide, block, or censor something, it always has the opposite effect and makes whatever it is larger than it was before, gives it power and grows it.

When it didn't pan out, it was like half a dozen other jobs that I thought were going to be The One, that big film that was going to catapult me to the next level. It wasn't just *The Fantastic Four* that had the propensity to give me an A-list career. But that's okay. I had a twenty-five year career as a working actor in Hollywood. I didn't have to have other jobs or other work to make my living.

Why was the film never released?

When we were told that the film was getting shelved, we were all in a state of shock.

Everybody was planning for it and looking forward to it being released. We all believed it was coming out. Over the years, fans wanted to know what happened. Articles exploring why the movie didn't come out started appearing in the same publications that were interviewing us before. This has gone on for almost thirty years. Mark Sikes and Marty Langford made the documentary *Doomed* that tries to take all the pieces of the puzzle that have come up over the years, fit them all together, lay out what happened, and explain why *The Fantastic Four* didn't come out.

Our basic understanding is that Eichinger had the rights, which were going to expire at the end of the year, and so he goes to Roger Corman and says, "Can you make this movie? It's got to be in production by December 31." The next strange thing is they budgeted it for a million dollars. The question in my mind is why they would spend that much money to make it. Why doesn't Roger just make it one of his $50,000 or $100,000 movies? When all of this first happened, I just thought it was all a ploy solely designed to keep the rights.

Now, I think Eichinger wanted to make this movie and have a finished product that he could release, or he thought, "At least I'll retain the rights," and maybe he could sell it to the highest bidder. I think he saw both as options. I don't know that he actually talked to anybody else or any other studio yet. It could be that he planned to release it. There would be no other reason to go to the lengths everyone went to like setting up premieres, creating charity tie-ins, and going to conventions if from day one he planned to never release it. That wouldn't have made sense.

So he would keep his rights by making the movie whether he released it or not, but pouring all of that effort into the activities surrounding the movie and allowing others to do so suggests that he was committed to releasing it.

If he only wanted to keep the rights, he would have gone into production. He would have done whatever he needed to do to satisfy his contract to keep the rights, and then they would have pulled the plug. I don't know what his contract was with Marvel. That's the big question. What did he actually have to do to satisfy the contractual requirements in regard to preserving his rights to the movie? Did he just have to be in production by December 31 and shoot one day of footage and be done? Did he have to have a completed movie? Did it have to have a specific budget?

What we really need to see is the contract. Someone — maybe more than one person — has got a copy of it somewhere.

What did you learn from working on *The Fantastic Four*?

It hurt us all when it didn't come out. It pained us. It was discouraging. It was a shock. It was a slap to the face. Anger sets in. You think Hollywood sucks. You want to think there's not that dark seedy side to it, but there is. At the time I really believed that all these people knew ahead of time it wasn't coming out, and we were laughingstocks because we didn't know. Then we realized it's just business; it wasn't intentional or personal. Eichinger may have had a love for film and Corman may have a love for film, but they're also businessmen. In some sense, you can't blame them for doing what was right — or what they thought was right — from a business perspective. The rest of us, unfortunately, got caught up in those moves. I came around from thinking that anyone was deliberately trying to make our lives miserable or fool us. Oley's got stories about talking and working with Eichinger later.

Does the movie have a message?

If there is a message, it's not so much the movie, but it's in everything else that's happened and the making of the movie.

What have you been up to since making The Fantastic Four? Other than being in the documentary Doomed!: The Untold Story of Roger Corman's The Fantastic Four (2015), any more films or television programs related to comic books or Marvel?

I used to joke and tell people that I would never work for Marvel again after calling Avi Arad a ding dong (laughs). Before I got the call to ministry I spent a little over twenty years in Hollywood as a working actor. I've moved on. I'm pastor of a church in a small California mountain community. God took me out of Hollywood almost completely. My connection now is mostly through Christian filmmaking, a day or two kind of deal. I don't have to leave my church or my ministry. I have had occasions when friends will say, "Hey, I'm making a Christian film; do you want to be a part of it?" All of that stuff shows up on IMDb. I don't know how they get hold of credits.

A friend of mine runs the film department at a Christian university and he'll call me up every now and again looking for actors for a student film. I direct school plays here in our little community. I'm hoping to inspire the next generation of young people towards performing arts the way I was inspired.

When I first made the change, I jokingly asked God, "So what was the first twenty-five years about?" referring to my Hollywood career. As a pastor I quickly realized so many ways how what I learned in Hollywood translates to what I'm doing now in terms of telling stories and figuring out what makes people tick so that I can help them. There are a lot of connections, actually. Everything worked out how it was supposed to; everything worked out fine. It all makes perfect sense in the bigger plan that God had for my life.

I'm thinking about the connections between some of the traditional figures of Christianity and the characters in *The Fantastic Four.* **Reed Richards, the thinker, the planner, the leader — God, in a sense. Victor Von Doom as the character that would like to be God and sort of falls from grace by fighting with Reed and thus becomes Satan. Ben Grimm/the Thing as the outcast is Christ, perhaps. I am not sure where Sue and Johnny fit in, maybe they correspond to Mary and the Holy Ghost. I have no idea for Alicia. I don't think I paid enough attention in Sunday school to take this very far. Do you see any parallels?**

The major parallel from a biblical perspective is the classic good versus evil. You see this in Tolkien, C.S. Lewis, and Harry Potter as well.

Please complete this sentence *"The Fantastic Four* **is…"**

…the original and always will be the first *Fantastic Four* movie ever. We are the originals. That's the one thing we have that they can never take away from us.

Marvel's Avi Arad claims that he "burned" the film, although it survives in bootleg versions. Do you think there is a print, negative, or other high-quality copy hidden or forgotten somewhere? Do you think it will ever be released? What would it take to release it? Is there profit potential?

Nobody burns the negative. What a ridiculous thing to say. It's in a film vault somewhere I'm sure.

If anything got burned it might have been that contract. That's the thing that is indisputable. Everybody read it and agreed to it beforehand.

Since everyone knows about the film, it seems it would take nothing and maybe even be of benefit for Marvel to release it. Maybe not as a standalone but why not put it on one of their releases as a bonus — "Roger Corman's unreleased 1994 version?" At this point, I don't see it as something that can be released by itself.

When I spoke with Oley, he seemed to think that the special effects are the main thing that could use redoing.

Here's where I would disagree slightly with Oley. The special effects are the main thing that obviously require more money, but because of the budget there's a trickle-down effect for everything: set, costumes, or even time for Oley to do all the shots that he would really like to have done. I'm not trying to slight, for example, the set designers. There just wasn't money for more than what we could do with Roger Corman's studio, which is this tiny, rinky-dink warehouse, so you can only build so much. You can only have so much money to make the sets or the costumes that way that you really want them. We did the best with what we had, but we didn't have a lot. The acting and the script wouldn't be affected. On the other hand, taking an unreleased film and releasing it hasn't been done much, so maybe it would do some business.

The legend and lore surrounding a movie can be a big attraction. The other day we were flipping channels and came across *The Misfits* with Clark Gable and Marilyn Monroe. It was the last completed film for each of them. That was enough to get us to watch and it turned out to be a great film.

We'd like to see them try something with getting this movie out. There's a sense of wanting a little validation and acknowledgement that we made this movie. I know each of us would love to see it come out in some format or fashion. You make movies for people to see.

The *Fantastic Four* films have not been as successful as some of Marvel's other movies. What is the difficulty with successfully transferring the *Fantastic Four* from the page to the screen?

They've made, what, three since ours? The *Fantastic Four* films should be one of their hottest franchises. Instead, it's a franchise that they would have to admit has kind of dudded out more than some of the others. They're no Avengers. All of them have been received as less than stellar in terms of acceptance by the comic community and just in terms of what the movies have brought in. Rebecca is great about finding mentions of us in the press and sending them out to us. There's been in the last few years — especially when the last *Fantastic Four* came out and really dudded — a lot of comparisons to our version. I've heard this comment from multiple people over the years: "Out of all the *Fantastic Four* movies yours really does stick closest to the story and does the best job of bringing the characters from the comic to life." I think that's great. I think that's a tremendous compliment about the authenticity of our version.

Rebecca Staab
Susan Storm / The Invisible Girl

Note: The credits just list Susan Storm. However, since the film begins with the origin of the Fantastic Four it seems more appropriate to refer to Susan Storm as the Invisible Girl than the Invisible Women since that change doesn't come around until issue 284 of the Fantastic Four, *which is also after she is married to Reed.*

Prior to the audition how familiar were you with the Fantastic Four? Did you read comic books? Did you research Susan Storm?

When a project is being cast, they put out what's called a breakdown that all the agents get. It describes the project, the character, and the type of actor that is needed to fulfill that role. The audition for *The Fantastic Four* was an audition like any other one: here's this audition, here's this movie. But it was more exciting because it was a comic book original. At that time in the early 1990s, the Internet may have existed, but it was basic, very rudimentary. I didn't have a computer and I wasn't used to doing research on a computer. The ability to research the Fantastic Four was somewhat limited. So I went and got some comic books to see what Susan Storm looked like, and what her character was like.

I read comic books as a kid. It was *Richie Rich, Little Lotta,* and those kinds, more along the lines of Disney. I didn't really read superhero stuff, so I wasn't familiar with the Fantastic Four. When I got the audition, I went out and got some of the comic books, and felt confident when I saw Susan Storm because I looked a lot like her.

Joseph Culp talked about wearing a heavy duster to his audition as a way of creating a sense of Doctor Doom's

Rebecca Staab as Susan Storm. PHOTO COURTESY OF MICK STRAWN

armor. Did you wear anything that might create a sense of Susan Storm?

For the audition, I wore a really tight black turtleneck and tight leggings so it looked like I was wearing something like a catsuit. I knew that type of costume would be in the Fantastic Four. I remember after I did the audition and was walking out of the room, Oley Sassone said, "Thank you for dressing the part." For any audition you want to do something visually representative of the character.

What memories stand out about making *The Fantastic Four*?

It was really kind of twofold. It was the best of times; it was the worst of times *(laughs)*. We were playing comic book heroes. Does it get any more fun than that? We got to play, literally, PLAY, which is the dream of any actor. The people involved made it such a lovely place to be every day. Oley is one of the most incredible human beings on the planet. I just love him and how he embraced this. To him it wasn't just a job. It wasn't just a movie. It wasn't just directing. It wasn't just the shots. He was into the spirit of it and the authenticity of it. He really wanted to capture the feelings and the sentiment. All of us wanted to be true to the story for the comic book fans. There weren't really comic book movies before this. There was *Batman*, but this really predated this whole rush on all of these superhero movies. It was one of the very first ones. So to us, yes, we were making a movie, but we were making a live-action comic book. There was a constant awareness and a constant adjustment to either story or situation so that it would be accurate because we know how loyal comic book fans are and wanted it to be something that they accepted and they embraced. That dominant feeling through all of production is what made it different than any other film that I'd worked on. We had a goal that was bigger than just making a movie.

Everybody was on board. That was the great thing. Mark Sikes did a brilliant job with casting actors that were so committed and such great people. There was no ego or attitude. We were there as a team and working together whether it was on the days that we were shooting or when we weren't shooting. To this day, twenty-five years later, we're all friends. There's really nothing else that I've worked on that I can say that about. We're so lucky that that stage was set and it still has an energy and a life.

What about the budget?

What was also memorable was the almost miniscule and nonexistent budget *(laughs)*. It was the epitome of low-budget. It wasn't just a low-budget film it was a super-ultra-low-budget film. We were aware of that and, of course, that affects everything. A lot of times it's frustrating. Time and money are the same thing. You don't have time for something because there isn't money for it and if you don't have money, there isn't time for it. It was frustrating from a loving point of view because you always want to do more. You want to make this better, you want it to look like this — "let's do that again." When there isn't money there isn't time and those things don't get done. That being said it somewhat unites the team even more because you realize you're also up against that beast of budget and time. It's like, "This is all we have but we're going to have to make it our absolute best." We never threw our hands up and said, "It's low-budget. Who cares?"

How were the conditions at the studio?

The conditions that we worked in were not great. I don't think I had worked on a show with that low of a budget. Even the studio that we were shooting in was actually condemned to be demolished. They told us that after we were finished shooting. Conditions in there were bad. Nobody had dressing rooms. We had one room all of us would hang out in when we weren't on set. Our only luxury was we actually had a television in there. As far as catering, craft services, and coffee runs it was bare-bare-barebones.

It shows in the film. Whenever Sue was wearing everyday clothes, they were all my own clothes that I brought in. The only real "costumes" were our Fantastic Four suits and the wedding dress. When those conditions exist and you have that low of a budget, you better hope that you have a really good team and that's where we were blessed. We didn't have the money, but we had the team.

The sweetest thing is that it seems like every time an updated version of this film is made, our film gains more clout because people go, "You know what? At first I thought it was cheesy and low-budget but, whatever, it actually had a good storyline. It had a lot of heart as well. If it wasn't for the special effects this is probably the best one."

So people come around. They see some of the flaws first, but then they begin to see past those and start to appreciate the film.

People come around. The respect for our version kept growing after every other version was released because the stable points which we based this movie on endured. Even without the special effects, it's still an enjoyable movie and there's still a story. The themes are timeless. It was a little time capsule because it was shot to look like a comic book, which didn't really stamp a decade on it. If anything, it was supposed to look sort of like the 1960s, like when the comic book came out, and I think it does look a little retro, which also makes it more embraceable.

One of the greatest memories I have was the night that we were shooting up in the high desert after the crash when we're all in our space suits and we're all just realizing the changes that have happened to us. I'm turning invisible. Johnny is shooting fire out of his hands. We had to shoot the day work, and then wait for it to get dark for the night work. We were sitting around the campfire with our faces all smudged up just looking around at each other. Alex Hyde-White said, "Look at us. We're playing. This is what you imagine doing as a kid. We're in space suits in the middle of the desert sitting around a campfire with our best friends." That was just such a really nice night and I love that scene for that reason. None of us really wanted that night to end; let's just stay here by the fire. There were a lot of memories like that.

One night we were in the studio and for whatever reason we're watching *The Deer Hunter* on the television. We were running back and forth from shooting our scenes to watch it. I don't remember what we were shooting that night, but I remember there would be a big scene on the TV, and they call us to set. We'd say, "Wait. Just a minute. Hold on. Can you wait till a commercial?" (*laughs*)

Jay Underwood who played my brother Johnny Storm was actually my neighbor. Jay lived, like, two blocks away from me. I would pick him up, and we would just drive to work together. It was really like being brother and sister. Plus, he looks so much like my real-life little brother. Jay is so much like Johnny. Jay was literally on fire. He cracked me up constantly. He's one of the nicest guys in the universe. He has that positive, combustive energy. It made so much sense that he was Johnny Storm. Carl Ciarfalio, who was the stuntman inside of the Thing suit, was also my neighbor. He also lived two blocks in the other direction. The fact that the three of us lived within a four-block radius of each other in Los Angeles — we're not talking about a small town — what are the odds of that?

I just had so much fun shooting it. It was one of those movies that I didn't feel a lot of pressure while we were making it. We shot it right at the very end of the year. We started right before Christmas. The nineteenth, the twenty-first? At that time of the year everything else was shutting down. Everybody's going home for Christmas. That created a different feeling on set because it just kind of felt like a vacation. Nobody else is in town. It's a holiday. There was an ease and a relaxed attitude about it.

I wish I had more photographs. The real beauty of taking pictures is that years down the road that's all that you remember because you have a picture of it. Again, to remind people of the time period, I didn't even take my camera to the set because I got a video camera for Christmas that year. That's when video cameras were coming out for the public. If you were somebody in the business, you had one of the early versions. I took that to set instead of my regular camera, so I don't have a bunch of still photographs. What I do have are the videos, but I haven't seen them in decades because I moved years ago and a lot of the stuff from that house went into long-term storage, so those videos were packed away about fifteen years ago.

That would be great material for the fans or as a bonus feature for any formal release of the movie.

I know! I didn't think about it at all at the time. Now I go, "Oh my gosh, they're so valuable, and I wish I had them." When Mark and Marty made the *Doomed* documentary, it would have been interesting for them to look at. But they're packed away in some trunk in a crate in long-term storage down in South Los Angeles. I have to pay to get in. It would take me three days to dig through these gigantic crates. There is a little time capsule tucked away that someday I'll open. But I have to pray that there's a way to watch them because the technology is so different from when I shot them and now.

Somebody will have the equipment somewhere. I read about rock bands that have live tapes from decades ago and have to go on a scavenger hunt to find the equipment to transfer it with, but the means are out there. In Los Angeles, especially, somebody knows or knows someone who knows how to do it.

There's a way to do it. I want to find those so badly but the time and expense to rummage through all of my possessions is a lot. But I'll get there someday. The good thing is that I know they exist; the making of *The Fantastic Four* exists. It will be amazing what memories those tapes bring back because there's so much of this that we don't remember. I always love the making of, behind-the-scenes stuff. For years, whenever anything was going on, I was shooting the behind-the-scenes material with my video camera. It will be quite a treasure when I do dig it out, so I should put that on my to-do list.

This add to the intrigue and mystique of the movie. Now we have unseen, unreleased footage somewhere about an unreleased movie.

Any encounters with Roger Corman or memories related to him?

Not while we were shooting anyway. He did come to the screening of *Doomed*, which I thought was great. He took a picture with all of us. I never had a one-on-one conversation with him about anything. I did other Roger Corman films. Here's the funny thing: They are probably my best memories of work and my career which is strange because they were so low-budget. I did another Roger Corman film that was called *Stray Bullet* that we shot in Ireland. Again, same thing, super low-budget. There was no money for it, but we had an incredible director who I love with all my heart and I did it with Robert Carradine.

The two Roger Corman films that I did were two of the absolute most precious and memorable working experiences ever. Either one of those movies I would go back and do tomorrow just to work with all the same people.

Please discuss the casting and the fit between the actors and their characters.

One of the most interesting things and why I think the movie works so well is the four of us were and still are so much like the characters. It's like they literally cast the characters, which is priceless. Alex as Reed Richards was really the leader. He was experienced. He was the one who could rally the troops. He was always nineteen steps ahead of everybody else. Alex was the planner and was always thinking. He always knew what was going on and who everybody was.

It was Michael Bailey Smith's first movie ever. He to this day is one of my favorite people on the planet. He is one of the most kind-hearted, loving souls. Ironically he is in this great big muscular body that just blows your mind. He's the epitome of the gentle giant, which is what Ben Grimm was. Casting Michael Bailey Smith in that role was such a coup. He was the last one of us cast because his role was the hardest to cast. They couldn't have cast a better Ben Grimm because he is exactly like that.

I've already talked about Jay and his incredible energy, always whizzing around.

Sue was the glue. She was a cheerleader; she was the heart and soul that says, "Come on guys, we can do it." She was sensitive about things. I was still inexperienced work-wise. That was one of the characteristics of Sue. She was bashful. She was shy. She kind of followed Reed's lead. She's the one that makes the suits. "Come on guys, let's be a team" — that's so me.

Joseph Culp who played Doctor Doom is a *genius*. This guy is such an Elizabethan actor to begin with. To have somebody play Doom who has this kind of gravity, mystique, and intensity is great. When you meet Joseph, it's so rich. This guy is just so multidimensional. When I'm with Joseph, I just kind of sit back in awe and I just love listening to him talk about anything because he's so knowledgeable. He was the perfect person to play Doom. He's always reinventing himself.

When you take that, those five people, you get something wonderful. We really were those characters in our own way. Then they let us play those characters and the movie kind of made itself. If we had had a budget, this could have been one of the absolute greatest films. It's not like the talent wasn't there. It's all there.

I just wrapped on a movie three weeks ago. There's only so much I can say about it, whereas I can sit and talk about *The Fantastic Four* until the cows come home because there was so much there for all of us every day before, during, and particularly after we finished shooting because here we still are. I literally just saw Joseph a couple of weeks ago. He comes to town and stays at our house. There's nobody else that I've ever worked with that I'm such close friends with. We're all still friends. We were at a screening for a different thing and Alex was there. My husband and I had just called a cab and Alex said, "I'll take you home." That's what I just love about all of this. I would drop everything in a second to go back and do it all over again, but I'd want all of the same people doing it. Otherwise, it wouldn't be the same experience.

When you were talking some about the connections between the actors and characters. I was also thinking about Carl Ciarfalio who played the Thing. We think of the Thing as sort of an outcast in some ways that the other characters aren't because he can't turn his power off. When I talked to Carl, I had a sense that he felt good about the people in the film, he had a positive overall experience with the film, but he also felt distanced in a way. He talked about being a stunt guy and how the perception of that role differs from being an actor. There's sort of an interesting inversion that he expressed. In the film, people are scared of the Thing and run away. Carl said that on set people wanted pictures of him when was in the Thing suit but didn't care so much about him when he was just Carl. Do you see a connection between the Thing and Carl?

Michael was the last person cast. They had to make the suit before anybody was cast, so since they didn't have an actor to build the suit on that's where Carl came in. They picked Carl and built the suit according to his dimensions not realizing later that Michael is taller than Carl. It's hard to see it on film but there's one clip when Michael/Ben Grimm morphs into the Thing. He actually morphs shorter *(laughs)*. Nobody really catches it because of the way that they shot it.

I love Carl. What a trooper. Since he was a stunt guy and didn't come onto the film as an actor, he probably felt a little awkward. We all loved him. He was part of the gang, for sure, and he stayed that way. Whenever we would go to comic book conventions or do screenings, Carl was always included and always there. You talk about a heart of gold; he was one of the nicest people and funny. I think he's the funniest of all of us. Carl is hilarious. There was always a weird dynamic with the identity of the Thing for both Michael and Carl because they were kind of half and half, sharing the role. Michael had to relinquish a lot by not playing the Thing. I'm sure he would have loved to do both roles. As far as Carl being the Thing, it was hard for him to have an identity because he was really only there as the Thing, the suit, as far as the audiences are concerned. He was there physically as Carl just as much as Michael was there as Ben. We all love Carl. I feel bad if he felt left out or excluded.

Have you talked with all of the Fantastic Four?

I have an interview scheduled with Michael Bailey Smith. I've talked to Jay, Carl, and you, of course. I have corresponded with Alex, but I haven't been able to schedule something yet.

Alex is a holdout, but sometimes he does it just to be dramatic *(laughs)*. He'll talk to you.

My understanding is that Michael and Alex seemed to have the largest feeling of investment in this movie.

It is true that Alex and Michael were the most invested. When you finally get to talk to them, you will get an earful. Have you seen the *Doomed* documentary?

Yes.

So you know what to expect. Those two are definitely the most invested, personally and financially. It really was the biggest deal to those two. They're both very knowledgeable. They remember details from it that I don't. Those guys were already putting puzzle pieces together while I was completely oblivious. They have a lot more to say about that kind of stuff. My memories are about making the movie and the people. I was never in the politics of it. Even when I found out it wasn't going to be released I was like, "Oh well. That happens." That happens in this business. I didn't feel like we were targeted or that it was this gigantic catastrophe. I felt this disappointment to know that things like that happen in the business, but I wasn't over-the-cliff devastated that the movie wasn't coming out.

Here's a connection I made with that. A lot of *The Fantastic Four* is about how these characters' weaknesses became their strengths. Their superhero powers really were their human weaknesses, which I think is the best message ever for anybody about anything. Ironically, for the movie, the weakness of being shelved and never being released has, in fact, become its greatest strength.

That's a great connection. People have speculated that if it had been released, we wouldn't be talking about it now.

To me that's a really heartwarming message. It takes the theory of it, and the story of it, and actually applies it. It's true. I don't know what would have happened if it had been released. I didn't think it was going to be a great big blockbuster hit. "I'll be a star. I'll make millions." I never thought that. I knew it was a low-budget movie and I could imagine what it would physically look like once we finished it. I know it would be big with the right audience. My hope wasn't so much that this would be huge but that we could do another one. I thought this would pave the way for the sequel and then we'll have money for that one. And we would go from there. I wanted it to be a series of movies.

We figured maybe they'll even make an animated version and we can do the voices. I wanted that. So my great hope was that there would be more. When it wasn't released, that was my disappointment. We can't do any of this again. We can't build on this. We can't show them what we really are capable of. I think that would have been really great. Maybe if it had been released and we did a second one or the third one, we would still be talking about it today because it would have been a gigantic franchise. Maybe there are different ways that we would have been talking about it.

The fact that it was shelved and it became such a cult hit tells me that we reached our audience. It was the comic book fans who we felt would come to the movie that have kept it alive even until today. They still ask us to come to comic book conventions. I would wonder, "Does anyone still remember this?" But, of course, they do. It never gets old because it is timeless. I think we accomplished what we set out to do. A lot of the fans now want to show it to their kids. My brother was young when we shot this but he shows it to his kids now. I like that it's moving on now to more generations. It just keeps growing.

Is to be better to release it as it is now? Or would it be better to improve it as much as possible with what's available technologically now? I know that Joseph more than anything would love to go back and re-record and improve some of Doom's dialogue. He was literally talking through a plastic mask the whole time and so it's hard to understand him. Joseph has one of the most powerful and commanding voices on the planet. To have him redo his lines would make that character so much more ominous and powerful. The special effects could be improved. If you made all these changes, would that make it a better movie or is it better to leave the movie as it is?

What do you think?

I don't know. I've never really thought about this. That's a good question. Part of me just likes the idea of leaving it in the form that it's in because it leaves more room for discussion. That's what keeps films alive — talking about them. Which would be better: an updated version with better special effects and fixes for things we didn't have time and money to fix, or the original version that has so much heart? I don't know. Think of how special effects changed so dramatically from the year that we shot that to just two years ahead. It's one of the last pieces of film they didn't have the luxury or option of using big special effects. Two years later it would have been a completely different movie due to advancements in technology. I like that the film is a little time capsule in and of itself. There's an innocence about it. This is before everything got so big.

It's very handmade. It's very organic. Perhaps it goes back to what you were talking about earlier with weaknesses being strengths. The special effects could be better, but in some ways that works well for the movie. It's not too slick or over-the-top. That's also one of the things that makes it endearing to fans. If you went back and improved the special effects, it might be better in one sense but it loses other things. It wouldn't be that same movie anymore.

What we didn't realize when we were shooting it and what I didn't realize until I saw it with an audience is how funny it is. That's the beauty of time. The stuff that was innocently cheesy. There was a comic book convention in St. Louis called Contamination that screened the movie in a big ballroom with an audience. They had incredible sound. It was amazing. I've only seen it a couple of times myself. There is the really, really bad VHS version. A VHS version on a TV twenty years ago already puts you behind the eight ball in terms of what it looks and sounds like. When the digital copies came out on DVD, the experience is better, but the DVD will only work on my computer, so I saw it on a tiny laptop screen. Cut to watching it on a big screen with an incredible sound system and an audience. Oh. My. God. It is a movie that needs an audience. Everybody's watched some crappy version on their own at home. Nobody's seen it in the theater. It's amazing what a difference it makes. I would love for it to be released theatrically because you can watch and critique it alone, but I don't think you can enjoy it as much as you can with a group of people.

The sound blows you away. The sound editors on this deserve an award. You can't get that on a laptop or a TV from twenty years ago. It was so funny. The stuff that's kind of cheesy is funny when you watch it with a group of people. The comedy is an unexplored treasure that only comes out when you watch it with a group of people. We didn't intend for it to be funny. Sometimes the sincerity of it is funny. The bad special effects are funny. I'm sitting here with the hugest smile on my face thinking about all of this. It was really great to watch it that night in St. Louis. Some parts make you teary-eyed. Some parts make you laugh. Some parts make you want to cheer. It's all there. It takes an audience to bring out the final factor. It takes an audience component to really make it work, so that would be the nicest thing about it being released, but it should be released only in theaters so that everybody has to actually go and see it.

Is there anything you would change about the movie?

What I would change is me. What I would give to be twenty-five years younger and go back and do it all over again *(laughs)*. I wish that I would have worked harder as an actor. Maybe I just did what I was capable of at the time so I shouldn't beat myself up. I'm not particularly enthralled with my execution. I would do so many things better. It's part of the innocence. We were trying to emphasize the shyness of Sue's character. She was meek. She wasn't a leader. I wanted to play the superhero. This film was really the very beginning. In it, we are people more than we're superheroes. The point of this movie was to set up how the characters became superheroes.

We figured that there would be a sequel where we really get to BE the superheroes. The confidence that I wanted Sue Storm to have doesn't really exist that much in this one. We're more regular people. When we are superheroes, we're still sorting out our powers. We're baffled by them. I wish I had been better in it. In trying to play the innocence and the shyness, Sue comes off kind of milquetoasty, but then I have to forgive myself because that's what the character was. In the sequel I thought we could watch her mature.

Do you think Bernd went into it knowing that it wasn't going to be released and that the only reason he went into production was to hold onto the rights?

That's my belief, yes. That's what we were told. I believe that Corman didn't even know. Bernd was just contractually fulfilling the requirement that it be in "production." Then he was going to shelve it. That's what I've learned. Whether that's actually true or not, I don't know. That's how it was explained to me over the years and talking to different people.

Then they shelved it because they didn't want it to interfere with their plans for a blockbuster that they hoped was going to come out down the line. We didn't know that. The sad part for a lot of people is that even after we were finished shooting, a lot of the post-production people worked for free never knowing that it was going to be shelved. I think that the guys who did the music did that for gratis. Oley begged, borrowed, and stole to get the special effects done. To me, the real stab in the back was that THOSE people were allowed to put their money, and time, and love, and passion, and energy into finishing it when it was just going to be shelved. It's one thing to wrap and then pull the plug, but they didn't do that. They drug it out.

The Thing with the Jeweler and other outcasts. PHOTO COURTESY OF EVERETT BURRELL

Does the movie have a message?

Using your weaknesses as your strengths is the most important message to me. That's what I would like audiences to take away, as well as the idea of friendship. No matter what adverse conditions you find yourself in, friends are friends. You think of the extreme situations that these friends went through and they stay friends and help each other despite the circumstances. I'll never forget shooting the scene — it's one of my favorite scenes — when we are all back at headquarters and the Thing is out wandering around lost and upset. When he comes in, Sue runs to him and hugs him and the rest of the team comes over. That's the whole point of it. That's when they join all of their hands together and they really become the Fantastic Four. Even when our dear friend feels disenfranchised, we accept him. He feels different after he becomes the Thing. No, you're not. You're better. We're better than ever before. Right now we need that message so much. I think about what kids and young people are going through. Society has gotten so vicious.

A lot of people feel like outcasts. It just breaks my heart when people don't realize their personal worth, their personal value, their uniqueness. It's hard when you're young to see the big picture. I'm getting choked up talking about it. That's what that scene means to me and I would love for so many people to see that and feel that. So many people feel that they are outcasts. I want them to experience that scene in the movie, to experience having your friends and loved ones embrace you and say, "No you're not all of these negative things." You are valuable, and you're loved, and you're important, and you're unique, and you have strengths and talents that maybe you haven't realized you had, but you're blessed.

You look at the Thing and you know he must have been going through some heavy stuff to feel so odd, awkward, like an aberration. He has the strength to come back. He doesn't stay out wandering the streets feeling like a reject looking to do something stupid. When he feels like a reject, he comes back. When you feel like that, come back to the people whom you know love you. Maybe it's only a couple of people, but come to them and let them know that you're feeling bad and destructive. The Thing had that potential.

The Thing on the run. PHOTO COURTESY OF EVERETT BURRELL

He could easily have turned into a villain.

Yes. Instead, he process his feelings of vulnerability and his weakness. He comes back to his friends, his family, to find support and draw from their strength. He realizes he can use this awkwardness for good. That's what made him a hero. Look at all of the members of the Fantastic Four. There's a way to use all of these shortcomings as blessings. The Thing makes the decision not to be a victim. He makes the choice to believe, "I'm worth it. I'm worthy. I'm important. I'm loved. I'll see the big picture at some point and kind of muscle through," literally — no pun intended. Don't ever give up. I'd like to think that watching the movie will give people confidence and strength.

Avi Arad claims that he "burned" the film, although it survives in bootleg versions.

Do you think there is a print, negative, or other high-quality copy hidden or forgotten somewhere? Do you think it will ever be released?

I would like to think that there is a good copy somewhere. I hope there is. Even if there's a bad copy, they can make it good and clean it up digitally. I hate to think that anyone would do that to any kind of a film. No matter what, it's always worth something. When, where, how, I don't know, but I do think that eventually it will be released in some capacity.

I wish they would make a version where all of the characters are now my age. We can all do it again! Let's revisit those characters twenty-five years later. Let us make it now! Sue and Reed have their little boy who is now grown up.

The *Fantastic Four* films have not been as successful as some of Marvel's other movies. What is the difficulty with successfully transferring the *Fantastic Four* from the page to the screen?

Every version they make of this movie never quite cuts it. Why is that? People work hard making the movie so I don't think that any single person can be faulted for it.

I didn't see all of them so I don't know what worked and what didn't work. I think it's possible for somebody to make one that does. With current films like *The Avengers* the point is that you have all of these superheroes in one film. The theory that the Fantastic Four has four heroes instead of one and that might be why it doesn't work doesn't hold water anymore.

The Fantastic Four may not be as universally known. That could be one of the issues. Also, it's just never had all the pieces fall into place perfectly. There was a campaign on Twitter to have John Krasinski play Reed Richards and Emily Blunt to play Susan Storm. Maybe if they got that caliber of talent it would be huge. To make a superhero movie work they have to have a gigantic budget. A superhero movie has to out-wow whatever the superhero movie was last week and now there's so many of them. That's part of the problem because the focus of the movie becomes outdoing the one before it whether in terms of explosions, or special effects, or 3D. Another problem is they have, or think they have, to get the biggest name actors to play these characters whether they're right for it or not.

Have you seen the latest *Avengers* movie?
No.

Are you going to see it? I don't want to spoil anything for you.
No, I probably won't because it's not really my genre, so go ahead. If I see it, I'll still enjoy it.

In the latest one the main villain, Thanos, is trying to acquire some stones that will give him the power to kill half of the people in the universe. I thought about that when you talked about how these movies are currently trying to outdo one another. Where do you go from trying to kill half of the universe? Unmaking reality?
These filmmakers are trying to satisfy an incredibly wide audience. They want it to be recognized as good filmmaking, but they still have to satiate all of these action fanatics. There are two different audiences. One wants to see a good film. One is more concerned about the action and spectacle. I would like to think that the filmmakers have a bigger goal than just making money. I hope that they want to create a film that leaves the audience as better people for having seen it.

Have you seen *Logan*?
No.

Are you familiar with the X-Men?
Yes, but I don't know a lot about them. I know Logan was Hugh Jackman's character. That was him before he becomes Wolverine?

It's the other end of the timeline. It's sort of what you were talking about earlier about shooting the characters later on in life. The X-Men have kind of fallen apart. Logan is sick and deteriorating. Professor X is losing his mind. I don't know if it's inspirational, but it's very powerful, very good. It's less about spectacle and more about character. Maybe that's a phase that these movies will move towards. We've seen a lot of the prequels and an examination of who these people were before they were heroes. Those have been successful, but you can only go so far in that direction, too. Do you start making movies about superheroes as infants?

That's great that they went there with Logan. Age is an untapped subject in superhero movies. It's something we all experience. Everybody gets older. Every generation is getting a little bit older. There's so much to explore with that. I definitely will see Logan. I love him, and I want to see what they did with the idea of him getting older. You can cover those kinds of topics and still be entertaining, poignant, and meaningful.

I'm thinking about what you're saying earlier with the spacecraft scene. They just acquired their powers. They're discovering them, figuring out what that's all about. It's sort of the same thing with aging. It's not so much an exploration of power as it is an exploration of change. I don't know that aging is strictly a decline as it is pretty much portrayed in Logan, but it does bring changes, trade-offs. It's that same process of discovering who you are now, how things work differently, changes to your body. Maybe that connection is there between the two films also.

Oh, yeah. Those connections are there. Things do change. Now I think, "I need a nap. Why am I so tired?" (laughs)

What have you been up to since making The Fantastic Four? Any more films or television programs related to comic books or Marvel?

Not really comic books. I did vampires with the revival of Dark Shadows. They had a comic book for that, too. The audience was somewhat similar. That was the first time I played a vampire. On Port Charles they had a whole storyline with vampires. I got to be a vampire for that too, which I really love to do. I always wanted to go on *True Blood* or one of those vampire shows. I want one more shot at being a vampire.

I've been fortunate. Part of the advantage that I had when we were shooting the film and one of the reasons that I wasn't seriously devastated when it didn't come out was that I was working. I was doing one project on top of another. When they announced *The Fantastic Four* wasn't going to be released, I had been working nonstop. I've been very blessed. I've worked consistently. I've been on a lot of classic shows. I like when I go into an audition and they look at my resume and say, "Oh, my God. You were Susan Storm." I like that as much as when they go, "Oh, you were on *Seinfeld*," or, "You were on *Cheers*." It's nice to have those milestones. It's not superheroes, but those projects are timeless. People recognize me from *The Wonder Years*, *Ellen*, *The Drew Carey Show*, *Beverly Hills 90210*, *Glee* — all of those kinds of things.

You've played characters on *Guiding Light* and *The Young and the Restless* as well as *Port Charles*. Are there any similarities between making a soap opera and the making of *The Fantastic Four*?

No. Not really. The beauty of a soap opera is you get to be the same character day in and day out, so you have a whole life of this character that you go through. In a film you have a finite amount of time. This film was during this particular segment of Sue's life. On the soap opera it's a lot of repetition. It takes a lot of time to get from point A to point B. In a film you have to move quicker. Doing a soap is different from doing most things anyway because of the speed in which you have to get so much material in. There are similarities with the budget. We had to do a lot in a very short amount of time. The beauty of the film is you have the luxury of time. You can shoot three or four pages a day in a film if you have the luxury. When I was on *Port Charles* we shot two episodes a day, so we were doing like eighty pages a day. You have a deadline. We had to be out of the studio every day at 5:30 come hell or high water.

With a soap opera you're running up against the clock. On a soap you often don't even get a block to rehearse. You get to set and it's "This is where you come in. You sit over there. After you pour the drink you walk out. Okay, and 'action.' " A lot of times you don't even get to walk through it. Plus, you're just memorizing boatloads of material. As soon as it's out of your mouth you forget it in order to make room for the next juggernaut of dialogue that you have coming up for the next day. That's the biggest challenge with a soap opera: There's no time, but there's so much material. You get one take and that's usually it. You don't have the luxury of doing anything over. That was the only similarity I would say between being on the soap opera and *The Fantastic Four*. We didn't have time.

Instead of it being a regular film where you shoot four pages a day, we're shooting like EIGHTY pages a day. I don't remember exactly how many it was, but it was a lot. We never had that luxury of trying things or shooting things again to make them better. You either have to get it right the first time or live forever with what you did the first time. That's about the only similarity.

I don't know a whole lot about shooting soaps, but I thought about the small budget, the frequent use of plot twists, the limited special effects, and the deep and extended character histories. Even if you can't get into all of that in the film, the Fantastic Four have decades of history like some of the soap opera characters.

Well, that is true. Those are some good connections.

And you've done other projects.

Then I had a period when I did all of the letter shows. *CSI*, *NCIS*, if it had letters in it, I did it *(laughs)*. I did *Dexter*. I was on *Masters of Sex*, *The Mentalist*, *Criminal Minds*, and *Desperate Housewives*. I was in *Nip/Tuck* with Julian McMahon who played Doctor Doom, so if you watch the show there's a scene of Sue Storm and Doctor Doom having sex on his desk.

That's funny because in the 2005 *Fantastic Four* Sue and Victor are in a romantic relationship.

Oh, they are? I didn't see it.

I'm working a lot in Vancouver. That's actually where I'm at right now. They do so many Hallmark productions up here that I've had the opportunity to do several of those. There's a huge following for Hallmark. I'm in the process of negotiating for another one of their mystery movies. Those movies kind of last forever as well. There are constantly new films and TV series that I'm working on. Fortunately, they keep adding up.

The *Fantastic Four* is the one that goes on the longest. The thing I get most recognized from is *Love Potion No. 9* with Sandra Bullock and Tate Donovan. I only have two scenes in the whole movie and they were added later. *The Fantastic Four* and *Love Potion No. 9* are the two most enduring pieces of work that I've done. I would do a Corman movie again. It's just fun working. It's not about the money or the prestige. A budget doesn't necessarily reflect the quality of the project. If it's a good story, actors will do it just because they want to be part of it. That's a good message for writers and independent filmmakers.

Write it and get it on the page because you may not get the biggest star to do it, but it'll get done. The only way to get the big stars to do it is to write it. Writers have to stick with it. Actors spend most of their time banging their heads against a wall, but it's probably worse for writers. Everybody wants to be on the next big hit show, sitcom, or movie, but it's just as exciting and fulfilling to be involved with something that has a great script, something that you're excited about. You think, "I don't care if it's just a little cable show; I want to make this." You can get frustrated when nothing's out there, but it's very rewarding when you read things that are good. If you want it done, just do it.

What else have you learned?

Don't get intimidated by the competition. It's not easy. There are a lot of winners in Hollywood. A lot of actors show up in Los Angeles thinking, "I was the lead in my school play, I was prom king, and I can sing, so I'm going to take Los Angeles by storm." They come and their eyes pop open because everybody was the lead in their school play, everybody's good looking, everybody can sing, and everybody was prom king. You have to compete with the best of the best. That's what it's all about. It's not easy. None of it's easy. You spend more time not working than you do working. That's the life of an actor.

It's tough as you get older because there's not roles for actors my age. There are a lot of actors who are a lot bigger stars than me and are considered first for roles, but I'm still here. I'm still working. I'm still plugging away. It's never really over as long as you keep doing your best.

Whether you are continuing to do what you love or striking out and trying to find your space, keep putting it out there. The rewards don't come for free.

A lot of times we don't show or see the work and the craft that goes into the final product, so people think if it looks easy, then it must be easy.

Michael Bailey Smith
Ben Grimm

What experience did you come with to *The Fantastic Four*?
It was one of my first films. I had done one film before that called *CIA Code Name: Alexa*. It had O.J. Simpson, Lorenzo Lamas and Kathleen Kinmont. I was hired to do a fight scene. I was a pretty good fighter. I had been studying pretty hard. I came from an athletics background. I was never in theater. I don't have any kind of degree or anything like that in acting. My degree is in computer science. I had only done one film and one TV show by that time. They liked what I did and said, "Hey, we're going to give you some dialogue." Next thing you know the fight scene turned into being the fourth lead in the film. That's all the experience I had.

What about *A Nightmare on Elm Street 5: The Dream Child*?
I had done one other little thing before that to get me kind of started in the whole business. I was lucky enough to land *A Nightmare on Elm Street*. I played a character called Super Freddy, a bigger version of Freddy Krueger. That happened by accident because I went with a friend of mine to an audition. I was living in San Diego at the time and he was coming up to Los Angeles to read for this movie. He said, "Let's go to Los Angeles to read for this film and then we'll go up to Gold's Gym and train." I was into bodybuilding. I was pretty big. I said, "Cool." So he went up there and I was just waiting and he did his thing. The casting director asked, "Why don't you audition?" I said, "Well, I'm not an actor." She said, "Why don't you come in?" So I met the director, laughed like Freddy Krueger for the part, and I got the job. That is when I realized I wanted to make it a career, so I moved to Los Angeles and studied

hard. I was taking acting classes three or four times a week and spending all my extra money on that because that's what I found out I wanted to do after I did the *Nightmare on Elm Street* film.

So you had a couple of scenes. How was that different from actually playing a character?

My acting experience was very limited with building a character and carrying a character all the way through. This was really cool to be one of the leads in a superhero film and actually have a character that had a lot of dynamics and emotions. Basically, it was me in real life. It was kind of nice to play something like that. I got to work with all these really seasoned actors like Rebecca Staab, Alex Hyde-White, Jay Underwood, and Carl Ciarfalio, this phenomenal, historic, legendary stuntman. I learned a lot from him. I was like a big sponge. Besides playing the character, actually getting to work with these phenomenal actors and just really appreciating the craft of acting, just being around these great people and learning how they work was the biggest takeaway.

How did you find your way to *The Fantastic Four*?

I went to a typical audition. They had a casting breakdown and I went to it and read. I was booked for another TV show called *Renegade* so I went down to San Diego to film that. I was Jesse "The Body" Ventura's brother and we were the Butler Brothers. It was a two-week shoot. Over the weekend they had me return for a callback. I read for Oley Sassone. The next thing you know they hired me. A lot of times it takes weeks, even a month or more, sometimes to get things going. This one happened really, really quickly. This is the end of November or start of December. Normally Hollywood shuts down the first or second week of December.

Did you have any encounters with Roger Corman or have any experiences related to him?

Before, no. It was more after the film than during the production. When Alex and I were doing publicity for the movie, I got to interact with Roger Corman because we asked him for stills and things like that. It was all black and white stuff that they gave us for free. He has always been very gracious to me and very nice to me, just a gentleman. He has his niche with the kind of stuff he does. He's been very successful and launched a lot of careers doing it.

What challenges or limitations did you experience while making the film?
As an actor I'm a physical dude. I've always been. I was in the military for a while. I played college football. I ended up going to the Dallas Cowboys. When I found out that they hired a stunt guy for the film I was like, "I don't understand; why don't they put me in the suit?" They told me later that their experience with actors was "Yeah, they want to get in the suit, but then they're not physically ready, they pass out, and they're difficult, so we hired a stunt guy who is used to doing that kind of thing." They didn't know me. Not being able to play the Thing was a limitation. To me the Thing is the coolest part of the film. I wish all the blessings and grace to Carl because Carl was freaking awesome. Since that film he's been a tremendous friend of mine and to my family as well. I've done probably four or five things with him since in my twenty-five years of acting. He did a stunt coordinating job when I was an actor.

So you've got two guys who in a way are sharing a role. How did you two work that out so that it seems like Ben Grimm as the Thing instead of two completely separate characters?
When the Thing was on the set, I wasn't there being filmed at the same time. I would go to the set, and I would help Carl. He had to do the acting portion, and I went over and voiced all of his dialogue. He did all of the physical stuff. He and I worked together. I showed him how I would have done the scene. He would copy that, but he would also add a lot of his own stuff in there, too, because he's a very seasoned pro. I really wanted to carry that whole character through.

It was kind of challenging to do the voiceover work for that because now you're acting in a dark room in a soundstage. That's a lot different than actually being on a set engaging with the other actors and seeing them. Things are meant to be and I would never have met Carl and built a great relationship with him otherwise, so it was a blessing in disguise.

Why did they use one person for Ben Grimm and another person for the Thing?

They cast us right before we filmed, probably three or four weeks. It takes longer than that to make the suit, so they had already decided way before that to hire a stunt guy. Carl was already going to fittings, moldings, and all those things like that.

So they wouldn't have necessarily known that they were going to end up with a really physical, athletic guy like yourself?

Agreed. It was just meant to be. I'm so glad that Carl could share that experience with all of us.

Knowing now what Carl went through in his suit — how hot and uncomfortable it was — do you still wish you could have played the Thing?

Of course. I'll say that forever. Of course. I've been in some pretty sticky situations as an actor. I just finished something where I was buried from the neck down for about three days out in the Mojave Desert. It would have been fun to be the Thing, but again I love that Carl did it. He did a phenomenal job. The only thing is that he's a lot shorter than I am, so there's a difference in height. Ben Grimm is taller and then he gets a lot shorter as the Thing. People explain it away by saying, "Well, rock is a lot heavier, so it compressed his body." Of course I would have done it, but it's a lot easier to just be an actor. I've done lots of stuff with prosthetics on. In Morocco it was 130 degrees out when I did *The Hills Have Eyes*. I was completely miserable during some of the things I've done. Carl is a lot like me. We're both guys that have been rough-and-tumble dudes. I have the attitude more of a stunt guy than an actor anyway.

What was your approach to playing Ben Grimm?

I looked at some books and things like that, but I kind of stayed away from that because I wanted to take my own approach and come from a fresh point of view. Ben is a lot like me in real life. He was a football player. He was an astronaut. I wasn't, but I was into computer science. We both were physical, into football, and we also were educated. He's probably a lot smarter than I am, but he's a freaking rocket scientist. He's a pilot; he's awesome.

I grew up being this tall, skinny, gawky individual with big ears sticking out, and I was picked on all the time in high school. It got so bad sometimes, especially my freshman year, that I would have to literally find a new way to my bus each day because I had people waiting for me to beat me up. I had to leave early or go late or try to avoid this one group of guys who were always wanting to beat me up. Ben is that. He's kind of that outcast when he becomes the Thing. I could relate to that as well as some of the emotion that he was going through. For him it's not understanding why and I didn't know why I was getting picked on. Why was I getting picked on? So my ears stick out and I grew up in the military, so maybe my hair was shorter than everybody else's in the 1970s. You wonder why. I have a friend like that. His daughter is actually thinking of killing herself and now she's getting some help. Same thing. You look at today's climate with kids. Most of these kids who do these things, who shoot up schools for example, are kids that have been bullied. I never thought about killing anyone.

What kind of helped me that I was good at athletics, so I just used that as my way to get back at the people who bullied me. That took me to the Dallas Cowboys. I just wish more people would figure out a way to deal with it positively instead of doing it through violence. And maybe find a positive way of building yourself up.

I'm in the business world now. I basically quasi-retired from acting back in 2014. Let me tell you there are some studs in the business world. They might not have been athletic studs, but they are multimillionaires. They know how to make deals. You walk in the room and you are in awe. I have customers that are from Amazon, Apple, Microsoft, and Google — the biggest players in the space. They are like movie stars. These guys are sharp. These are probably the guys that were picked on and beat up. Maybe, I'm not sure. I look up to them and think, "You guys are awesome." I want to be like them.

I really appreciate the honesty of that answer and you sharing your personal ordeal.

I'm giving you a lot more than you asked for. I'm sitting here talking about this and I'm having, like, tears running down my face.

It's such a moving answer.

That's how Ben Grimm is, I think. There's a lot of him being the outcast. He's not part of the clique, but Susan and people like that try to bring him back into their group. I think that's good. She's the mother of the group, so it's kind of nice.

I teach at a college for students who have learning disabilities. So I've seen a lot of people who have been picked on and felt the brunt of that. I think a lot of people can really relate to your story. I certainly can. Thanks for telling it.

The thing is people say to me, "You're such an overachiever." I just live my life. I've always said to myself I want to do everything a hundred percent, give everything I have, my passion and my drive, to whatever I'm doing. I'm going to do my best to be the best that I can be and try to be the best at whatever I'm doing. And if I can't be the best, then guess what? I'm okay with that because I gave everything I have. If I come in second, I'm okay with that because I did the best I could. I'm this big guy. I used to be a pretty good martial artist, a fighter. You think you might always be the toughest dude on the planet, but there's always someone tougher. You'll always find someone a little bit faster, a little bit smarter, a little bit more whatever, but that's okay as long as you give a freaking hundred percent and do everything you can do to be the best you can be. It's cliché to say, but it's true.

You're okay, and I wish people that aren't in the clique, that aren't the pretty ones, could realize that they're fine as they are. I wish they could just cut out all that bullshit and try to work to be the best they can be. Everybody has something special and unique to offer. They really do. They just have to find it. Everybody has their weaknesses, too. No one's perfect. If they could just work to be the best and give their passion and drive to that, then I think a lot of those negativities and ideas of wanting to hurt people will go away. I really do.

You've spoken about moving away from acting. Maybe you should consider becoming a motivational speaker. I can also see why you would have been one of the best people to promote the film. On that note, I understand you and Alex really got into promoting the film. How did that get started?

After the film, we started looking at comic book festivals. For some reason, they were going to show *The Fantastic Four* trailer. I went to this. They showed the trailer. You would not believe the line of people that were out the door and down the street waiting to see this trailer. We knew we did something. We didn't know the whole story behind this. We didn't know anything about how Bernd and Constantin Film just wanted to make this movie to keep the rights. We were these actors that did this great little film and we were just naive and kind of innocent. Alex was the most seasoned in the business, so he kind of knew about what to do.

After the screening I turned to Alex and said, "This is pretty crazy." He says, "You know what? We need to leverage this." I said, "What do you want to do?" He says, "Let's hire a publicist." I turned to Alex and I said, "Let's do this." He and I went at it. We hired the publicist. We started setting up all these showings. We went to comic book stores. We went everywhere, and we started bringing the cast along, too. One of my acting coaches told me whenever you get your break, you need to do whatever you can to really capitalize on that break, meaning if you need to spend money, take the money you've made and put it back into promoting the film. Whatever you need to do, do it because this will catapult you. I ended up paying for a publicist. He was a startup publicist, but he wasn't cheap.

How much did all this cost?

I don't know how much I ended up spending. When it was all said and done, it was probably close to $15,000 out of my own pocket over probably a six or seven month period.

Why was the film never released? Who knew what when?

It's business. It's not show friends, show fun, or show anything. It's show business; it's all about making the money. That's the reason why. It's not okay that they did it to us, but I understand it from a business point of view. Maybe what they should have done is told us at the beginning, which they didn't. They didn't tell anybody. I think Roger Corman knew, or maybe he didn't.

So you folks didn't know anything until after filming was done?

Yep. I didn't know about anything until probably right at the end of this whole thing, about a year later. We were told to cease and desist on any promotional activity in November or December of 1993. We had already set up a premiere. It was supposed to be in January at the Mall of America. Alex had set up a thing with the Children's Miracle Network, Ronald McDonald House, and a bunch of different radio and television affiliates. National stuff. We were in magazines and such. There were trailers being played. I heard there were trailers being played at the theater where it was supposed to premiere. I don't know if that was a rumor or not.

When do you think Bernd knew? What do you think his intention was?

It was purely a business thing. Again, I understand. What he didn't know or understand is the drive that we had as actors. I did a movie with Jean-Claude Van Damme called *In Hell*. We shot that in Bulgaria. I respect him for the way that he got his career started. I don't remember what movie it was, but he stood out and was pushing the film as hard as he could. He was selling copies out of the back of his trunk or something crazy like that, just doing whatever he could to promote the thing. That's kind of how he got his career going, and it demonstrates the drive he had. That's the same thing we did as actors and Oley as well. Even when he was working on other stuff, he was finishing the film by having footage snuck in to him. That's the beauty of Hollywood: People give their time and money for certain projects. Right now I work in the business world. That's pretty black and white. You don't see a whole lot of people doing things for free. In Hollywood people will do things for free in the name of the art.

When do you think Roger knew?

I don't think he knew at the beginning. We were going around the country and doing all this promotional work. If he knew, then why would he give us promotional material for free? It doesn't make any sense. It would be a waste. Why would he do that if he knew this was going to be shelved? That's a good point to think about. He probably found out before we did, probably not until the end. I remember we were coming back from somewhere, Florida or New York, and I had the trailer. They play videos on airplanes, and back in the day it was VHS. I got them to pop in *The Fantastic Four* trailer and play it. They played it and the whole plane cheered. It was awesome.

When do you think Oley found out?
I think he probably heard rumors. I think the hope was that we were going to promote this so much, get it so big that they couldn't refuse to release it because it had so much momentum.

If Oley heard rumors, when do you think you might have heard them?
He probably heard some stuff at the beginning. I think Alex knew more. Alex is pretty movie savvy. He grew up in the movie business. He knows about these things. Not me, I was clueless. Me and Alex did most of the promotion. It was good. It was fun.

Referring to the film's cancellation, you said in 1994 that "It's like knowing you had the winning lottery ticket and then lost it in the laundry." How do you feel now?
(Laughs) I have to tell you I've lost a lot of lottery tickets in the laundry since then. You kind of learn. I've done television shows where I had recurring roles and they told me that next season they're going to bring me back as a series regular. Then the show gets canceled. Or they tell me that they're going to make me a series regular and move the show up to Canada. Then they move up to Canada, but they don't take me. Other times they tell me that they're going to bring me onto this film that's going to be huge, but then they don't. Or I lose out because Schwarzenegger calls the director and gets his buddy into the film. I've had these kinds of instances happen. It's part of the business. When it's the first time, it has the biggest impact. That's probably why I said that, and it's true. I mean, I might have exaggerated a bit because maybe it would have been released and people would have panned it and it wouldn't have gone anywhere. But at the time it really felt like I lost something big.

I had hair back then. I was kind of pretty. (laughs) When I started as an actor, I put on the mirror of my Hollywood apartment "Michael Bailey Smith — Hollywood's new leading man." That's what I wanted to be, this big muscular good-looking dude. At least I thought I was kind of good-looking; I used to get the chicks back in the day. I'd be that kind of guy, a leading man. That didn't happen. I ended up playing bad guys, which is better. I think playing good guys is sometimes kind of boring. I had a lot of fun playing bad guys, and I made a good career out of it.

What did you learn from the whole experience?

I learned how much you don't have control over your career, especially in terms of what a film does, what the life of a film is after you finish. It showed me what I could do, what I can do. Me and Alex started this thing, and we got everybody else involved and got the momentum built. Another thing I learned on the opposite side of that is when you finish a film, you have to walk away and hope for the best because it's not up to you. If they give you an opening where you have some control, boy, take it, and see what you can do with it.

I've done that with a couple of things. I did a film short called *Blood Shot* with a friend of mine, Dietrich Johnston, who's the director. I knew him from when he was in film school. I would do his film school movie skits and projects like that. We shot it over the weekend. He put it together and put it out at some festivals and I won best actor. He won best writer, best director, and things like that. It's about a vampire who works for the CIA and kills terrorists. It's a little bit tongue-in-cheek. You can go on the Internet and watch it on YouTube. He ran into some guys, they gave him about $3 million, and he made the film.

You learn how to hustle. I've learned from the many times that I've auditioned and been told no countless times and been told yes countless times. I take that and use that in other parts of my life. Right now I head up all of the development for this company and I handle all of North America. I travel a tremendous amount, and I walk into the room with probably the biggest players in the world when it comes to the technology business and I'm not phased by it whatsoever. Most of the time I win them over. A lot of that is because of the twenty-five or more years that I've been in Hollywood.

I learned how you can take something small and really make it into something bigger. We made something from nothing with *The Fantastic Four*. We could have just let the trailer play during that one film festival, left it at that, and not done anything else. Then it wouldn't have went anywhere. Me and Alex started getting this thing going, got everything else involved, and next thing you know momentum started building. Then everything stopped.

It's almost a blessing that it got shelved, if you think about it. It's been all these years and people are still talking about it. There was a documentary made about it. On the Internet and Facebook I see petitions to get it released. If it had been released at the beginning, none of this stuff would have happened and you wouldn't be talking to me right now.

What themes do you see in the movie?

There's definitely the love story between Reed Richards and Susan Storm. There's themes about teens with Johnny trying to find his way. There's the struggle of Ben Grimm and what he goes through with wanting to get back to the way he was and finally accepting what he is. Actually, I don't think he really accepts it at the end, but he figures something out because he comes back to the group. Of course, there's the bigger theme of good versus evil with Doctor Doom.

What did you think of Joseph Culp's performance?

Joseph is so meticulous and artistic. He does a phenomenal job. He is Doctor Doom. Other people have played that character, but no one compares to what he did.

You've played a lot of villains. What is the psychology of a bad guy?

Most bad guys don't think that they're bad guys. Most people who do bad things don't think that they're doing bad things. They have a purpose and a reason behind it. They can explain what they do. And it makes sense, at least to them. Doctor Doom is the same way. He has a purpose and a reason behind what he's doing. For me, who went from playing Ben Grimm to then playing a whole lifelong series of bad guys in films and TV shows, I learned a lot from that. Bad guys don't actually think they're bad. They think this is what they're supposed to do. It's their mission. There's a reason why they do this; it's not just because they're bad. If you play a bad guy from the perspective that they're just bad, then it's not going to be real. As a bad guy if you really believe in what you're doing because it has purpose and it's for a greater good or greater goal, then it'll come off being real.

The best way, then, to play a bad guy is as if the bad guy really thinks that he's a good guy?

Yes, agreed. When you do that, you add so much more color and depth to that character. You can play it to the point where the audience might start feeling sympathy, or empathy, or pity for you. That sounds kind of crazy, but I played enough bad guys to know that. You got an acting lesson out of that, too.

Thank you. What you say makes a lot of sense. It's interesting also because I've found in doing these interviews that the characters that people tend to talk most about are the

The heads of Doctor Doom and the Thing. PHOTO COURTESY OF EVERETT BURRELL

Thing and Doctor Doom. They seem to be the most complex and complicated characters. I've thought the Thing has gone through a lot of the same circumstances that create villains. Maybe that's true for lot of heroes, but it seems more so for the Thing than the other members of the Fantastic Four.

Marvel's Avi Arad claims that he "burned" the film, although it survives in bootleg versions. Do you think there is a print, negative, or other high-quality copy hidden or forgotten somewhere?

He might have burned it. Not to disclose too much, but I know that there are probably some pretty good copies of it floating around.

Do you think it will ever be released?

I hope. Probably not. I signed the petition to get it released. I even announced it to my Facebook friends when I was pushing the *Doomed* documentary that was coming out.

I still think they should release it. Fix up some of the special effects because, come on, man, it was released during the same time as *Jurassic Park* or right around then. If *The Fantastic Four* had some of the same special effects as that, it would have been pretty darn good. I'm not really happy with my performance compared to what I can do now, though.

What's your opinion of the 2005 version?

That's the first one that was made after ours, right?

Yes.

It's funny. I've never seen any of them. I've seen bits and pieces, but I've not sat down and watched them. I just haven't. Julian McMahon was Doctor Doom in the 2005 version. He and I share a similar story, or shared path. Three of four years before he did that film he was on *Charmed*. He played Cole Turner and I played his evil alter ego Belthazor.

You said that you had seen bits and pieces of it. Do you have any opinion of those bits and pieces?

It looks great. I don't know if the story is very good. The visual effects are phenomenal. I think the Thing costume and the Doom costume were both so much better in our film than anything that's been done since. Everybody else has done it digitally, so it looks a little funky. Our Thing looks like the original right out of the comic book, so does Doctor Doom.

Can I share a story about the 2005 *Fantastic Four* and Fox?

Please do.

After the film was shelved, we heard that Chris Columbus and his production company were going to do it. I had an audition at 20th Century Fox. I knew that they bought and shelved the film and they were making a new version. I always had this thing about going to audition for anything on Fox's lot because these jerks killed my film. I had an audition there, and I was reading for some film. It was in the Chris Columbus building. I was walking down the hallway. I passed by an open door and looked in. I saw something that said "F 4 pics" on the floor leaning up against a desk. I stopped, and I gave it a second look. I thought, "Well, that's interesting." I walked into the office and said, "Hello." This lady comes around the corner and says, "Yes, may I help you?" I said, "I see you have something that says 'F 4 pics.' Is that from the new *Fantastic Four*?" She picked it up off the ground, and held it like I was going to steal it. She says, "Yeah, and why are you asking?" "I was in the original *Fantastic Four*." She says, "We are doing the original *Fantastic Four*." I say, "No, there was an original one done in 1994." By this time it was the early 2000s. I told her, "You are incorrect. We did it. It was done by Roger Corman. I played the character of Ben Grimm." She said, "Oh. Well. We're doing it now, so...thank you." I just walked out.

The *Fantastic Four* films have not been as successful as some of Marvel's other movies. What is the difficulty with successfully transferring the *Fantastic Four* from the page to the screen?

The *Fantastic Four* is a family film. To a certain extent it's an action film. When it gets really commercialized, and they add in all the fancy visual effects and pomp and circumstance, you lose some of that family feel, some of that heart that makes it so special. They got away from the original story as well.

What have you been up to since making *The Fantastic Four*? Other than being in the documentary *Doomed! The Untold Story of Roger Corman's The Fantastic Four* (2015), any more films or television programs related to comic books or Marvel?

In 2014 I wanted to step away from acting for a while. I got to the point where I wasn't appreciating what I was doing, and I wanted to do something different. I started complaining to myself. I drove in for an audition for a commercial. All I had to do was slate, which means basically just to say, "Hey, my name is Michael Bailey Smith." They want you to turn to your side. They said, "Thank you so much." I was walking back to my car saying to myself, "Are you freaking kidding me? Is this what my life has ended up being now?"

When I first started acting, I would go to an audition. I was young, full of excitement. I would see these other actors. They were older — sometimes much older — people I had seen on TV back in the 1970s or 1980s. I'm thinking, "What happened to his career? Why is he auditioning with me? It doesn't make any sense. He must be doing terrible, or he's at the end of his career." Well guess what? Now I'm at the end of my career and I'm going to auditions seeing these young dudes and I've realized that I've become that guy that I commented about. That really bothered me for a while. That along with just wanting to do something different, something more had led me to take a break from the business. I've done this. I've taken it as far as I can go.

Rebecca Staab talked about how it's tougher to find roles as you get older. In a sense, it seems kind of like starting over.

I might come back to Hollywood later, maybe in a different aspect. I've written about ten to twelve screenplays. I have one that I'm working on right now that I'm turning into a novel. I have a publisher who wants to get it published. I'm still staying creative but I'm not doing the day-to-day auditioning and hustling. Instead of waiting tables as an actor, I worked at a test laboratory for a computer products business. I became an expert in wireless technologies and have my degree in computer science so it's a natural progression for me to move into the tech space. I've taken that expertise and when I wanted to leave acting, I became head of development for this company called Osram Sylvania that deals in lighting and connected lighting. It's in the same space as IoT (the Internet of Things). I did that for a year and didn't really like the company, so now I work for a company that manufactures IoT products. I'm known for taking companies that have no presence in a certain area and building them out to be millions of dollars. That's what I'm doing now with this company. My next adventure is to start my own company. I want to ride this to the end and see how far I can take this. I want to see how successful I can be in the business world. I did pretty well in the acting world.

I love my wife and family. About five or six years ago I told my agent that I don't want to travel. I want to stay around Hollywood as much as possible and focus on my family. It was important to me for my kids to be well-rounded and good human beings. My wife is totally supportive of what I do as long as it's supporting the family.

I'm head of development for this company called Leedarson. I travel probably half of the time or a little more.

I love it because it reminds me a lot of acting. I get on the plane. I get my rental car. I go to the customer and it's like auditioning. I'll try to win them over. I'm older now, so people ask me, "When are you going to retire?" I tell people that I already had my retirement in the beginning when I was an actor. That was fun. Now it's time to get serious. I'm going to bust my ass until I fall over.

Jay now is a preacher, which is awesome. Rebecca is still doing it, Carl is still doing it, Joseph is still doing it, Alex is doing more production stuff but he's still associated with the business, and Oley is still doing it. I consciously made the decision to pay attention to my family. I could easily still be doing movies and going around the world, but then I'd be this lonely actor with nobody. I'm a family guy. We have TV shows that we like to watch and a pool in the backyard and a little barbecue. I stuck my toes in the acting world. I got to walk the red carpet a few times. I won some awards and things like that. Now it's back down to reality.

Every so often when I see a project that looks nice, I'll do it. I just did this project called *Miracle Desert* coming out in a few months. I just saw a little clip of it, and it looks pretty good. Mark Hosack wrote and directed it about ten years ago. I read for it, he wanted to hire me, and then funding fell through. It never happened. He called me up out of the blue a couple of months ago and says, "Hey Michael, I'm going to do this film, just a film short of it. Would you mind doing it?" I hadn't been an actor in front of the camera for about three and a half years so I said, "Yeah, I'll do it." My manager is very happy and asks me if I'm going to get back into it. I said, "We'll see — if the right project comes along." After I wanted to walk away and take a break for a while, I've been turning down movies and TV shows. Some of it has been pretty big. I might be open to it and come back. My wife thinks I'm crazy.

You never know. You might feel refreshed and recharged and want to come back to it. You sound like you're in a really great place where you can pick and choose what you want to do and don't have to jump immediately at everything that comes by.

Agreed. Right now I'm working on the funding to start a new company. I have some good ideas for the IoT space that might make some money. I'd like to have more control so I think that's part of why I've gotten way from acting.

When you say "control," what exactly do you mean?

The supply chain: manufacturing, distribution, shipping, and actual product placement in the store. It's like being an actor. Every actor wants to have more control over things like the editing process and how the film is distributed. They'd like to have that control, but they don't. It's like flying in a plane. The most terrifying thing about flying in a plane is not being able to fly the damn thing and not being able to look out the front window. Give me a parachute. Everybody wants to have a little more control over their destiny. With the work ethic, passion, and connections that I have, I think I could do really well with my own business.

Please complete this sentence — referring to the unreleased version — "The Fantastic Four is..."

A great little film that nobody ever saw.

This is where I thank you for your time and willingness to do the interview, and ask if there is anything else you want to add or talk about.

There's one other thing I want to mention. This was disappointing. It hurt my feelings. I was really shocked. Stan Lee came to the set. We thought it was a big deal that he was coming to the set. He was there and he seemed excited, happy about what was going on and what he saw. If this was supposed to be shelved, why did he come to the set? The answer is no one knew. Roger Corman didn't know. The director didn't know. No one knew. Bernd knew this and didn't tell anybody. He didn't even tell Stan Lee. This is before Stan Lee became a movie mogul, of course. I remember he came up to me and he says, "Hey Michael." I say, "Yes sir." He says, "I have to tell you that you are what I envisioned for Ben Grimm." I'm like, "Wow, that's really phenomenal! Thank you sir. I appreciate that." I felt awestruck. He told me that when we were in downtown Los Angeles and we're filming the scene in the movie where Alicia Masters bumps into me and knocks over the statue. I pick it up and give it back to her and that's how I meet her. That's the start of the relationship.

We flash forward to six months after the film. It was July or August. I'm at Comic-Con. They had us all there. We had a table. Stan Lee was there doing a panel. I was listening to him and waiting for him to say something about *The Fantastic Four*. Someone asked him, "So what do you think about *The Fantastic Four* film coming out?" I'm paraphrasing but he said something like, "Yeah, I don't really give it much hope. It's not that good of a film. I know people tried hard." I'm like, "You just killed us." That really hurt me when I heard that. I can't believe he said that.

That must have been tough to hear after you put all of that effort into making the film and promoting it.

I think maybe Alex had even more interaction than I did. I remember going back to the table thinking, "He just destroyed us." Disheartening. I know Stan Lee was trying to be as politically correct as possible. I think what happened by that time is that the whole Marvel thing started. Hollywood was going to start throwing a lot more money at superhero projects. I think that was the last of the low-budget superhero projects. If Stan Lee didn't want it to happen, if he knew it was being shelved, then why did he come to the set?

Maybe Stan Lee didn't know that the movie was going to be shelved. Maybe later on he takes a position that supports Marvel's then-current intentions of burying your film and moving forward with the 2005 version. That opinion may or may not have been and may or may not be reflective of his actual opinion. Either way, I know that was painful to hear him say. It would be insightful to know what, in his heart of hearts, he thought of the 1994 film then, what he thinks of the various films since, and what he thinks of the 1994 film now after seeing the various films that came after. I don't know that we will ever find that out, though.

Final thoughts?

I'm going to say something that I always say as an actor. If it was a bigger film, they probably would have gotten a bigger name and a much better actor, too *(laughs)*.

Kat Green
Alicia Masters

What was the audition like for *The Fantastic Four*?
It was very competitive as there were a lot of people auditioning. I know that there were some bigger name actors who auditioned for some of the roles. I had just moved back from New York where I was studying acting and theater. I put my whole self into the audition for Alicia and they seemed impressed with my theater background. They also asked me about playing Sue Storm and if I was willing to dye my hair blonde. They ended up casting me as Alicia.

What memories stand out about making *The Fantastic Four*?
There are many great memories. The sets blew me away and the costumes, especially for the Thing. There wasn't a lot of CGI and I knew it was expensive to do, so I thought, "Wow, Corman is going all out on this." The cast and everybody that worked on the film were great; it was such a terrific team.

One of the memories that stands out is a scene with Joseph Culp as Doctor Doom. When Doctor Doom captured Alicia, he felt it was necessary to make the scene feel very realistic. Joseph pressed a gun very hard to my head so I was crying because it was hurting me. It looks like I'm overacting, which I probably was *(laughs)*. It's just a funny memory because I realized Joseph is *really* a method actor and was very serious about portraying the Doctor Doom character authentically.

Were you familiar with the *Fantastic Four* comics prior to playing Alicia Masters?
Only a little bit. Once I found out I got the part I figured that I'd better find out more about the comics and who this blind girlfriend truly is. So, I went to this comic book store in Santa

Doctor Doom pressing a gun to Alicia Masters' head. PHOTO COURTESY OF MICK STRAWN

Monica which I think a lot of us did. Once I realized this is a huge deal I asked the producers, "Is there going to be an Alicia doll? Do I get any merchandise?" *(laughs).* I thought, hey, I might as well ask.

Always good to think ahead, and I think other people thought about and hoped for the possibility of merchandise, sequels, and so forth.

Any encounters with Roger Corman or experiences related to him?

Not really. I was introduced to him, but I didn't have any kind of interaction or relationship with him.

Did you have any contact with Stan Lee?

Yes. He came to the set a few times. This was a very important movie to him. I think Fantastic Four is one of his favorites. Meeting Stan Lee was very cool. He's a very nice man, and introduced himself to me and was really excited about the film. Everyone knew how iconic he was, and his presence there made us feel like the film was important.

What challenges or limitations did you experience while making the film?

I had to supply a lot of my own costumes, which is very unusual but I suppose they needed to save money. For the princess dress, I wore a dress from my mother's closet that was like a hippie dress from the 1970s. It didn't even remotely look like a princess gown at all. I'm still not sure why I picked it and why they approved it *(laughs).*

What was your approach to playing Alicia Masters?

Alicia is blind so I researched and studied the behaviors of the blind. I went to the Braille Institute in Los Angeles, observed and spoke with people about their experiences. I watched them very astutely. Studied how they walk, how they use the cane, and how I would attempt to mold clay. My mother is a potter. I practiced with her clay, blindfolded myself, and got into it.

But yet...If you look at the first scene where the Thing meets Alicia in the lobby of the building, I'm coming down the stairs. Nobody questioned it. Being the newcomer I was afraid to say anything. Here I am a blind person walking down a giant staircase with a walking cane. Not holding the railing. No blind person would be doing that. They'd be taking the elevator *(laughs)*. I think there are a lot of silly moments like that in the film. I had to think about whether to play her super-realistic or a little more lighthearted and camp.

If there had been more films, what would you have liked to see happen with the character of Alicia?

I'd like to have seen her have a bigger role in the production and develop her character and backstory.

The way that the comic book storyline goes we know that Alicia has her romance with the Thing. Later on, she becomes involved with Johnny Storm. Which of those two characters would you like to have seen her ultimately end up with?

(Laughs) Oh, always the Thing. Definitely the Thing.

How come? You seem really sure.

Well…he's strong. He's sensitive. It's just classic. We can't have Alicia ending up with Johnny Storm. When you think about it, here is the bottom line question: Who would she rather have sex with? *(laughs)*

What's your understanding of why the film was never released?

It was never released because it was never intended to be released, which I came to learn later. At the time Marvel was practically giving away rights to their properties so Constantin Film purchased the rights for next to nothing. Their option was getting ready to expire unless they were in production on the movie by the end of the year. So they needed to get this movie in production all the while knowing that they wanted to do a big-budget version of this movie. So they hired Roger Corman to produce it on a low budget. In my understanding Roger didn't know that they weren't going to be releasing the movie when he started. Everybody thought this movie would get released. But the German production company apparently knew they were never going to finish it.

As soon as the year was up and they got the renewal, they pulled the plug. They shelved it. It's an interesting story and I wonder how many times this has happened before in the history of making movies.

How big did you think the film was going to be?

I thought it was going to be pretty big. *Batman* had come out and there was a big push to make comic book based movies.

The Thing stripped down to his drawers and rock hard. The answer to Kat's question is obvious, no? PHOTO COURTESY OF EVERETT BURRELL

I think we all thought that this was going to be a theatrical release.

What did you learn from the whole experience?

I learned that the movie business is just that — a business. The passion or the art often goes out the window. As an actor you're not in control of much. Don't get your hopes up about any project. Just do your job and move on. Whatever project you're working on whether it be as an actor, producer, director, do the best you can, complete it, and then if there are other powers-that-be that are involved, just let it go. But we were all vested in this movie and it was an emotional disappointment for all.

Do you think it will ever be released?

Yeah, I do! Eventually, they should release it. It has such a cult following and cache to it. It would be so great to play the midnight movie houses. Like *The Rocky Horror Picture Show*. And have audience members act it out. That would be hilarious and awesome. This version of *The Fantastic Four* has a charm to it that the other versions have not been able to capture. Even though it was so low-budget, the director really tried to stay true to the characters as they are in the comics. There's humor in the original comics and each character felt very human and had their own personality, backstories, and insecurities. I think that's what made this version so likeable to diehard comic fans. They really feel that this one captures the essence and the heart of the original comic books.

What's your opinion of the 2005 version?

Most of these comic book movies rely so heavily on special effects and action that they lose the integral essence of the actual comics and the characters. That's the biggest flaw of the newer version of this comic. They take themselves too seriously.

Since being in *The Fantastic Four*, what have you been up to?

I'm a film producer, director, and recording artist. Actually singing is my first love. I've produced movies for the Hallmark Channel as well as independently. I directed a short, and I direct music videos. I record and produce my own albums so directing videos for my own art is very satisfying.

Final thoughts? When you think back to the 1994 version what's something you might say about it in a single sentence?
The original *Fantastic Four* is extremely charming.
Will you do this as an audio book, too?
I haven't thought it out that far. You never know.
I think that would be great. You can get Alex to read it.

Alex Hyde-White
Reed Richards/Mister Fantastic

You had some previous roles in sci-fi and Marvel comics television shows and movies such as *Battlestar Galactica*, *Buck Rogers in the 25th Century*, and *Captain America II: Death Too Soon*. Please talk about those a bit.

I started my career when I was nineteen as one of the last contract players at Universal. I was hired along with a couple of others to fly jets in space on *Battlestar Galactica*. That show ended after a year. Then, I was on *Buck Rogers*. Really, it was the same thing; they just turned some of the sets upside down. While I was there I also did the *Captain America* movie, so it was serendipitous, a happy accident. They were fun.

How did you find your way to *The Fantastic Four*?

Hollywood casting breakdowns went out. In those days it was headshots and resumes and relationships with casting directors. I had been in *Pretty Woman* and I'd done a couple of lead roles in TV movies, so I had credibility and I was well-represented. Roger Corman wasn't really at his peak. But he was still going with the Venice studio. I suppose his peak might have been the Jack Nicholson and Jonathan Demme days, but he was still vibrant. It was a very legitimate career move for me to play a lead in a Roger Corman movie. It was kind of considered farm team as opposed to major leagues, but a lot of the time if you do well in the farm system, then you get called up to the majors, so there were guys who went on to be recognizable.

So it was a good thing to do a Roger Corman movie, and it was a fun part. I didn't really know too much about it. Being an independent movie, it was one audition. That's the great thing about auditions for independent movies: It's meeting the director and producer, and then Roger signed off on it.

I'd done a couple of sort of character parts for Roger Corman movies up until then. Roger's the kind of guy who wasn't afraid to take a risk. He didn't need a movie star. It was very much a conventional story of an audition except that there were no callbacks — just one audition. That either means I was really right for the part or else they couldn't find anyone else *(laughs)*. I ended up being pretty right for the part.

The Fantastic Four. PHOTO COURTESY OF EVERETT BURRELL

You said the part "rescued" you. How so?

It was weird. I had an earthquake. I had a divorce. I had a two-year-old child and I was doing really well. My wife kind of freaked out. She woke up one day and I guess didn't want to be married to an actor. That was a long time ago, so we get along now. That part came along to end a drought and, personally, give me something to really rally around. It was a sad period in my life, personally, but it ended up being the beginning of a very empowering and long developmental period. Sometimes in order for the phoenix to rise, the phoenix has to roll around in the ashes for a while. That's what I mean by "rescued." The part put me back in the game.

I heard somewhere that you named your son Franklin. That name, of course, is connected to the Fantastic Four because Sue and Reed have a child named Franklin.

Oh no. That would have been really weird. I have two sons. One is named Garrick William and one is named Jackson Connor. I have a friend named Franklin, but I don't know if I would ever name a son of mine Franklin. Franklin Hyde-White? Goddamn, it sounds like a street corner in Hollywood.

(Laughs) I see your point. What stands out about making The Fantastic Four?

Pretending that it was a real movie in a way. Like I said, it was getting out there in Albuquerque in 105 degree heat and taking some swings. Yeah, you're in the Dodgers organization but you're playing in the middle of the desert. You kind of have to visualize, "Hey, wait a minute. I was number one on the call sheet. I was the team captain." The character lent itself very much to being an overwatch on everybody, being responsible for everybody. Reed is intense when it comes to a cause. He's not a like a suffragette or an emancipator. He's not like John Brown. He's not crazy like that, but Reed is tuned to a frequency that not many people are.

That was a great through-line for me to play, so the fact that it was in a low-budget movie wasn't going to stop me from pretending that I was in a bigger film. It was rushed, but it gave me a team captain kind of experience that I had a little bit before but not on a project that meant so much to the filmmakers. There was a feeling that this film meant a lot to Oley, the director, and Steve Rabiner, the producer, and even Roger. I've only had that experience on the really good sets of Spielberg and Lucas. Garry Marshall, maybe. To play the lead role under those circumstances made me sort of forget that it was low-budget and the sets were creaky and the film stock had already been used once. All of those realities went way down the list. It was a great opportunity to be an optimist as an actor. You don't always get that.

How did they create the effect of Reed stretching?

It was three parts. There was a mechanical device. I would put my arm behind my back. They had a dummy arm that would literally extend on an escalator-vise sort of thing for about three feet. That started the shot and then it would go into a matte shot from the side where it would extend. If it had to be a long extension, then they would just do a video effect for the last part of the process — very first-generation feel to it. It was like a stunt suit in a way. It was a metal contraption with hinges. Like if I'm throwing a punch, like a jab, with the fake arm, that would start the shot. Then, they would continue it from a different angle and they'd have to make a special effect out of that. It was fun. That's probably the way it would be done at that time in a $20 million movie.

So even though it wasn't the best technology by today's standards, it was the best available for the time.

Well, yeah, in a way the only way you could have made a low-budget version of *The Fantastic Four* was if nobody had ever done it. They were trying to do *Spider-Man* with James Cameron, but the computing power wasn't there. Going back to my *Buck Rogers* and *Battlestar Galactica* days, it wasn't much different really. It was a practical set. By "practical" I mean lumber and metal, real stuff, real materials. They've been making movies like that since 1903. That was a neat part of film history. It sort of takes the edge off the fact that it's really low-tech. I don't know if it was the highest available technology at the time, but it wasn't that hard to do and it wasn't expensive to do.

Thoughts on Roger Corman?

I was at Sundance when they debuted his documentary at a midnight screening about five or six years ago. Roger and his wife Julie were there. It was a lovely documentary about him. That's great that it's out. That's part of Hollywood history, and that makes me feel good. Even though I wasn't a part of that documentary, it doesn't matter. I was part of Roger's life and Roger was a big part of my life. He knows that and I know that. I wish him well and Godspeed. He's a true pioneer. I am part of a very long list of very, very talented Hollywood people who tip their cap to him and say, "Thank you."

I've seen him through the years. My old manager is a friend of his. Every few years I'd call him up. "Hey, Roger. It's Alex. Can I direct a movie for you?" He's always says, "Alex, you'd make a good director." I just missed it. He sort of stopped making movies after he sold the lumberyard in Venice where we made *The Fantastic Four*.

Did you have any contact with Stan Lee?
Yeah, he visited the set one or twice. He brought donuts and shit. On the set he acted like, "Hey, good to see you. We're happy about this." Marvel was a real small company on a lifeline almost at that time. I don't fault him at all. I appreciate that he came. It was fun at the time.

Poor old Stan, man. He's lived a long time. Looks like what's happened to him is what happens to a lot of older folks. He doesn't really have anyone around who loves him or cares for him. It's a sad story.

Later through the years it almost felt like it was a business decision for him to have to say, "Well, you know that film was never meant to be made." You don't need to say that. I've forgiven him. It's wrong for me to hold onto that because Stan means a lot to a lot of people. It just shows you sometimes the potential cruelties of this business when ego and narcissism get in the way.

What challenges or limitations did you experience while making the film?
The rush. The speed. The pace. "Alex, you're so good. You can get everything in one take." I'd ask, "Can we do another one?" "No, actually we can't" *(laughs)*. That kind of thing. Sometimes I think that these low-budget movies I've done as a lead actor would have been better if there had been more attention paid to the actual take, particularly in sound. The camera work is usually pretty good. Sometimes in independent film because you get the shot, you think, "Hey, we're really doing a good job." But there's a lot of value in saying, "Maybe we should only really film about four to five pages a day — not twelve." We missed the ability to craft the production more. Then, they came back about a month, or maybe two or three months, later and did a couple of reshoots right at the end, which was encouraging.

They wanted the final scene with me and Victor when he falls off the castle to be different. They put a little bit of money into it. That kind of attention. That was like, "Okay, we have a night shoot for you," and that's great. It was like a minute of film. That was nice. That's how the big boys make the movie, but you can't make a movie for a million dollars on that schedule. Going back to the analogy of AA or AAA baseball, that's what happens. The pace of the production made it almost impossible to devote enough energy and attention to the actual shot. It was just sort of "Hey, that's good. Let's move on."

What was your approach to playing Reed Richards?

I internalized a sense of salvation, purpose without relying on an emotional hook. The childhood relationship that was in the script between Reed and Victor and the responsibility of that kind of shakes him. I think Reed Richards is a living embodiment of the second law of thermodynamics. He's trying to create order out of chaos and in order to do that he has to stretch himself.

What else would you say about Reed's personality?

He tried to enhance the lives of everyone he meets. He's not vengeful. He's a very positive person. He might come off sometimes as a bit ADHD, but it's just because he feels he's already solved that equation or addressed that situation and moved on. He's almost at 45 rpm when the rest of the world is at 33 rpm psychologically, not physically.

Why was the film never released? Who knew what when?

Basically, it wasn't released because it wasn't very good. Marvel didn't want to release it. It was a good business play for Eichinger. Once he flipped it, Fox realized that they now had to play ball with this producer because he sort of conned Marvel into giving him the rights, so it was a con job. It's almost like having a child out of wedlock. If the child ends up successful and wealthy, then everybody wants to be his parent. But if he ends up being an outcast or a convict, then nobody's going to want to know him. The fact that the whole beginning of the film was a bit of a con… . Marvel didn't make the movie. Roger ended up at least giving the film and giving the people around him a real experience of filmmaking. I'm thankful for that. As a business person you can say, "This guy did what he had to do," but it cast a bit of a pall, a dark cloud, over the whole project. In many ways it's better that it didn't get released and get shot down and get dismissed within two years. It's gone on to live in infamy, and the actual story about the film is very interesting and multifaceted.

They wanted to give Chris Columbus a shot. He'd just made *Mrs. Doubtfire* for Fox and he was the darling director on the lot.

Why do you think Bernd waited until the rights were almost going to run out before he started production?

He was probably trying to negotiate with Marvel, and Marvel probably didn't want to work with him. Marvel didn't want him anymore. Marvel may have felt they could go to somebody else. These things happen last minute. I can visualize him saying to Marvel, "Hey, I have really good ideas. I need another year." They respond, "Fine. Give us some more money."

Then, he went to Roger. Roger says, "Sure" because Roger has a studio. The guy did what he had to do. He beat Marvel. He beat Marvel out of the rights to the Fantastic Four. When Roger got involved, he played both sides. Roger is smart. Roger is a vendor. The client is Neue Constantin. "I will make your film according to your specs, according to your deadlines," but what he didn't tell him is "I'm also going to make this film just in case it ends up that I own it or that I can release it, and I want it to be a Roger Corman film."

How big did you think the film was going to be?

I thought it was going to be an interesting news item, kind of fun. I thought it would have a quick life because of the nature of the fans around it. They were very excited about it and very forgiving, which I thought meant that we'd have a good ride. I thought it be good with the comic book core, the base audience. I didn't think it would really inspire much else. It would have been a fun little TV series. It was just a little too early, a little before its time. My expectations were tempered by reality.

Did you think there was any possibility of a sequel?

No.

I understand you put your own money and time into promoting it.

Roger gave me a thousand stills. I got a publicist. We ended up contacting comic book stores. They would guarantee, like, $500 to go and spend an afternoon. When I'd go to New York, I'd try to put three of those together, and then I'd buy the plane ticket and put myself up. I didn't make any money. I put a little bit of money in it. It was a good old grassroots PR publicity campaign very much in the same manner that Roger ran his studio — "I don't mind putting my own money in, but I'm not going to lose it." He liked that approach. He gave me another lead role in a movie a year or couple of years after, so that was cool.

I get a sense in the documentary that you perceived a slowdown in the finishing and release of this movie and maybe promoting it was a way to force a release. Was that some of the motivation?

Yeah, absolutely. That was kind of a bargaining chip that probably enabled Bernd Eichinger and Fox to do a deal. I supported Roger's bluff — "I made this film. It's a complete film. My actors are on the road producing it." In the same way that Bernd was sort of holding a gun to Marvel, Roger could say, "Hey, this movie is ready to go. We're going to premiere it." Everybody did a deal. Everybody got paid, and the film got shelved.

I believed in myself as an actor. I believe the hero was a real American hero type of character. I was proud of it, and I just wanted to get out there and talk about it. It was an easy decision to make. Rather like Reed himself, perhaps, once... it was a very easy thing to visualize and it was pretty easy to put together because I had the support of the necessary powers. If that added leverage to whoever was in negotiations, more power to them, but I did it because I wanted at least the fans to feel a part of it before it was taken away.

What did you learn from the whole experience?

That I could make movies. That I could direct, that I could produce. I ended up making a couple of films. I never made one for Roger. It wasn't a revelation, but it was confirmation that I could create entertainment. It's just a matter of finding material that deserves to be made. I do that with audiobooks now thirty years later. It validated me. It was finishing school for me. Playing Reed in *The Fantastic Four* was like getting my master's degree.

What themes do you see in the movie?

Collaboration. Not to be afraid of boldness. Be fearless, inspiring, and collaborative.

Do you think your film, the 1994 *Fantastic Four*, will ever be released?

No. That's the first time I've ever said that.

Why not?

Fox is selling their assets. Maybe if Comcast buys Fox's film library, we might see it come out. But if Disney ends up owning Fox's assets, they're not going to go anywhere near that original *Fantastic Four*. They'll probably try to make a new one. Every time I've talked about this on and off through the years, I'd say, "Yeah, this movie's gonna come out because it's valuable." Now, I don't think it will.

I'm sure you're aware of that quote from Avi Arad that he "burned" the film. Do you believe he actually did that?

No. He'd blow himself up. It's be like Richard Pryor with the pipe. If you try to burn nitrate film... that's a mistake. I don't know Mr. Arad, but it's a stupid thing to do. I don't know a filmmaker alive who would burn a film. Martin Scorsese would shoot him on sight *(laughs)*.

Have you seen the 2005 version that eventually came out?

Yeah. I saw the first one. Was that the one Mark Frost wrote?

Yes. What's your opinion of it? What did you think of it?

It felt contrived. They say a camel is a horse made by a committee. It was a $100 million flop. At least our movie was less than a $1 million flop. It's not even a flop because it never got released. They're talking about our movie in very kind terms, but they're not talking about that movie in kind terms. The people that did the 2005 version didn't get it right, obviously.

What do you think some of the problems are? In general, it seems that they keep trying with these films and they can't produce a version that really seems to work. What do you think the issue is?

Maybe it's hard to have four characters be leads. Maybe they should have done it more like *Gilligan's Island*. I mean, who the hell's the hero? Is it Reed? Well, it is — maybe. No, it isn't. In one of them they tried to make the Thing the hero. Then, they make Johnny Storm the hero. They're all heroes. It goes back to the question of the theme of the movie: collaboration and boldness. There's no boldness. There's no real sense of collaboration. The chemistry is an issue. Maybe it's casting. But those things are usually the director. I know that sometimes you go to a studio with a franchise and the director — unless he's a really good director, politically, and it's somebody they want to work with — is someone that they don't want to have ideas. It's a franchise. They say, "Look, it's our dime and just follow our lead." It's the opposite of the organic nature in which our *Fantastic Four* was made, which was a result of passion and desire. That's what these characters operate on, especially Reed. He has passion and desire. He leaps before he looks and that's why he has to stretch.

Please complete this sentence — referring to the unreleased version — "*The Fantastic Four* is…"

A cheesy, can't-look-away pop culture mess that brings a smile to your face.

Other than being in the documentary *Doomed!: The Untold Story of Roger Corman's The Fantastic Four* (2015), what have you been up to since making *The Fantastic Four*?

I've raised two boys. I've driven a truck to New Mexico, produced two movies, done maybe fifty TV shows. I've created and produced an audiobook company called Punch Audio. No so much independent film anymore, there's not much of it around. I've done a lot. I was in some nice movies. I was in *Catch Me If You Can* and *Gods and Generals*.

What have I done since *The Fantastic Four*? "What have you done recently," says the executive to the movie star when he walks into the room. "Nothing," says the movie star, "It smelled like that when I walked in here" *(laughs)*. You figure it out. You can put whatever you want on that.

I'll leave that as is. Anything else you want to add?

I like audiobooks. What I'm doing now is producing audiobooks through Audible and other publishers. I'm bringing all sorts of stories and turning them into audio. I feel like I'm the Roger Corman of audiobook production, which is absolutely lovely because there's no camera and there's a lot less drama. We produce about fifty to sixty audiobooks a year. We've been doing it for about six years now. If you're an independent author or you know independent authors, you would want to know a company like us because we would bring voice to your work and that's very satisfying.

Kat Green and I were talking about Punch Audio doing *The Fantastic Four*. That's one way to get the movie released in some version. I know Joseph Culp would like to redo his lines, and I have a copy of the screenplay…

Joseph Culp
Victor Von Doom / Doctor Doom

How did you find your way to *The Fantastic Four*?
The Fantastic Four found its way to me. It was purely through an audition. I was almost thirty years old and had been doing film and TV off and on. I came from theater in New York and Los Angeles. I was called in to read for Doctor Doom, and I immediately said, "What? What? The Fantastic Four? Are you kidding me?"

Were you into comics as a kid?
I was not a huge comic person in my childhood, meaning I followed certain comics, but I was mostly into movies, monster movies, and that whole genre. But of all comic books, the *Fantastic Four* had to be my favorite. It was the most interesting. These four superheroes have these strange powers, and they were kind of freaks like many superheroes. I had a better memory of and appreciation for the *Fantastic Four* than almost any other comic. I was excited. I was trying to remember Doctor Doom so I went down to the comic book store and I started looking at back issues and thinking, "Wow, I like Doctor Doom. He's the major Marvel supervillain."

Tell us about the audition and what your approach was to playing Doctor Doom.
On a very rainy day in Los Angeles I went in for the audition wearing this long, Australian oilskin duster that my dad, Robert Culp, had given me years ago. He had been to Australia to make a movie and he brought back some dusters that the cowboys there wore. I thought, "I need something. I need some sort of flair, some sort of panache as Doctor Doom." A shirt and coat wasn't quite it. I thought the duster was kind of a cape and kind of like armor, too. I came in and pulled out all the stops from my Shakespearean training. This character is

large. This character is magnificent. The character is a tyrant and king in the grand tradition. That's how I saw him in all of the comics. He's brilliant, and he's narcissistic, and wounded in a certain way. In the audition I just went for it. Oley got very excited and said, "Do it again!" I think maybe there was one callback, so I came back and did it again. Maybe I was the actor most willing to go that far in terms of the size of the character. Before I knew it I had the role. Oley encouraged me to really have fun with this and take it as far as I possibly could as an actor.

I did have questions. Who's making this? Roger Corman is making *The Fantastic Four*? I paused for a moment. Huh. I'm a big cinephile. I have a pretty encyclopedic knowledge of movies. I love all the old, bad Roger Corman films starting in the 1950s and all the way up. *Attack of the Crab Monsters*, *Little Shop of Horrors*, all that stuff. I'm wondering what he's going to spend on the movie. It had to be low. No one would give me a straight answer. How are they going to do *The Fantastic Four* as a Roger Corman low-budget film?

After that I started preparing for the role. There wasn't a lot of time.

What recollections do you have about making *The Fantastic Four*? What stands out to you about making the film?

What I remember the most was my experience in acting the role. The production around it I took as best I could. We had a limited time to shoot. We had the resources of the Roger Corman studio, which were funky, at best. I had this little dressing room I could hide away in and prepare for the scenes. What I remember overall is the absolute sense of purpose and camaraderie that everyone had on the project. We all knew this was special, for better or worse, whatever the budget was. Everybody was at their best. I don't remember people acting out or being prima donnas. They really were enjoying this opportunity. From the crew, to the director, to the cast, we were all in it. This was cool. We're doing something cool. It may be impossible or foolish to do this, but we're doing it. There was a kind of joy around that.

So you're happy to be in the film, but what about being in the costume? I understand the suit was not very comfortable.

The experience of putting on the costume every day, the physical process was rather extraordinary. That took effort. It wasn't something you could just slip on. I had to have a couple of guys from Optic Nerve who made the suit help me get it on. They took body casts to make it and get it as close to my measurements as they could. Wearing the mask was another part of it. It's metallic, of course, but made of a hardened, very durable plastic so that had to be strapped on my face. All the pieces had to be fitted on my body with a bodysuit. It was all incredibly uncomfortable. I was sweating. I could feel the plastic pinching into my skin. I developed a wound in the back of my leg. Every time I would walk, the costume pinched into that wound. It was so aggravating it gave me a kind of emotional condition — a kind of rage — that was very much in line with Doctor Doom. Within this incarceration of the suit also had to come the voice and the intention of the character. That kind of all went together.

So you're in a suit that is physically painful and also very restrictive in terms of physical movement and facial expression. How did you work with or around all of that?

I went into my process to physicalize this character. That was probably the greatest challenge because when you're wearing an iron suit, the question is how you are going to communicate the complexity of this character, articulate his emotions and his intentions. Usually, an actor relies on facial and physical expressions.

Acting in a costume that is supposed to be essentially a metal suit of armor had incredible limitations. My fear was that I would just be a piece of metal or that I'm reciting dialogue and no one can understand me. Before shooting, I worked by myself in a theater working on the physicalization of the part, and that's not something that you often think a lot about if you're just doing a naturalistic performance in regular clothing. I said to myself, "No, no, no. This is a stylized performance. This has to be articulated through my physical gestures and his emotions. It's okay for me to be demonstrative by throwing my hands in the air or making sweeping motions with my arms, hands, and fingers. How I touch things can convey meaning. How I interact with people." All those things I could work on physically in terms of his physical behavior. I worked on that

Doctor Doom pledging allegiance to no one but himself. PHOTO COURTESY OF EVERETT BURRELL

intensely and I think viewers notice it in the film. I wanted to capture what was in the comic. The beautiful artwork of the comic gives Doom grand gestures and an imperious delivery. I wanted to mimic that and bring that spirit of the comic into the character. Doctor Doom's character has a link to many archetypal villains and monstrous people in power.

Who are some of those villains and people?

One is Kronos the Titan who castrated and overthrew his father, ate his children, and has a kind of destructive energy. The Phantom of the Opera is another reference point. I thought about the role of Shakespeare's Richard III who seeks power and is kind of a mutant, kind of a freak. There is an anger and a sly power that fueled him. There is no question in my mind that Doctor Doom is the precursor to Darth Vader. Doctor Doom came first. He is a brilliant, power-hungry father figure, a bit like a king, encased in a suit of armor.

And both are disfigured.

The connections to archetypal characters are why I thought he should be done on a classical scale as a tyrant-king, a wounded lover of some kind. The big-budget version didn't show that side of Doom. He was more of a naturalistic, modern villain. I feel that they lost something there from the original comic. We want characters of this large size. We don't always want to bring characters down to earth and make them regular guys with an agenda. It's much bigger than that. It's why we love comics. They have an extremity to them. They touch our collective unconscious where dreams are. Doctor Doom is that world of the great archetypes of the power-hungry tyrants and kings.

I'm also thinking of characters Doom might contrast with such as the Tin Man whose search isn't for power but for a heart, compassion. Even the dull gray of Doom's armor contrasts with the shiny, polished silver of the Tin Man. Could you see Doom as the flipside, the foil, of the Tin Man from The Wizard of Oz?

Certainly. The Tin Man is searching for a heart in a very amiable and sincere sort of way. The Tin Man is less than human in a way. I see Doctor Doom as very human. He's part of the human experience. He feels deprived of something. He's a kind of wounded child or lover. He's the id. He's the power-mad part of our psyche. I was clear that that's who he should be in this film and the Fantastic Four encounter that on a metaphoric level.

I am reminded of something you've said in the past about Doom. "Doom is all that we wish to be and all that we cannot face." Very human, indeed. I've heard variations of something like, "Anyone who seeks power should usually not be given it." Whereas Doom's search for power is doomed to fail because he can never have enough power, the Tin Man's search and desire for a heart proves, ironically, that he already has it.

Can you speak about Doom's emotions and voice?

He is full of rage and desire in several senses: There's a sensual aspect to the role that I thought was there and a desire for power. At the base of it he is a lonely, pained person who's been really wounded in some way. Even that should be there in his mad laughter. There's a part of Doom that's kind of crazy even though he's brilliant. He's one of those classic villains who's a little twisted. All of that came out from the work I did as an actor on the emotional content of the role, but I will say that the suit had a lot to do with it. It was very easy to access certain emotions because the suit was so bloody uncomfortable. It was a challenge. Doctor Doom's challenge is to vanquish the Fantastic Four, to get their power. I was challenged moment to moment by the physical imposition of the suit. The two go together, as I discovered.

The voice was important. How I would project the voice, how he would command, how he would deliver things with irony and with a sly twist. Those are the things I was going to have to really rely on. I used my voice and physical gestures to compensate for the restrictions of the suit.

Why was the film never released?

I don't think anybody really knows. It was a big surprise to me after we were doing press junkets, interviews, and magazine stuff that all of sudden we got this call that the film was being stopped and shelved indefinitely. We were all stunned. I didn't know if it was just going to take some time for it to come out. I thought maybe there was some legal stuff holding it up and then slowly more months went by and then another year went by and it was clear. This is really over. This film is not going to be seen. I shrugged, thought the situation was really strange, and went on to look for the next role. I wasn't crushed.

What really happened? This was purely a financial situation. Bernd Eichinger had the right to buy back the film and try to make another deal, which he did. Ostensibly, the film was locked away somewhere. Was it a big hoax of some kind? I don't really buy that. I think Eichinger was hedging his bets and he did what he wanted to do with the film. I think we were going to release it and then he had the ability to stop it, so he did. As far as there being some big plot to make a film that was never going to be seen, I'm very doubtful about that. I don't think human beings do that very much. I think circumstances unfolded that allowed him to make a bigger deal with Fox to release a big-budget version and part of their deal was not releasing our film.

So you don't think he went into the film with that strategy? He planned to make it and release it and then after having made it, he then decided it would be a better business move to let himself get bought out, shelve it, and do the 2005 release.

I don't think anybody really knows that he had the sole intention the entire time to just let Roger Corman make a film with the expressed purpose of buying it back. That's a tough one to believe. Eichinger was in a lot of negotiations with Fox and he was hedging his bets. I think his strategy was "I don't want lose this, so let's go into production, make a movie, and see how things go." Not releasing and making a big deal could have been in the back of his head. He could have thought that making the movie would make for a bigger, better deal with Fox. These are businessman that have all kinds of ideas; I don't pretend to know what their intention is. I just think that we were very close to releasing the film, and Corman was ready to do it. Why would we have gotten to that point if not releasing the film was the original intention? The decision or announcement about not releasing it could have come down before it was finished. Instead, we went on for many months promoting it.

Corman was going to start making money on it; that's what Corman does. I'm sure he would have made his money and then some.

It's one of the strange stories of Hollywood. I really can't think of another instance of this kind of thing happening. There are some movies that were not released until years later or films that were stopped, but nothing like this. This had a fan base that was growing and really wanted the film. Very strange.

Michael Bailey Smith compared the cancellation of the film's release to losing a winning lottery ticket. How big did you think the film was going to be?

I hadn't pinned all my hopes on *The Fantastic Four*. Looks like we had some fans. It was going to be fun. I knew it was a smallish film, and at that time I wasn't convinced of how well it would even do in the marketplace. I saw it. I thought we did a terrific job considering what we had to work with, but I also thought it's more like a really great, fun TV movie of a comic book.

Even though the comic had legions and decades of fans that would be interested in the film version, it was still going to be a tough go to hold it up against something like *Superman*. Would it have been the lottery? I'm not so sure. It certainly would have been good for the actors to be associated with a genre film like this one, maybe given us a little heat, and helped us land another project. I go with what I said before, though. I didn't feel like it was going to be *Titanic* by a long-shot. I was proud that I was associated with it and got to be the first actor to play Doctor Doom. That's something I still feel very proud of.

What did you learn from working on *The Fantastic Four*?

From the film itself, I learned that I could risk playing a character, a supervillain that perhaps was very broad in the size of the character and in the style of acting. Every actor can worry about that and how they are perceived. I got away with it. It worked. Years later I would get the opportunity to hear from fans who liked what I did with Doctor Doom. The movie confirmed for me that it's good to take risks as an actor. Even though you think you might fail, fail big. I think I learned that even with a short amount of time and little preparation, I could be up to the task of such a role. Being in the film gave me confidence.

I learned how strange Hollywood and the trajectory of a film or any project can be. You really cannot pin all your hopes on anything. The thing that you think might be of the most artistic merit may not get seen by very many people. A project that you think is not really that interesting or that you think is subpar might end up being that thing you are most known for. I learned a lot about the irony of Hollywood with that project. I was really pleased to know that we did something that was very difficult. Everybody sacrificed a lot and gave of themselves. Even though the film didn't get an official release, all of that work was not for nothing. It was for the future and for all of the Marvel films that we might even take for granted now. In a strange way we were the cornerstone of that movement with *Avengers* films and everything else that Marvel dominates the world with today. We were the humble beginning of that in our own special way.

All the work that we did was not lost. Many, many people saw the film. I would venture to say that more saw the film in its bootlegged version than might have ever seen it if it had been released in the theater. I believe that is true. There is a specialness to it. As we know people have many stories. "Oh yeah, I remember when I first got my really bad VHS copy of *The Fantastic Four* movie. It was kind of grainy and it had been duplicated a million times. It was kind of fucked up, but, man, I enjoyed watching it. It was really my prized possession." Better copies began circulating. The movie got upgraded to DVD. There's something kind of wonderful about the fun of that. It was contraband. I may have more fans for that film than anything I've ever done. Even the obstacles and business mechanics of Hollywood that basically killed the movie could not stand in its way. Have faith, ultimately.

Does the movie have a message?

Looking at the characters of the Fantastic Four and perhaps even Doctor Doom and the Jeweler who is an amalgam, a stand-in for the Mole Man, the message is that the thing that makes you different may be your greatest strength. The thing that might even be a defect of character or a flaw or a weakness may end up being your greatest strength.

What a great, great reading of the film.

Sue Storm is shy, so she becomes invisible. Mister Fantastic is too spread out, so he can stretch in any direction. Johnny Storm is a hothead but that's also a kind of strength when it's needed. Even Ben Grimm who is a tough guy and kind of inept can bash through walls of rock. Doctor Doom is a brilliant scientist but can also end up destroying the world. This all shows us that there's amplification of these aspects and that they can be strengths as well as deficits. I think the film has a good message.

Since we're talking about the individual traits and characteristics of the main characters, this seems as good a time as any to bring this up. I realized that the characters have corresponding elements. The Thing corresponds to earth, Sue Storm to air, Johnny Storm to fire, and Reed Richards to water. Do you agree with this?

Yes.

What elemental substance do you think Doctor Doom would be?

What is his motivation and what is he obsessed with? He's obsessed with something, which you could call cosmic power, the universal energy of the cosmos. He seeks to recapture that power, which is Colossus, from the Fantastic Four. Cosmic power is all of the elements and more. It's beyond the elements in a way. Doctor Doom is trying to harness that and even own that, which may be impossible. Maybe that's what drives him mad. That's the archetypal problem of a lot of human beings. They want to have that power of the universe like God. They can never really have it, and that may always be a conflict for them.

I'm thinking about metal, not just because of the armor but also because Doom seems so rigid, inflexible, and unyielding. I also have this image of Doom as a cracked, black diamond — brilliant and rare but also damaged and flawed. Electricity and gravity don't seem quite powerful or vast enough to describe what you are talking about. Something like chi, maybe. Aether or quintessence might be the corollary to the cosmic power that you connect to Doom.

He is certainly the element metal. Inflexible, strong, armored. He says he wants to drain the power of the four. There is a desire to capture the cosmic energy, that invisible, powerful, all-encompassing energy. That is man's obsession with becoming like God or as close to infinity as possible. That runs throughout the entire story. Even though Doctor Doom

Doctor Doom pointing to that which is ever beyond his grasp and which we mere mortals cannot see. PHOTO COURTESY OF EVERETT BURRELL

may identify more as metal, his obsession is with this element that is beyond the elements.

What have you been up to since making *The Fantastic Four***? Other than being in the documentary** *Doomed!: The Untold Story of Roger Corman's The Fantastic Four* **(2015), any more films or television programs related to comic books or Marvel?**

I am an actor and also a filmmaker. I also appeared as the father of Don Draper in *Mad Men*. I gained quite a bit of attention for that. I've done some thriller and horror stuff, but I haven't done many genre films since *The Fantastic Four*. I've been making films for a number of years both as a producer, writer, and director. I've made several independently produced films. One is called *Hunger*, which was based on a famous classic Norwegian novel of the same name. I made a film called *The Reflecting Pool*, which was the first investigative thriller centered around 9/11. It was played internationally and was a rather controversial film. I've also been involved in doing original work with my theatre group for many years.

Most recently, in release now is *Welcome to the Men's Group*, which I wrote, directed, and co-starred in. It's a film about men seeking community through the modern phenomenon of a men's group, which is where men actually get together to talk about their feelings and try to learn to support each other. It's a drama as well as comedy. I hope everyone will look for it because it's an interesting exploration of men's issues today.

Do you think Victor Von Doom would benefit from participating in that group?

(*Laughs*) I was going to make a post about that on Facebook with a picture of me as Doctor Doom and a picture of me in the men's group asking how things would have turned out if Doctor Doom had been part of the group. I don't know. I think Doctor Doom would have a really hard time sitting in the men's group because he'd want to take it over. But, yes, I think he might have benefitted by getting some feedback from other people about some of his more hostile feelings about life, and that would be pretty funny if you think about it. He might say, "I hate Reed Richards so much. I want to destroy him." The other men in the group would say, "Well Victor, why do hate him so much? What is it about him? He's good-looking?

We know that you have to wear your suit of iron. How do you feel about that?" Reed has a beautiful wife. I think maybe Victor covets Sue Storm or would like to get a date with her. His jealousy issue could be sorted out a bit with a men's group. He might get some healing on those issues surrounding his father and his mother. He wouldn't naturally gravitate to a men's group but, yes, I think he might benefit. He would blow them all up in the end or turn them into his robot minions.

Please complete this sentence "The Fantastic Four is..."

The best film version of the original comic book to date. Why shouldn't I say it?

Be proud of it.

The thing that I got from many fans over the years who knew The Fantastic Four movie is they felt that it was closer to the spirit of the original comic book and it had a kind of fun, dramatic, but tongue-in-cheek humor. That's what they really appreciate about it, and they don't even mind that it doesn't have really big special effects or even very good special effects. They felt like it still captures the original feeling about these characters. I got the opportunity some years ago to finally see it screened with a bunch of people. They were just cheering and laughing and clapping and having the greatest time with this movie. All I'd ever heard from people is that fans are disappointed with all three big-budget versions of the Fantastic Four.

Marvel's Avi Arad claims that he "burned" the film, although it survives in bootleg versions. Do you think there is a print, negative, or other high-quality copy hidden or forgotten somewhere? Do you think it will ever be released?

I don't believe for one minute that it was burned. Nobody burns film. I'm sure the original exists in a vault somewhere. Even if you don't want it seen, you don't burn up film. If someone did, that would be obscene. I just don't believe it. I think the original master, negative, and all of that do exist somewhere. That's for sure. Wherever those versions are, they're retrievable.

The lack of an official release has become more and more ironic. It's probably the most bootlegged film of all time. I get fan mail and have gone to Comic-Con many times. I have legions of fans for my role as the first Doctor Doom for a movie that was never actually officially released. It's almost unheard of. I can't think of another instance.

Do I ever think it will be released? Yes. Yes, I do. I think that everything eventually finds its way. It will get released. It may take a long time, maybe after we're all dead. At some point someone will say, "I'm going to make a print of this and we're going to release it." It's a fully realized movie. Even if something was banned for many years, it gets released. Things get out eventually. I hope they do it sooner than later because people would enjoy watching it, money could be made on it, and it's silly to waste all of that. I used to think it would be great if they would release it as a special feature on a DVD of one of the modern *Fantastic Four* films. My hope for the film is that someone will get to that. I think it will get released. I just can't say when. Until then you can watch it on YouTube. That's the great thing about the world. We can watch it right now if we want and have a great time. You can't stop movies even if you try.

The *Fantastic Four* films have not been as successful as some of Marvel's other movies. What is the difficulty with successfully transferring the *Fantastic Four* from the page to the screen?

I would just say that most big-budget Marvel films today attempt to modernize the style of the comic book. When I say "modernize," I mean the attempt to put it in a modern day kind of naturalistic idiom. The way the characters talk and the emotions that are allowed are examples; it's all too pedestrian. The filmmakers try to make it more reflective of our world today, which means humor and pop culture. I don't know if I can speak really intelligently about the new films. I just know that there is an attempt to put them in a very current context — the characters, the way they speak, the way they joke, and that I think fans are looking for something that hearkens back to the original style. Something is missing or else the other *Fantastic Four* films would have been more successful.

Mind you, I like some of the new superhero films a lot. Some of the *X-Men* series, and *Logan*, *Black Panther*, and *Guardians of the Galaxy* I enjoyed immensely. That's just a bit of PR when someone says that the versions they're making now are the best; they're not. One thing is sure: It doesn't matter how big the special effects are. There are also elements of the story and style that are not there. They reimagined the story and I think people want to see the original story. When you depart from that with something as graphic as the Fantastic Four, fans get disappointed. Why would people prefer the low-budget version? They feel like it's got a lot of heart. We didn't have great special effects but we did put a lot of our heart into it. That reads, that comes across in the film. You have a fun time watching it even if you shrug and say, "That special effect was not very good." CGI was still years away from being really good and we had very little money to include even the best of it then. Yet people seem to excuse it because they love the spirt of the movie. It gratifies them.

What else can I say?

David Keith Miller
Trigorin

Although Doctor Doom probably considers everyone inferior to him, he does have a lot of lackeys, servants, underlings, henchmen, and so forth. Please tell us about the character you played and the scenes you were in.
As I recall, Doctor Doom has two henchmen who were from Latveria, which is the eastern European country that he rules over. I was Trigorin. Howard Shangraw played Kragstadt. He was a really nice actor who was the principal person that I hung out with on set; he was very funny and we'd crack each other up. The idea of Trigorin was basically a kind of a not terribly effective Boris Badenov character who thought he was more effective than he was. I recall a scene where we were briefed by Doctor Doom, and then we were sent out to complete the mission. We had a scene with the Jeweler who had gotten ahold of something we needed. I believe we failed in our attempt and we had to go back and report to Doctor Doom and incur his displeasure. I think there was another scene where we did some reconnoitering. That was really the extent of what we did. I spoke with a heavy eastern European accent. Me and my partner exchanged significant glances quite a bit with raised eyebrows. That was sort of the extent of our performance *(laughs)*.

Truthfully, I wasn't a very good actor. I'd just moved out from New York where I'd been doing a lot of stage acting and, actually, I'd been singing on Broadway. I was doing really well there, but I had a really fluke accident where my vocal cords were physically injured and I couldn't sing anymore. I had a really astounding voice. Mouths would drop open when I sang. Often people would touch their chest because the resonance would go right through them. It was a really beautiful and powerful bass baritone.

The loss of my voice was pretty devastating. I probably should have immediately gone to business school or something, but I tried to hang on as an actor for a while.

What were you told about the role? Did you audition for it?

I did. I believed I had auditioned for something previously for Oley. Or maybe after *The Fantastic Four;* it was a long time ago. But, yes, I auditioned. I came in there with voices, faces to put on.

When I saw the tape years later, I was really pretty appalled (*laughs*) at my level of acting because it's simply too big for the camera. I was still doing stage acting tricks. I don't think it happened on this film, but on other film shoots I would get applause from the crew when I did takes. I didn't realize until much later that that was the kiss of death because if what I was doing projected to the crew across the room, then it was too big for the camera.

Were you familiar with the comics before taking the role?

I had read the comics as a kid. I knew that somehow Roger Corman and Constantin Film had gotten involved. I knew it wasn't going to be an A-level production and if it was, I wouldn't have been cast in it. I think I was probably told that I was an eastern European spy from Latveria doing the bidding of Doctor Doom and, probably, that I wasn't a very effective spy. In fact, I think that Doctor Doom's hiring practices needed to be overhauled if he was taking on the quality of spy that I was (*laughs*).

That's interesting because Doom is such a perfectionist. You would think as time progressed that he would have refined and tightened his hiring process and screened his workers a little bit better.

Absolutely. He was too busy trying to destroy the world.

Well, that's what happens when you're a perfectionist obsessed with a single goal. Other things are slipping through the cracks. His spy program was perhaps one of those areas.

Absolutely.

Were you supplied with Trigorin's (pronounces *Trigorin* with a hard initial i) clothing or did you supply your own as some of the other actors did?

It's Trigorin (pronounces *Trigorin* with a soft initial i) by the way, which is a character from a Chekhov play. I think it's *The*

Seagull. I don't recall. Kragstadt comes from an Ibsen play (Nils Krogstad is in *A Doll's House*). My costume certainly wasn't anything special. It was just a tweed jacket with perhaps a sweater underneath.

What are the qualities of a good Doom henchman?

(*Laughs*) Fanatic loyalty mixed with heart-stopping fear of one's master are definitely de rigueur. The ability to be inconspicuous. That's certainly one thing Doctor Doom lacks. Certainly, ruthlessness. We have to represent the values of Doctor Doom, which are utter heartlessness towards others, so we had a corporate ethos to stand up for *(laughs)*. Then, of course, where we fell down was in the area of effectiveness and actually accomplishing our mission.

Do you remember how much you made?

I don't. I'm sure it was pretty low. I don't think it was union scale at all. It was simply an opportunity to get filmed. Of course, I was under the impression this would actually make it to the movie theater. I was under the mistaken impression that I was any good in it and that it would actually benefit my career if it was released *(laughs)*.

Could you have seen a bigger role for Trigorin in a sequel?

I do think it's an interesting role because it seems to me it was written to give comic relief. Howard certainly was comic. Comic relief can be pretty tricky in a mythic or superhero movie. Look at Jar Jar Binks. I would hate to go down as Doctor Doom's Jar Jar Binks. The tone of humor that they managed to set in the later Marvel Movies is of a whole different nature. It's not so broad. It's knowing banter and it's very character based, so it makes a lot of sense. There could have been a future role for the henchmen if they had actually been effective, a little scary, and not so silly. As pure comic relief, it's just a dumb idea.

Did you think this role might bring you larger or better work, or did you just see this as an end in itself?

I thought it would help, especially because as far as I knew it was going to get a theatrical release. Initially, I did think this was a big opportunity for someone who had just come to Los Angeles or only been there a little while. I was still arrogant enough to think that it was sort of to be expected that something like this would fall in my lap.

It turned out to be a less exciting experience than I'd hoped. It's when I discovered that acting in film meant waiting around a lot. It's also when I began to see the reality of the caste system in casting. We were playing small parts so we were not treated like the leads. Really, it makes sense. There's limited time on set, so the crew has to focus on the people who have the most to do. The lead actors hang out with each other because you hang out with the people you have lots of scenes with. I was used to the theater where the cast is together for extended periods, and the whole thing is more socially egalitarian. There are the occasional exceptions in Hollywood. But Howard was a great companion on *The Fantastic Four* set. I regret having lost touch with him.

Oley had a good word for everyone. He was very human on set. I didn't feel ignored by him. He was a good man and a good person in terms of granting people their humanity. Oley worked under the production constraints he had, and he put together the best film possible.

Certainly, everyone was highly invested and working hard. No question about that.

Joseph Culp had a difficult role. Playing your role in a mask and being forced to act with your hands is an unenviable job.

Definitely. Plus, I'm not sure how well someone can move in that costume, and his voice is muffled. At a certain point, it may be like asking to somebody to act from inside of a closed closet. He definitely had a challenge. Anybody would have had a challenge.

I think he struggled with the limitations of the costume and poured that frustration into the acting, which is the best thing you can do with it because it gives the work immediacy and authenticity. It struck me that I recognized his father's technique in that, to grab what was happening in the moment, on the set, with the other actors, not just as characters acting a fictional story but as people right there in front of him, and react to that in his performance. I never heard either of them talk about their technique but it seemed to me that was what they did, father and son.

I read an interview in which he talked about kissing a medallion around his neck as a reference to Victor's mother, magic, and his complicated backstory. It's right at the

Doctor Doom clenching his fists. PHOTO COURTESY OF EVERETT BURRELL

nine-minute mark when he and Reed are trying to capture the power of Colossus. That wasn't in the script, but Oley liked it and kept it. His performance is full of nuance and detail. I think he got *really* into this role.

What do you think would have happened to the film if Marvel hadn't bought it up?

If there hadn't been this chicanery from the beginning, I think it would have gotten a theatrical release or at least gone straight to video. It would have done all right. It wasn't a slick studio movie, but you can't compare it to those movies that came after. This was a long time ago, and those superhero behemoths were not yet dominating the landscape. It was an honorable try. Of course, ultimately, it's a darn shame. But personally I feel I was spared the humiliation of having everybody see my work in that film *(laughs)*. So there you have it. Maybe I'm too critical of myself, but I don't think so. I was once a hell of a singer. I was a good stage actor. I was a lousy film actor. And I like to think I'm a good writer and getting better.

Robert Alan Beuth
Dr. Hauptman

How did you find your way to the film?
That was during a period of time when I was auditioning a lot for low-budget Roger Corman films. Mark Sikes would bring me in all the time. I knew Oley because I was friends with his ex-wife — she and I were pages at NBC together in the late 1970s and early 1980s — but I also happened to audition for this project when I was busy going in for other Roger Corman films, so the stars aligned perfectly and I was able to get this role. Oley is a great guy and a very talented director. I was very pleased and flattered that he cast me in that part, and I feel really grateful to him for that.

How were conditions at the studio?
It was an old converted lumberyard, so if the planes took off from Santa Monica airport, you had to keep quiet and wait. Once the helicopter or the plane would go over, then they would continue shooting. It was that sort of setup. I did a subsequent Roger Corman movie there with Martin Sheen called *Demolition Day*, but at the time it was called *Captain Nuke and the Bomber Boys*. I recall one of those rare evenings where it was raining in Los Angeles. I walked outside the soundstage, and there was a large puddle with an electrical cable laying right in the middle of it (*laughs*). I remember thinking that one day this little studio is going to blow up or something. It was charming. They turned out a ton of little movies there.

What were you told about the role?
I was told nothing. Because I did comedy for years, I knew when I read it that that Dr. Hauptman was the comic relief. I just knew from the scene itself that I was supposed to have some really funny reactions to what was going on and be the

comic foil for the Fantastic Four's special feats. I just knew that it was going to be my shocked reactions to everything unexpected that would end up being funny. I got the role, read it, went in, and I did it.

At that point in my career, I'd done a lot of sitcoms, so I was always playing the goofy guy who is off to the side making comments and things like that. I had been with the Groundlings for about four years, which was a great place to do comedy in Los Angeles when I first got here in the late 1980s.

Dr. Hauptman is a hilarious character in the movie. Was it your decision to play him that way?

Yes.

There was an interesting conundrum that I had. I think we did a table read on the movie.

There were a couple of guys there who were henchmen. They were doing Russian accents. I wanted to do a German accent for Dr. Hauptman, but in the last minute I kind of panicked and thought, "Well, someone else is doing an accent. I really shouldn't." Now, if I were to go back in time, I wouldn't even worry about it. I'd just say, (adopts German accent) "Of course, I'm going to do a German accent." But I didn't, and that was one of my regrets from doing the part. I think the part came out fine and worked without the accent. I just think it would have been a little bit more funny and interesting with the accent.

Oley was not on the set for my scenes, which was probably why I didn't do the accent. Had he been on the set, I would have asked, "What do you think of me doing an accent?" Most of that scene was shot with the second unit. I think Oley was off shooting some other stuff. I was on my own with that whole sequence.

Was it Ian Trigger who played the Jeweler?

Yes.

I have an interesting connection to Ian. God rest his soul. I know he's been gone for a few years now. I had worked in regional theater with Ian in 1982 or 1983 in Pennsylvania at the American Shaw Festival. They had done an exchange with British and American actors. I needed my equity card. I was living in New York City at the time. A friend of mine who

The Thing and Ian Trigger as the Jeweler. PHOTO COURTESY OF EVERETT BURRELL

was the non-equity stage manager of the Fulton said that the American Shaw Festival needs an equity stage manager. My buddy Barry knew that I needed my equity card, so he asked me if I was interested in stage managing up there. I ended up getting the job, so I spent the summer in a place called Mount Gretna, Pennsylvania. It's a tiny, little place with a lake and an outdoor theater. It's lovely. It was my idyllic summer. Ian was one of the actors. He played Gunner in the Bernard Shaw play *Misalliance*. Unfortunately, Ian, at the time, had a very, very bad back. I got to know him since I was the stage manager and I was always driving him twenty-five minutes into Lebanon, Pennsylvania to the chiropractor. Years later, I came out here, got cast in *The Fantastic Four*, and realized Ian was also in it. I remember bumping into him one day, and we were both sort of in shock that we were both in that. He also had no idea that I was an actor because I spent that summer pretending to be a stage manager when I was really an actor.

In the early 1980s, he was a lovely, lovely very gracious, very gentle Englishman. He was a terrific stage actor. Just a very, very pleasant guy. I think I got to know him more than anyone else during that summer because he had a bad back. I just felt awful for him. He was a tiny man bent over with bad chiropractic pain. It was quite a lovely and lucky coincidence that we ended up being in the movie together. I didn't work with him in the film, but when it came out it was neat because I knew him. He was the only person in the actual film that I knew.

Other than Oley, no one has really talked about Ian. That's so great that you have some memories of him. I didn't put him in my list of questions for you because I figured that since you wouldn't have been on set much, you wouldn't have had any significant contact with him. You never know what and who people know.

Were you given a backstory for Dr. Hauptman?

I was not given a backstory for Dr. Hauptman. What I basically knew was that he was the resident scientist helping Doctor Doom. That's all I really knew about him. Of course, had we had the Internet I would have gone on and really found out who he was and what he was doing. Because I wasn't really familiar with the history of Dr. Hauptman, I was sort of blindly going forward into doing the part. I look back at that now as a more mature actor and I go, "What in the world was I thinking?" I was flying by the seat of my pants and doing the best I could at the time.

So you weren't aware of any of the history of Dr. Hauptman from the comic books?

No, I was not aware of Dr. Hauptman from the comic books. I had heard of Doctor Doom, but I didn't really understand who he was. I did know who the Fantastic Four were. Growing up in the 1960s, I'd comes across the Fantastic Four and all the Marvel heroes of the time.

I'm going to fill in a little bit of information here that I researched just so that readers will have the backstory. In issue eighty-five of the *Fantastic Four*, Gustav Hauptmann — with an additional "n" — appears as a Nazi war criminal working for Doctor Doom who kills him in issue eighty-six. Gustav's brother, Gert, substitutes for Gustav in issue 196. He dies in issue 258 after Doom forces him to test a method on himself that he developed for capturing the Power Cosmic.

Were you supplied with his clothing or did you supply your own as some of the other actors did?

I think the glasses were mine, but the costumer gave me that giant magnifying glass, which I thought was brilliant. It really helped. It just ended up being a great prop. The white lab coat was theirs.

Do you remember how much you made for playing Dr. Hauptman?

I wish I could remember how much I made. I have no idea. Back then I had a day rate of about $1200, which was great. I also remember it was a low-budget thing and most actors don't really care about the money. If they get a chance to play a fun part like that, they're not worrying *too* much about the money. I know that because I was working constantly in film and TV back then, and I didn't worry too much. I would imagine I got $500 a day for that movie and that I was contracted for two days.

Dr. Hauptman just kind of disappears in the movie. Could you have seen yourself playing him again in a sequel?

That is one of those questions that any actor who had a fun role like that would have to say "yes." The only problem would have been that I had established the character as not having an accent, and I would love to have had an accent in any subsequent portrayals.

I would have loved to have done the sequel, but it just wasn't in the cards.

You went on to a lot of roles after the movie. Do you think your appearance in *The Fantastic Four* helped, hindered, or had no effect on your career after?

I would love to say it helped me. However, it had zero effect on anything. Part of that was that the movie was never distributed, and no one ever really saw it. As a matter of fact, I thought that it had been buried completely until a friend of mine went to a Comic Con and told me they were selling bootlegs copies. I remember getting a copy of the movie.

What's your opinion of the 1994 movie?

A lot of times someone will ask an actor, "What do you think of that movie?" Because they were a part of it, they go, "Oh, wow. It was great! Fantastic!" Bullshit, bullshit, bullshit. Considering the very, very limited budget that we had, I feel like the movie held together. I don't want to sound like Pollyanna here. "Gee, I was in it, so it was great." I just thought it was a very, very good representation of the Fantastic Four. Needless to say, if you've got Universal or Disney or one of those companies behind you, you can turn around and produce a product that is a hundred times more impressive than what you see onscreen in our little film. I liked it. I thought it was charming. I thought the special effects were definitely cheesy, but there was something kind of charming about that. I thought it was a terrific film given the limitations of the budget and the timeframe that it was being shot in.

When we first made it and it wasn't released, I was genuinely disappointed. Oley told me that Marvel bought it back from the studio because they didn't want it released. I completely get it. It's the nature of the marketplace. If you've got a legendary character or set or characters, you want to have complete control over who's making it. Who would have imagined twenty-five years ago the juggernaut that Marvel Comics ultimately became? It's absolutely exploded.

I understand both sides. I understand wanting to get it made, and I understand Marvel going, "Wait a minute. We really need to have more quality control over what we're putting out." It's really fun to have been a part of it because I know that it has a bit of a cult following. When we made it, we all did it with the best of intentions. That's what shows up onscreen. I certainly wasn't embarrassed by it. I've done a couple of goofy things over the years that I don't tell anybody about. I just wish that they had released *The Fantastic Four*. I think that people would have enjoyed it. I can't imagine that Marvel would feel that it would threaten anything that they would put out now.

Glenn Garland
Co-Associate Producer, Film Editing

Please speak about your role as co-associate producer of *The Fantastic Four*.

During the making of *The Fantastic Four*, the editorial process became a lot more than just editing the film because of the many visual effects. The normal post-production schedule for a Roger Corman film was to edit the entire film in eight weeks. This film took months and months mostly because of the visual effects. I helped supervise both the sound and visual effects and worked very closely with Oley to make sure the film was as good as it could be considering the budget constraints. I got very attached to the project working as Oley's right hand, and, as a result, Oley gave me an associate producer credit for my efforts.

Please speak about your role as film editor of *The Fantastic Four*.

I had edited six films for Roger Corman when I was recommended to Oley to cut this *Fantastic Four*. I thought it was an amazing opportunity because I was a fan of the comics and also of Oley's work. As the editor, I was in charge of assembling all the footage, finding the best performances, discovering the best and most interesting shots, working with Oley on unearthing the best story and characters for the piece, and creating an audio template for both the composers and the sound designers.

Please describe the editing process. Given the mismatched film and antiquated equipment it was shot on, were there any difficulties? How tough was it to edit the film?

In those days, we edited everything on 35 mm film. Now, everything is cut on computers. At Corman's studio, we edited on a machine called the Moviola. Moviolas are large, loud, and cumbersome machines that many times would rip the sprockets from the film. Editing was extremely labor-intensive with heavy reels that would need to be rewound. Also, every edit was spliced by hand with a Revis splicer and tape. When the tape went through the Moviola, it would sometimes make the film jump and cause a "smacking" sound. Therefore, you didn't want to make too many edits that didn't work. You really had to think about the scene before you started cutting because it would be a lot of work to take out the splices and recut everything. It was actually great training since I learned to think about the motivations of the characters in a scene before I made a single edit.

One of the biggest challenges with editing *The Fantastic Four* was just to get as good visual effects as we could on such a small, limited budget. We had no money, so it was really a labor of love to try to get the visual effects as good as we got them. Unfortunately, I don't feel the visual effects in the final film were great. One of our visual effects houses — Mr. Film helmed by Chris Walker — worked their tail off and did amazing work for the budget, but the budget was nonexistent. Also, at that time, CGI was in its infancy, and CGI effects hadn't come that far.

Earlier on when you were talking about the difference between editing then and editing now, if I made the analogy that film editing twenty-five years ago compared to film editing now sounds like typing something on a typewriter versus using a computer with a current word processing program, would that be a valid comparison?

Yes, except a better comparison would be to also remove the keys of that typewriter and rearrange them. It was more labor-intensive even than a typewriter versus a word processor. However, it is similar in that with word processing, if you want to change something, it's very easy. With a typewriter, you have to start over.

Was anyone else involved in the process? Did anyone else look at versions of the film or segments of it and offer feedback or suggestions?

I'm certain that Roger Corman watched it and gave us notes. When Roger would watch a film, he would also have various people in the office watch it with him. Afterwards, they would give their thoughts, and then Roger would give his final analysis. I assume we also screened it for friends and family, but I don't remember the screenings very well at this point.

How finished is the film? We know Oley had to sneak footage in and work on the sly to put it together. Is there more that needed to be done?

I don't think that we were completely finished, but we had a version that was very close. At a certain point, we were rushing to get it done because Roger said that he was very excited about the film and wanted to put it on a bunch of screens. The number was probably still small in comparison to other film companies, but Roger really wanted a larger theatrical release than he was used to. I remember we almost finished everything when we heard Marvel had bought the film from Roger or Neue Constantin. It was all sort of vague. The film was immediately taken from our hands.

Are there any deleted scenes, outtakes, or unused footage?

There probably are. I have no idea what happened to them. Whenever I cut a movie, there's always scenes or parts of scenes that aren't strong as others. Often those scenes are put to the side in a "lift" bin. I can't remember any deleted scenes, but I'd be surprised if there weren't any. As far as what happened to those deleted scenes, they're probably in a vault somewhere.

What's your theory on why the film was never released?

My theory is that Neue Constantin had originally made the film with Roger Corman because they were worried about losing the rights to make future versions of the *Fantastic Four*. Neue Constantin had to begin filming by a certain date and have that film finished by another date in order to retain the rights to the film franchise. When Roger then touted how pleased he was with the film and how he was going release it in a lot of theaters, I heard Neue Constantin got nervous. They worried that if there was a low-budget version of the *Fantastic Four*, it might compromise their ability to do a big-budget version in the future. The story I was told was that they went to Marvel saying that in order to protect the franchise, they needed to buy the rights away from Roger and shelve the film; otherwise there might not ever be a big-budget version. At that time, Marvel had a right to be concerned. Several of their comics had been made into movies with limited success such as *Captain America* and *The Punisher*. It seems strange now since they are such a successful juggernaut of content, but that was not always the case. I don't know what Marvel and Neue Constantin offered Roger for the rights, but I believe it was far more than he himself put into the film. I think he made out like a bandit.

Who knew what when in your opinion?

Oley and I were completely blindsided. I think that Roger was probably in talks with Neue Constantin and wisely inflated his desire to give the film a big release. Either way it was a win-win for him. He had a very low-budget version of a very big-budget franchise. If it played in theaters, the film would probably do very well for him. If Neue Constantin and Marvel purchased the rights before it could be distributed, he'd probably make a lot of money. Oley and I found out pretty much the day it was taken away. We were just told, "By the way, Roger sold the movie to Marvel, and they're planning on shelving it."

If you had known that the movie was not going to be released, would you have still taken the job? Why or why not?

That's hard to answer, but, yeah, I probably would have still done the movie. I was a very young film editor with an opportunity to work on something really special. The opportunity to work on a project as seminal as *The Fantastic Four* was something I couldn't pass up. For me, it was a dream come true.

Now, would I have put my heart and soul into it as much as I did knowing it wasn't ever going to see the light of day? Probably not. I did know that the movie had to get made by a certain date or Neue Constantin would lose the franchise, so I knew that they were doing a micro-budget version compared to the version they wanted to do. But I believed it would be distributed. *Film Threat* had even dedicated a whole magazine issue to the filming of our *The Fantastic Four*. Their spread was fantastic. We were all super-excited.

You have worked on lots of project since. Any connections between those projects and *The Fantastic Four*?

I wouldn't say there's any connection, necessarily. I do think it's something that people love to talk about. There's a lot of goodwill towards Oley's version of the *Fantastic Four*. Many people feel it's the truest version to the characters from the comic. It might look low-budget, but it's found a place in people's hearts. That's really special. As far as whether editing the film has helped me, it's a good conversation piece in job interviews but probably hasn't gotten me any work. Many films I've worked on since have a sort of cult status, and I think *The Fantastic Four* has that as well. Maybe some of *The Fantastic Four* rubbed off on me and gave me a cult-type creed. Perhaps people like working with me because they want that cult classic feel.

So maybe *The Fantastic Four* set you on a certain path?

It might have. It's hard to say. I mostly take jobs based on directors whose work I respect and great scripts I connect with. Perhaps having worked on *The Fantastic Four* indirectly influences those choices a little.

What's the most important thing you learned from being involved with *The Fantastic Four*?

One was that I had never spent so much time editing a film up to that point, so it really taught me patience and to hone my craft. It also taught me to work with visual effects. I hadn't worked much with visual effects before that.

Also, it made me less innocent. At that time, I felt like, if you had worked really hard on something and put your heart and soul into it, the project would see the light of day. When the film was taken away and shelved after all that work, it definitely made me more jaded. That's unfortunate, but it's the nature of the business sometimes. It's not only about trying to craft the best artistic piece; it's also about money and politics. It's unfortunate that it ended the way it did.

I believe our small version could have existed with the big-budget adaptations. In a way it has because of the bootleg copies that ended up getting out there. I have no idea how that happened, but I feel it's fortunate it did. Oley worked so hard on the film and had nothing to show for it. He'd interview for directing jobs, and because the movie was shelved people thought it must be terrible. But it didn't get shelved because it was bad but because of the politics of the situation, and that hurt Oley's future as a director.

Can I talk some about the visual effects?

Of course. Please do.

The visual effects were challenging because the original visual effects artist, Scott Billups, promised us the moon but couldn't deliver. He claimed that he had worked on *Independence Day* and that he was an amazing visual effects artist. Then, we started getting the visual effects, and they were dreadful.

Was any of Scott's work salvageable?

I think there's hardly anything in the final that Scott worked on. There might be a few small shots that were somewhat acceptable after months of trying to get him to do what he promised, but I don't remember how many.

Finally, we found Chris Walker and his company Mr. Film. I can't say enough nice things about Chris. We ended up finding this young, visual effects guy who really put his heart and soul into it. For practically nothing, his company kicked ass. I think that some of the visual effects are not fantastic, but I do feel like Chris did as much as he could with no money. He did a very commendable job, and it's important for people to know. I believe he went on to do a lot of visual effects for many films including two of the later *Fantastic Four* films.

I did not know until very, very recently that there are two Chris Walkers. There is the Mr. Film Chris Walker who worked on the 1994 *Fantastic Four* film and there is another Chris Walker who worked on the first two big-budget *Fantastic Four* films.

Oley and I did end up working together after that. I have very fond memories of working together. He had tons of enthusiasm and a huge love for the characters of the Fantastic Four. The Wurst brothers also did an amazing job with their music. They really brought it. Their stuff is beautiful. I just feel like everybody who worked on the film really gave it their all. Everyone felt like they were working on something very special, and it shows.

Craig J. Nevius
Screenplay
Part II

You didn't participate in the *Doomed* documentary. Why?
I did not participate in the documentary for several reasons. I didn't to revisit it all to tell you the truth. I literally just saw *Doomed* a couple of weeks ago. I was so impressed by the eloquence and passion of the cast, Oley, and Glenn. I was also aware that some people may have blamed Roger and/or Stan Lee when I'm not quite sure that was entirely accurate. I wasn't sure how Roger and Stan Lee would be depicted. I enjoyed a good relationship with both men, worked with them both after *The Fantastic Four*. There were a couple of harsh comments about Roger. I don't think that they were inaccurate. I don't think he liked those comments very much from what I hear. I've not spoken to him about it. I thought he was depicted accurately.

I was not a producer on *The Fantastic Four* because there were so many producers to begin with. I was not a full producer at that time. As a writer, I was a bit more isolated from the group experience. I was there but not every day.

I really had no idea that the cast felt as I did all these years. I thought Joseph spoke wonderfully and I thought Alex spoke emotionally. I was surprised and gratified that they all told our story so well and accurately. It's as fresh to them as it is to me. That was also a surprise to me. Had I known that before, I may have participated in the documentary. That was gratifying to see the documentary, to hear everybody speak. I certainly think that there's a story here worth telling again as a collective. As a group we sound less like conspiracy nuts because we're all telling the same story, basically.

Alex seems to have some issues with Stan.

Alex maybe thought Stan was in on it. Alex seemed a little angry with Stan Lee. I get what his perception is. I didn't know about Stan Lee's comments at the time. That was complete news to me. Stan and I only had one conversation about *The Fantastic Four* because I worked with him on a wonderful project in subsequent years which unfortunately did not sell, although maybe it would have a better chance now.

What was that project?

It's the story of his life, the creation of Marvel Comics, and the creation of all those characters told in kind of a Walter Mitty format. It was called *Secret Identity: The Real and Not So Real Lives of Stan Lee*. The whole thing was about how this Jewish kid from New York didn't see the world as it was. He saw it as he wanted it to be, as it should be. He saw things like Walter Mitty does. He had adventures in his mind. We see his real-life inspirations for these characters, all of the major ones like Spider-Man, Hulk, and the Fantastic Four. We pitched it a few places including 20th Century Fox who seemed to want it, and then they didn't. I don't really know why. That was right after the first *X-Men* movie premiered.

What was the one conversation you had with him about Roger Corman's *The Fantastic Four*?

I said, "I don't know if you remember me from *The Fantastic Four*." He said, "That was an experience, wasn't it?" I said, "Yes." We left it at that. I didn't want to delve into it any further because we were starting anew. I didn't hold him responsible for the movie not coming out. I still don't.

Do you recall what his status with Marvel was at the time?

According to my recollection at the time, he was not necessarily at Marvel anymore. I think he may even have been suing Marvel at the time or was in some sort of legal talk with them. I don't know the specifics. I believe this is before he became their contracted face of Marvel, their spokesperson for the upcoming movies. I think this was before *Spider-Man* even. *X-Men* was before *Spider-Man*, wasn't it?

Yes. *X-Men* was 2000 and *Spider-Man* was 2002.

I think that's about the timeframe. He was kind of an island unto himself. He wasn't contracted as far as I know with Constantin although he certainly was in contact with them.

He certainly was in contact, if not conflict, with Marvel. He was adrift, a free agent.

When do you think Stan knew that the movie wasn't going to come out?

I don't know what he knew and when he knew it. I don't think he was in on anything to begin with. I think he probably got wind of what was going on before we did, but I don't think he knew it when he showed up on that set. I'm not even sure he knew it when he made those remarks about the film never being meant to be seen. I'm sure he knew before we did, maybe not before Roger did. I don't think Roger knew from the beginning either. I really don't.

I think Eichinger was smart, brilliant actually. I don't like being on the short end of his brilliant maneuver. He kept his cards close to his chest. Roger is two things. He is a maverick filmmaker, an original mind, but he's also a businessman. There is an art to the deal with Roger. There's a reason he can make so many movies.

At a certain point I think Eichinger said, "Listen Roger, this is what I want to do. Really, I am the controlling guy here. Yes, you are the co-executive producer, but my name is on the contract with Marvel. I'm going to remake the movie or sell it." Again, they were already dealing secretly with 20th Century Fox, supposedly on the heels of the *X-Men* movie being set up. Rather than fight, I think Marvel said, "Okay, boy, the cast is promoting it. They're going to conventions. There's a trailer in the movie theaters. There are posters. There are buttons. They're about two months away from the target release date. We're in bed with 20th Century Fox on *X-Men* and other titles that are coming down the pipe. Let's get Eichinger and Fox together and that cuts us back in, too." It was a brilliant chess match. I'm not sure it was good faith. Is it actionable? Who's going to sue? Me? The actors? And Roger's happy. The rest of us were paid. We were contracted to do a job. There were no guarantees in our contract.

Would you have done the movie if you knew it wasn't going to be released?

Nah. I can make the money elsewhere with something that would see the light of day. Would those actors have done it? I don't think so.

So to clarify: Bernd always presented this as "We're going to make this movie, and it's going to be released?"

Yep. And Roger did, too. He acted as if it was going to be released. I don't think that was an accident on Roger's part.

One more footnote about Roger. He's a consummate businessman. I think part of him got really excited about the prospect of making money on the movie in a way that no other producer in the history of Hollywood ever has. He made money on the movie by not releasing the movie. That's a completely unique approach. Has anybody ever made a million dollars or more by not releasing a movie?

Corman has talked over the years about locating and developing new revenue streams. Making money on a movie by not releasing it is certainly a new one. I can see that as being appealing to his maverick sensibilities as well.

Absolutely. It became a piece of history, not necessarily even because of that deal — although that deal is certainly part of the lore — but because the movie eventually got seen. Bootlegs were being made and filtered through the comic book conventions. You can see the whole thing on YouTube, now, even all these years later.

The fans gave it distribution.

Although it didn't receive a formal release, it was very gratifying that our movie found an audience. I would rather have seen it in a theater with a premiere. There was a growing audience that first embraced it and then disavowed it as other more sophisticated movies, more expensive studio fare was coming out. Suddenly, it was an embarrassment, but it's suddenly been embraced again.

Why do you think that is?

Partially because of how awful the big-budget *Fantastic Four* movies are. I didn't hate the first one as much as everybody else did. Story-wise and character-wise it's certainly not better than what we did. In terms of the effects, yes, obviously, but I think our Thing was better than any version in the big-budget movies. Ours was more human.

And that's really important. It's the man still inside the monster that really makes the Thing who he is.

Certainly everybody points out that ours looks very cheap and looks even cheaper today than it did back then. You can't really compare it to the current Marvel movies or other movies with CGI. In terms of fans, forums, and online but also in terms of reporters, critics, pop culture journalists, there's kind of been a reembracing of the Fantastic Four, particularly of our *Fantastic Four* and particularly on the heels of that disastrous reboot.

They said, "Looking back, you know what? It's not that bad." Yes, it's cheap by any standard, but the heart, the sincerity, and the story are there. So there's a new respect, even a begrudging respect, for it. At first it was just cool to see this thing you weren't supposed to be seeing, so there was excitement about that. Then it waned, and the movie was rejected kind of like the Adam West *Batman* series was later on, which I always found unfair because times change. Things evolve. People evolve.

All things go through stages, so to do comic books and the film depictions of superheroes and comic books. All these things are equally valid. They just have to be put into the right time frame. I will defend the Adam West *Batman* series until my dying day for many reasons. There would have been no Dark Knight without the starting point of Adam West. I think Tim Burton would have done that earlier version of Batman had Batman never been done before, but basically that had been done to perfection with Adam.

So they looked for the next step in the progression.

It evolved. The comic book evolved. Tim Burton and the studio thought, "What's going on in the comic books? Now, it's time to take it to a new place." I think our *Fantastic Four* has to be looked at in the timeline in terms of Marvel movies and film depictions of comic books.

There were four Christopher Reeve *Superman* movies. I know several others have played Superman before him and after him, but there's never been a better Superman that Christopher Reeve.

I agree. He is the Superman I grew up with. For someone of a different generation it might be another actor like George Reeves from the 1950s television show or Henry Cavill.

That was the part Christopher Reeve was born to play. I don't think there will ever be anybody better than him, but who knows? There is an innocence about those movies, a certain true blue almost corniness, but a justified one. Part of that is truth, justice, the American way, and the idea of an alien, essentially an immigrant, coming to a new world and being accepted as a hero. Without those Christopher Reeve movies, would we have seen *Batman v Superman*?

I would have been okay with not getting that movie, but I see your point. I loved the *World's Finest Comics* DC series that showcased Batman and Superman. I wanted to like this movie, too.

It should have worked but it didn't, and I'm not quite sure why it didn't. The *Supergirl* series is uneven and definitely has problems. Aside from two fantastic actresses, what I like about the show is that there is the true blue, old fashionedness about it. There's room for that, but it is somewhat of a throwback. There is a sincerity to that show in spite of its flaws. I like its spirit.

I like the dark stuff, too, by the way. There's room for *Logan* which I saw several times in theaters. *Wow.* What a movie. I love *Logan*. I adore *Logan*. It's dark, brilliant, and wonderful in a different way.

I completely agree.

Our *Fantastic Four* was definitely the first step outside of the cartoon. It was the first step in the evolution of the Fantastic Four, an evolution that has yet to be fully reached in terms of what the Fantastic Four can be. We were the necessary first step. It's not the same time as the 1960s *Batman* but it's like that and to a certain extent *Supergirl* now. While it may not compare to the $100 million versions in some ways, it's been embraced by fans who understand what its place was. I watched a good portion of it after watching the documentary. Some of the effects especially the stretching is cringe-worthy. Even back then it was. Some of the effects are passable, a little cheesy but okay. The rays and the lasers are fine, not the best, but, again, passable. There are scenes — and, yes, I wrote them, so maybe I'm too close to it — that still give me chills. There's an emotion there.

What is your favorite scene or moment in the movie?

My favorite scene is where Reed says, "We know that our DNA has been altered by Colossus, but I think it's also touched our psyches. I think it's made us feel that our greatest weaknesses are in fact our greatest strengths." It's such a great analysis and thematic through-line that hasn't been done in any of the movies. I can't remember if I made that whole thing up or if it was embedded in the comic books themselves. I know Johnny Storm had a hot temper; that was definitely in the comic books. Ben Grimm was a tough guy; hence he is rock hard. I don't know if Sue storm being shy and feeling invisible around Reed was in the comic books. I'm pretty sure that I coined the idea of Reed spreading himself too thin trying to do everything for everybody. It's not been done in any other version. I don't know why because it's such a central idea.

It seems so essential. Everything comes together so well in that scene.

The music from the Wurst brothers during that scene is exceptional. Throughout the movie, the music was fan-fucking-tastic. Still is. I love the way Alex did the scene and I love the way I wrote it.

I'll admit that part of me is in love with my own dialogue but another favorite scene is when Ben Grimm comes back into the fold after Reed has figured out that Doom is Victor. That's when we have the image of the four hands on top of each other, which is straight from a panel in the first issue where I ripped it from. That scene was in every draft. There are moments like that that still ring emotionally true for me. Yes, maybe they're a little on the corny side tilting toward a Christopher Reeve *Superman* movie. I don't care. To me it works and there's an emotional truth there.

I think those scenes are highlights for a lot of viewers.

Based on the trailer, I saw *The Greatest Showman* with Hugh Jackman on opening day. I couldn't believe the horrible, vicious, angry reviews it was getting. Then this movie rose from the dead and became a hit. Some of the critiques of that movie are that it's corny. There's a moment towards the end of *The Greatest Showman* which is corny beyond belief, but I buy it and I love it. All three times I saw the movie in the theaters the audience burst into applause. At the end he turns the circus over to Zac Efron and goes off as he says, "To watch my girls grow up." He's late for his daughter's recital. They are waiting for him outside in the snow wondering where he is. He's rides up on a goddamn elephant. Does that ever happen? Not in a million years.

No, it's not particularly realistic, but it does make you feel good.

It's a wonderful, heroic reentrance. He's just given up the greatest show on earth in order to go to the smallest show, which is really the greatest show — his daughter's recital. It's incredibly corny, but I buy every moment of it, and the audience did, too. That's a scene I would have written. How ridiculous is it that I'm bringing up a Hugh Jackman movie that's not *X-Men* or *Wolverine*?

I completely agree. As different as the two movies are in some ways there is also a similarity in that they are about family and have final scenes in which Jackman's character recognizes and shows how deeply he cares about his daughter in each movie.

I am unapologetic for any perceived corny moments in our movie. I do apologize for the effects, which were not my doing.

Eichinger hired me after *The Fantastic Four*, which people don't really know. That was another reason I didn't really want to do the documentary at the time. The story has a happier ending for me then I think it does for most of the people involved in that it led to *Black Scorpion*, which was two movies and a series. Within six months of *The Fantastic Four* not coming out, Eichinger hired me for a pretty decent sum of money to rewrite an A-list screenwriter's adaptation of a Chinese graphic novel called *The Laughing Sutra* that Constantin had optioned or bought. The major instruction Eichinger gave me — and this is the only time we discussed *The Fantastic Four* after the fact — was don't do what you did on *The Fantastic Four*. I said, "What did I do?" He said, "Don't be faithful to the source material. We just like the main character. Disregard anything you want."

Obviously, he felt confident about your abilities, but do you take any other meaning from him hiring you after *The Fantastic Four*?

It was interesting that he hired Oley again, too. This tells me it was strictly a business maneuver on his part. I don't think there was any maliciousness. He's clearly the villain here because he clearly did not disclose everything. He got people working under false pretenses.

Just to be clear, by "him" you're referring to Eichinger?

Yes. The fact that he hired Oley and me again on different projects certainly said that he did not think that the people who made our movie were untalented or that the product was bad. It was intended to be what he needed, to get what he wanted, which was a deal with Fox and the sequels.

I was told the whole story. It came out in dribs and drabs. I think Rabiner filled me in on the whole picture behind the scenes. Rabiner and I were good, not that Roger and I weren't, but Roger held his cards closer. Rabiner was very forthcoming with me about everything. The funniest thing is I knew the story, that this was a plan. Steve wasn't saying that he was in on it. He was telling me in hindsight what had gone on. It did not matter how well we did our jobs or how horrible we did our jobs. The movie was not supposed to be seen. It was a tool.

Eichinger called me directly about hiring me. Clearly, he didn't think my writing was bad. Clearly, he didn't think Oley's directing was bad. All of that just confirms the whole thing more so, the whole plot, to me. Oley and I were the defining people. You got the guy who wrote it, and the guy who brought those words to life.

You won't hire them again just to fuck something else up (laughs).

(Laughs) No. Let's make sure they fuck this one up, too (laughs).

Working for Eichinger again is not something I've really disclosed to people, either. Not that I was ashamed of it.

It's a touchy subject. People might assume that since he hired you again that somehow means that you knew something or that you were in on it in some capacity. It's a situation in which if people don't know the truth, then everybody's looking at everybody else.

Paranoid. I think some people have given Stan a bad rap. I think Stan was adrift among all parties. This was one of his babies and he didn't want to be far from it. He was finding his way back into the Marvel fold. I don't think he would have been on the set had he known this was a sham. I think he found out sooner than Roger did, but as I've said I don't think he was in on it.

I read that *The Fantastic Four* led to *Black Scorpion*. What is the connection between the two projects?

When I told Roger how upset I was that the movie didn't come out, his very quick response was "I understand. It was business. It had nothing to do with your work." He said, "If you love superheroes that much, I've got a deal with Showtime for a summer series of movies called *Roger Corman Presents* where every week it's a different genre of movie." He said, "I need a thirteenth movie, and we can create our own superhero." That's where *Black Scorpion* came from, which was heavily influenced by *Batman*.

I describe the *Black Scorpion* movies — and particularly the series — as landing somewhere between Adam West's series and Tim Burton's reimagining, meaning we weren't quite as silly or funny as Adam's show, but we did have some tongue-in-cheek humor. We did have some crazy, colorful villains with humor. We were also serious and dramatic, but we weren't quite as dark and brooding as the Tim Burton Dark Knight and what those movies became. There is something to be said for both, but certainly the primary inspiration was Adam West's *Batman*. I loved *Batman* for so many reasons, Adam being one of them.

What is it about Batman that grabs you so much?

I just love Batman for Batman. Batman is a mortal. Batman didn't have powers. He was a millionaire. He had brains. He had a personal agenda towards crime because of losing his parents. He had James Bond gadgets. He was fallible. That's why in setting out to create *Black Scorpion* he was my model.

***Black Scorpion* features a female protagonist. Was Batgirl also an influence?**

Always loved Batgirl. Season three of Adam's show, which introduced Batgirl was my favorite. It was the lowest rated. It was not a fan favorite. I remain attracted to that idea of a powerful heroine. I knew that the Black Scorpion we would create for *Roger Corman Presents* would not have superpowers. We didn't want to spend money on those kinds of effects. We had effects already in terms of the car, the explosions, and the transformation into the hero. But if she had to fly, forget it. I wanted her to be fallible. She is essentially Batgirl.

How did Adam West get involved?

I didn't have much power over the casting of the movies other than Garrett Morris playing Argyle, our version of Alfred. But by the time we went to the series, other than Roger vetoing something and the group selection of the heroine, I had a lot of control. I always wanted Adam West to play her archnem-

Craig J. Nevius and Adam West. PHOTO COURTESY OF CRAIG J. NEVIUS

esis, the Breathtaker, in the first movie. I remember suggesting it at the time. That was dismissed. For the series we got Adam. He was damn good in it. He was evil. He was sinister. He didn't even need direction. He knew how to do this instinctively. He told me that he wanted to chance to have some of the fun that he saw Gorshin, Romero, Meredith, and Newmar having all the time on his show. He said, "Don't get me wrong, I love being Batman, but they seem to have a lot more fun." He relished this. I loved working with him. I was glad to be a part of his resurgence.

The connection between the two projects is I was heartbroken that *The Fantastic Four* didn't see the light of day. I think I expressed my extreme disappointment to Steve Rabiner, though it was not aimed at him. I could talk to him. He would tell me things I wasn't supposed to know sometimes. Roger and I have never exchanged a terse or tense word. He gave me a lot of latitude but he usually had strong ideas about what he wanted to see happen with any project. I can't say he and I were warm and fuzzy or personal. We were at a couple of Christmas parties together. It was very much a mutually respectful business relationship. It was always "Hi, how are you? Nice to see you. Now, let's get down to business." To a certain extent I appreciated that.

The only time I expressed anything to Roger about *The Fantastic Four*, I just said, "Roger I want to express my heartbreak over the fate of *The Fantastic Four*. I understand the decisions you made were motivated by business, but this was more than a job to me. This was my childhood." I reminded him of the dolls I had brought into the audition. It was heartbreaking to me not only professionally but personally.

Mark Sikes
Casting Assistant, Roger Corman's Receptionist

Please tell us what you did as the casting assistant for the movie.
I would call and schedule the actors for their auditions and then get them prepped when they came in and make sure they had the right materials. I got them down to the room and read for them. Once the audition process was done Laura Schiff took over. As the casting assistant, I didn't really handle negotiations or anything of that nature. From the very start they knew that I was a comic book geek so they wanted to know, at the very least, what I thought visually of people as in if I thought this would work for the comic book. Both Laura and Oley were very cool about that.

What was your official job at Concorde?
You wear a lot of hats when you work for Roger, of course. My official job at Concorde, what I was getting paid for at the time, was receptionist. I was his receptionist, and we had interns. What I would do is train the interns to cover the phones for a couple of hours and I would go into the casting sessions with Laura.

I was also his projectionist. Roger was obviously in every screening. I screened the film at least two or three times for him in various drafts. As usual, Roger would be in there. It was just Roger. It might have once been Roger and Steve Rabiner, the producer, but we never had Bernd Eichinger in on the screenings. Roger and Steve were really the two people that seemed to be in charge of making the movie and delivering this film for Constantin. Roger would have notes. They would then send it back down to the studio for another pass. I was literally dealing with the print of the film and the projection. This was not video of any kind. We had two projectors. You'd run them through all the reels. Roger oversaw all that all the way through.

As if all of that wasn't enough, you also played the Thing in a few places for the movie. Tell us about that experience.

This happened more in post-production. They were done shooting the film and Steve Rabiner came up to me one day and simply said, "How would you like to be the Thing tonight?" I was just shocked because it had been Carl in the suit up to that point. I guess they wanted to save a little money and not pay the stuntman. I jumped at the opportunity. I didn't even stop to think, "Hey, that costume is not going to fit me." It had been specifically molded for Carl, and it didn't fit me at all. Putting on the suit, I ripped through one of the feet. The feet probably don't even exist anymore. I had destroyed them because my feet were bigger than Carl's. Fortunately, you don't really see my feet. We drove from Roger's Venice stage where I put the costume on and then we drove up to Hollywood Boulevard. It was really, really hot. I don't know how Carl did it for as long as he did it. I was in the suit maybe a total of five hours. We didn't have permits. They weren't looking to do any reshoots or pick-ups, but they needed this, I guess. Oley wanted this information in the film. They wanted to see the Thing on Hollywood Boulevard even though I don't think it was meant to be Hollywood.

I was walking at Hollywood and Vine across the street disgusted with myself and how I looked now that I was this thing. Oley may have said in the *Doomed* documentary that they just paid the cop a few bucks to just sort of look the other way. We shot a couple of hours of me walking down Hollywood Boulevard, picking up a broken mirror, seeing myself for the first time, and literally scaring tourists. Their reactions were so natural and completely genuine. Those were not movie extras; they were actual tourists on Hollywood Boulevard. This is way before the days when everybody dresses up like a superhero on Hollywood Boulevard like they do now, so it was really unusual to see some idiot in a full body costume walking back and forth across the street. It really startled quite a few people. I think you can see it in the movie. On more than one occasion during the takes I had to really rush because the suit was very hard to maneuver in and I had to get across the street because we didn't have a permit and we didn't control the lights. I had to keep doing it because there'd been no rehearsal, no planning. This was just something they threw together at the last minute. Oley was great, but it was scary and exciting all at the same time.

What was co-executive producer Roger Corman's role?

Roger was the day-to-day physical producer. He was there through the whole process.

At this point Roger wasn't on the site as much. He worked a lot from his Brentwood office where we did the casting and all of the marketing. Roger had Steve Rabiner as the guy on set, the guy making sure the days were made and everybody was on schedule and on budget. Roger really was the guy in charge of making this movie for Constantin Film. It was a co-production, but it was all done at Roger's studio with Roger's crew. Obviously his casting director and our marketing people worked on it.

Can you talk some more about Roger's involvement in *The Fantastic Four*?

In terms of the production really we dealt with Oley and Steve, mostly. I don't really have a great recollection of Roger talking about the movie. I dealt with Steve a lot, and Steve dealt with the office. Roger was overseeing four or five movies at a time in various stages of production or post-production. I'm sure he visited the set, but when I was on set I don't recall him being there. The most input I got from Roger was when Marty and I were doing the documentary and we interviewed him. We didn't really talk to him much back then.

Do you have other memories of Roger even if they're not specific to *The Fantastic Four*? I would imagine there are other things about him before and beyond *The Fantastic Four* that might explain his approach to *The Fantastic Four*.

I've been a casting director now for about twenty-six years in the independent, low-budget film world. After Corman, I went off to PM Entertainment for four years and since then I've done a lot of low-budget films, a lot of horror films. One of the things I've always remembered and taken with me is something he said once. "We do very low-budget films, but we take them very seriously." It was one of the reasons why you never really saw him doing much in the way of comedy.

Hollywood Boulevard was a very rare film because Roger typically didn't like to make fun of himself and his genre of low-budget filmmaking.

I'm looking this up as we're talking and it seems that the agreement was that Jon Davison had to make the cheapest movie ever for New World Pictures, so he was given $60,000 and ten days. He was allowed to use footage from various New World films.

I wasn't around in the days he made that movie, but I would imagine it probably wasn't an easy sell for Roger because I remember a number of times when I was there that parodies or comedies were talked about and he really wasn't interested in them. It's probably part of why he's so successful. He took these feelings very seriously and he demanded that of the people who worked with him. It's not that he didn't have a sense of humor, but you better seem like you're taking your job seriously, which was great. It's something I've always carried with me as a casting director auditioning people. Hey, I know we're making a $1 million horror film, but I have to know that the actors auditioning are taking this seriously because it is a job and there is a million dollars at stake here. The producer with a million dollars has just as much at stake as the producer of a $10 million film because that's all the money they could raise in the world.

So you think he didn't make comedy because he would have seen it as undermining the low-budget genre as a whole. If people do comedy, that means they're not taking things as seriously as they should?

I think that was definitely part of it. Plus, Roger often liked the edge of tapping into something that was really hot at the time. When I was there, two things were very hot and that was kickboxing and kickboxing movies. Jean-Claude Van Damme was doing movies that were big movies at the box office, so Roger was doing movies like *Fist of the Dragon, Bloodfist, Angelfist,* and *Live by the Fist.*

Lots of things with fists.

Whatever martial art was popular, we were doing it. Kickboxing was just crazy in the late 1980s and early 1990s, and so Roger was pumping out three or four of those a year, easy, whether he was shooting them in Los Angeles or the

Philippines. We had Don "The Dragon" Wilson on something like a three-picture deal at one point. Don went on to make fifty, sixty movies. The other thing that was popular at the time I was there were stripper movies. They had been popular like the kickboxing movies for several years.

Roger also didn't really do romantic comedy, even if it wasn't a parody of low-budget films. If you went through Roger's entire canon, you would not find many comedies. Probably, the risk was a concern. Romantic comedies are very risky. These were the days before cable was so big. You weren't going to sell a film to Lifetime or USA in the 1980s, not a low-budget version anyway.

So he didn't see comedies as being profitable then? Avoiding them was a business move in some ways.

Absolutely. Everything was a business move with Roger. He's like the Terminator of producers. He's a computer. If it doesn't make sense financially, then it doesn't make sense. Obviously any time you spend half a million dollars there's risk, but Roger had such a great formula. Steven Spielberg's going to do *Jurassic Park*, so we announced *Carnosaur*. If you look over his resume, you can see a hundred examples like this. When you think about it, *Battle Beyond the Stars* was super-ambitious for him. That was a lot of money to spend, but he did it after *Star Wars* of course.

He knew the interest in that kind of film was there and he had a model available to him.

Part of the magic is that he was a little studio. I don't know how much we spoke about this in our documentary, but this is something that went on in the 1980s and 1990s. I don't know if it went on in the 1970s, but I talked to a lot of people who've worked for him and many attest to this. He'd build a set and then he'd use that set for six movies. One of the ways he breaks even is he cuts his expenses way, way down. He hires me as a casting director, and I get charged to every movie I'm working on. There was a month where I did three movies for him and I get worked into the budget of each movie, while he's only paying me once. The cost comes way down when you're basically a factory, an assembly line.

That's the formula he followed for a lot of things: recycling costumes, sets, even footage. One of the best examples I can

think of is *The Little Shop of Horrors*. **Principal photography was shot in two days and a night on a leftover set.**

He's incredibly opportunistic, which in a producer is a great quality. I don't mean any of this in a negative way. I know that way of working is hard to imitate. I've worked with a lot of producers since and if they had a production slate in which they were making seven or eight movies within a year, odds are they would be much more successful following his formula then if they're making one a year. Very few people could match his formula successfully. The other thing is they can't do it without getting into a lot of trouble. For example, Full Moon Entertainment had something going for a long time into the 1990s and even to this day, but there are a lot more stories of financial issues with Full Moon than you'll ever hear about Roger because Roger always paid everybody.

You never got screwed by Roger. You got paid very little, but he paid you what he agreed to pay you. And his checks *never* bounce.

Why was *The Fantastic Four* never released?

I think it's exactly what has been said. I'm going to give you a longer answer to this only because I think there were some things taking shape then. There are some people who want to think that this was a big conspiracy and they never planned to release the movie. I don't think that's true. I think very simply Bernd Eichinger was going to lose his option. That's a fact. He came to Roger. He had to go into production at the end of 1992. Fact. Roger was the guy to do it. He started the movie. They did it. They were investing money in it. They were spending money. They made a movie, albeit extremely low-budget. As someone who saw this movie at several little projection screenings, I can say they were making a movie that you could have released. It's not a high-end film. You've seen it. It's not a big-budget film. Would it have made $20 million at the box office? No. But it was a movie he could certainly release to home video. Somebody like HBO or Showtime might have taken it, some kind of a cable station. They could have made money on it one way or another.

They didn't release it simply because Marvel had the ability to come in there with their property and say, "Hey, here's a bunch of money. You're going to keep your option, damn it."

We don't have this official from anyone, but we know at the time Marvel would have just liked to get their option back, taken Constantin's money, and never had them produce a film on a low budget. They thought if anything this guy was going to go out and do a studio film when they gave him the option.

It never would have occurred to them to think he's going to go to Roger Corman with the property of the Fantastic Four. It's a fairly crazy idea. Marvel came in with, I want to say, a ballpark figure of $3 million of which Eichinger paid Roger a million. Roger walks away having probably spent three or four hundred thousand of his money, getting a $1 million return, and they're not having to spend any time selling the film, which saves him money because he doesn't have to put it into AFM, the American Film Market. He doesn't have to sell it anywhere. He doesn't have to spend any more money on materials to sell it and so forth. He's in a good place. Plus, in his contract I'm sure that was a possibility. Could Eichinger and Corman have had a discussion early on that it's possible Marvel may by it up from us? Sure. But I don't think there was any way they could count on that guarantee. So anybody who says that they made this movie never expecting to release it, I would have to hear that from Roger's lips. Even if it's true, he's never going to admit that because it would cast him in a very bad light. They didn't behave that way anyway as I've proven to many people. I can walk them through a lot of expenditures that Corman made that didn't need to be made.

Marvel didn't want this low-budget version out there because they were hoping to make a bigger film with Chris Columbus. They didn't want this low-budget version out their confusing audiences, confusing the public, and sort of sullying the brand of the Fantastic Four and Marvel.

At what point do you think Roger knew the movie was not coming out?

I honestly don't think he knew that until very late in the process because he did know that the actors were traveling around promoting it. I took it personally to the Los Angeles Shrine Auditorium where they had the monthly Los Angeles comic book convention and I introduced Los Angeles to the cast and the trailer that summer. There was no reason to be doing these things if you weren't promoting a movie that was actually gonna come out. The trailer for *The Fantastic Four* is on the screener for *Carnosaur*. Why would you do that if you're not gonna release the movie? If you know it's not going to come out, then it's a big joke on everyone. "Ha Ha Ha, we never plan to release this movie. Oh, but I put the trailer on one of my other films." That's just not Roger. That's just not that Terminator producer who doesn't waste money, time, energy, and resources. I would say Roger knew a day or two after Bernd Eichinger was approached by Marvel about the buyout. I don't think Roger is some Machiavellian villain in the background twirling his mustache, screwing over the actors. They could have been treated better in the final analysis. At the end of the day they were hired to do a job. Expectations weren't met. It stinks but it happens.

Does the movie have a message?

I think Oley's version of *The Fantastic Four* has the message to the fans of what a loyal, respectful version of the Fantastic Four can look like. I think Craig Nevius wrote a very loyal, fan-friendly version of this film that is probably the best of the four we seen so far. Optimistically, I'm hoping that somebody will come along, get it, and do a loyal version of the Fantastic Four unlike the ones they've been doing. They kind of Frankenstein it and take pieces of this and pieces of that, but they haven't really embraced the property. The message is you can be loyal to the source material which was thirty years old at the time we made our movie and fifty now. You can be loyal to that source material on a $1 million budget with a very simple script. Hollywood is throwing a lot of money at these newer versions, but clearly where the attention needs to be paid is the script. People can say, "Roger Corman is King of the B-movies. Roger Corman is a low-budget producer," but Roger Corman produced the most loyal version of the Fantastic Four that has yet been made.

In the process of doing these interviews I came across a professionally done fan film on YouTube called *Von Doom* that's about fourteen minutes long. Have you seen it?

No.

It's good. Ivan Kander made it pretty inexpensively, but it's very faithful to the spirit of the comics, and I think much

more in the spirit of the Fantastic Four and the 1994 movie then the later big-budget versions.

There isn't much legally out there. Audiences obviously aren't loving what they get.

Marvel's Avi Arad claims that he "burned" the film, although it survives in bootleg versions. In an online interview you stated, "There is a really nice ¾ inch copy of *The Fantastic Four* **that I do know exists." Can you elaborate?**

Well, have you seen my movie, *Doomed*?

Yes. Excellent, by the way.

Not wanting to get anyone into any legal issues, I would simply say that if you watch *Doomed*, the footage of *The Fantastic Four* movie isn't from YouTube. It's nice. I'll go this far: I think they are at least half a dozen really great quality copies of the film out there.

There was a very short window back in I would say late fall of 1993, maybe. I remember this distinctly in the office because all of a sudden the word came down that the film was going to be shelved and not released. All of a sudden everybody in the office was really sad and felt a little screwed. I'm not even talking about the cast, but everybody was like, "Oh, this was going to be a bigger movie; this was going to be something we could all take our friends to." Normally we make stripper movies and kickboxing movies on tiny budgets *(laughs)*. This was something special. Even though this didn't have a big budget, everybody thought it was going to play in theaters. There was a lot of sadness and disillusion going around the office for a brief period because then it was over. In those few days a lot of people like myself were very... opportunistic and we're like, "Hold on. We'd like some record that this movie existed." Marvel is going to buy it up. The rumor was Marvel wasn't buying it up to give it a big release. They were buying it up, and it might never be seen. We didn't know that "might be never" would be "never." I guess we thought maybe it won't get released for years, but it'll come out at some point. People were grabbing anything they could.

Such as?

Posters, props, buttons — anything that happened to be hanging around the office. I have Doctor Doom's cloak.

Nice.

That was hanging up in the marketing office on a hook on the back of the door because I think they had done some kind of photoshoot or something with it. I won't say who but an executive came to me and said, "Marvel's coming tomorrow to pick up anything we have in the office on *The Fantastic Four*, so if that isn't there tomorrow, they're not going to know to look for it. They don't have a checklist. They're just going to pick up everything that's visible and right at hand. So if that walks out of here tonight, and I don't see it walk out of here, I'm none the wiser." I took that as my cue, and I think everybody grabbed stuff.

But to get back to the main point about copies of the film, when the word came down the film might never come out that also meant the actors would, obviously, never see residuals, so there was a very disappointing financial outlook for them, but at the same time you want a copy of your work. You want footage. You want something to put on your demo reel. You want to maybe even show people a copy of the movie. They were really nice copies of the film, really nice, like ¾ inch, whatever they would take right off the negative. There were multiple copies of the film. Again, I don't know who was doing it. I know who was in power, and I know who could have prevented it if they didn't want that to happen.

During the interviews with all the cast, it became very clear that somebody got at least some of the leads footage for their reels. Somebody feel guilty, which would be a good thing and they made sure that the actors at least have some kind of proof that the movie existed. In some cases I think they were even given really nice copies of the movie and told, "Please don't duplicate this, bootleg it, and put it out there." Even if the movie doesn't come out, that would be a problem. You're not going to see one of the stars of the film at Comic-Con selling bootlegs of the film, but a bootleg or two definitely got out there.

So if Avid Arad did burn the film, he didn't burn all the copies. Perhaps he burned a copy.

I think Avi's quote was that he burned the negative.

To get a little more specific, the article's quote is that "he bought the film 'for a couple of million dollars in cash and burned it.'" The article says that the quote came from "a 2002

press junket for *Spider-Man*." A little later the same article says that he "ordered all prints destroyed."

This has been talked about a great deal. I think it might have been one of the questions that we asked every cast member because Avi so famously said this in *Los Angeles* magazine. I think he said this because they were in the throes of making *Fantastic Four* movies. I think he said it around the time the first big version was released.

Yes. The *Los Angeles* magazine article is in the March 2005 issue, so all this comes out before the film's release.

Avi had an agenda. He wanted to make it clear to everyone that there was only one *Fantastic Four* movie and it starred Jessica Alba, Michael Chiklis, and that cast. Don't expect to see some micro-budget version of the Fantastic Four. To end any discussion of it, he says he burned the negative. What better thing could you say to make people go away, to make people give up hope that they will ever see Roger Corman's version of the Fantastic Four?

That statement ends, or tries to end, all discussion of it coming out, which seems to have been Avi Arad's goal. If no copies exist, then there is nothing to talk about it terms of any future release. End of story.

While I suppose it is possible that he burned it, I don't necessarily think he burned it. Legally, I'm not even sure he could burn it because, technically, I don't know his power level exactly. I know his title. I know he's the guy behind a lot of this stuff, but at the end of the day someday Avi Arad is no longer going to be there and the entity of Marvel has to have all its business and properties protected. It's not a good move to take a film that they spent $3 million on that might someday, at the very least, become a Blu-ray extra or an extra disc in a box collection and destroy it. I find it very hard to believe that they would just burn it or let him burn it. I don't believe he burned it. I believe it's sitting in a vault somewhere and that he will do everything in his power to make sure that nobody ever sees it legally.

Do you think that the movie will ever be released?

I do. As I alluded to earlier, Avi Arad can't live forever *(laughs)*. I don't know if it's personal to him or if it's strictly business. I don't know the man like I know Roger, but he's obviously a very shrewd, very smart businessman. We started a change.org petition to ask Marvel to release it, but this isn't the first item on anybody's agenda. There's not millions of people clamoring for the release of Roger Corman's *The Fantastic Four*. It's probably going to have to be something people view as a financial advantage to release. Probably they're going to need to come up with a really successful franchise and somebody's going to have to step in there and do three great *Fantastic Four* movies like the Sam Raimi level *Spider-Man* movies. Love them or hate them, they were successful. People liked them at the time. We'd never seen anything like it. When that level of success happens, I think Marvel will be a lot less concerned about the Fantastic Four brand.

They're not going to release it right now because, frankly, the brand is shit. The comic book is just about to come back. The comic book isn't even a monthly comic book. Marvel is so focused on figuring out how to make more *Avengers* movies and more *Spider-Man* movies and how to make more stuff on Netflix on a low budget. They don't care about nostalgia. I don't think this movie will come out until there is a financial reason for them to put it out. Maybe it will be in a box set. I was hoping when Ron Howard alluded to the film in a fun way on *Arrested Development* that might open up the door and people might be like, "Gee, there really is a movie in the 1990s about the Fantastic Four that nobody's ever seen. Gosh, that would be fun to put out." But it hasn't.

So do you think Avi Arad is going to have to pass on to the Great Beyond before we see it get a formal release of some sort?

I think he'll have to pass on from Marvel. He'll have to become somebody that is in no way connected to anything having to do with Marvel. And even then it would take time after that.

I don't even know what his power level is to this day. Is he somebody who's directly involved? Is he someone who is just more interested in the big picture and the box office, marketing-type things? Or is he really involved to this day? We thought Stan Lee was still involved for decades, but gradually people realized that he's a figurehead now. I think he was a figurehead a long time before we knew he was a figurehead. Avi Arad's name is very synonymous with Marvel starting to step it up and do bigger films. You don't think of Avi Arad in connection even with the *Fantastic Four* that Corman did.

Sadly, I don't have any insight into that other than, again, they wouldn't release it for all those years, and when they bought the Corman version, they weren't very close to making the first *Fantastic Four* film at the studio level. Think about it. By the time they bought it up it was late 1993, and the first one came out in 2005. So it was over ten years. You could have released Corman's *The Fantastic Four* as a kid's movie, as a Saturday morning movie, or a cable movie. They could have put it out on Nickelodeon or the Disney Channel movie in the 1990s at any point and not hurt the brand because they could have said this was an older version or a low-budget version. The nostalgia has to catch up with them before they can embrace those early films like *The Punisher*.

What do you think of those early films?

Frankly, those 1980s Marvel movies are not good. Maybe Marvel will do a box set nostalgia collection someday of the first *Captain America*, maybe a couple of the *Hulk* TV movies, and *The Fantastic Four*. Then we'll see if it's burned or not.

***The Incredible Hulk* TV series — not so much the TV movies — there's something there. That was more serious, a little darker in some ways. A lot of that stuff in the 1980s and early 1990s does not completely satisfy the fans. The studios, in general, were still finding their directions and were also hampered by the state of special effects at the time. Some of the current films are still hit or miss. The effects may be there, but the story is lacking.**

They missed a great opportunity because we just passed the twenty-fifth anniversary for *The Fantastic Four*. They were in post at this time twenty-five years ago for the film. Unfortunately, that's been missed.

***The Incredibles* obviously draws from the Fantastic Four. A lot of the character names are similar, and in terms of powers, they switch out the Human Torch for a speedster and the rest is very much the same. Does it occupy the spot in the popular consciousness for a superhero film about a family unit with superpowers?**

Yeah, and I also think it wouldn't be a terrible idea for one of the studios to do a live-action, original content piece about a superhero family that fills that space as well. They might get sued by *The Incredibles* or the *Fantastic Four* studios, but maybe those same studios could do it.

The Fantastic Four itself was drawing from other things as well. You had Challengers of the Unknown over at DC a good two or three years before the Fantastic Four. It was also four people. If you look at *Challengers of the Unknown* comic books and you look at the first ten issues of *Fantastic Four*, the Fantastic Four went a little further into superpowers but it's four adventurers that go off and go on these crazy adventures. You can definitely see the influences in *Fantastic Four* from these other books. You had the Doom Patrol, which definitely involved superpowers and there was one girl and there were three guys. One guy was in love with the girl, and there was a bearded scholar. Doom Patrol and the Fantastic Four have major parallels. I heard that they're finally developing a *Doom Patrol* live-action TV series, which I've been waiting for because it seemed like such an obvious void that could be filled.

My understanding is that the Fantastic Four precedes Doom Patrol, but Challengers of the Unknown does come before the Fantastic Four. This material gets so intertwined. I'm looking at some notes here. For example, DC's Plastic Man appeared twenty years earlier in *Police Comics* #1 from 1941. Also debuting in that issue are Phantom Lady, Human Bomb, Firebrand, and Mouthpiece who have some parallels to the Fantastic Four. Or, again, in the case of Mister Fantastic, he debuts in *The Fantastic Four* #1 in November 1961, but DC's Elongated Man appears in *The Flash* May of 1960. Outside of comics, you can find precedents such as *The Invisible Man* written by H.G. Wells in 1897. The Incredibles is just a current version of the Fantastic Four, which itself is a version of something before it.

I don't think that the similarities between the Fantastic Four and the Incredibles were lost on anybody. If anything that, too, could have been the Fantastic Four. With the Lego movies being so popular, and so funny, and so successful, you could have done a Fantastic Four animated version like a Pixar *Fantastic Four*. That might have been the way because there is so much expensive CGI involved in a live-action version. There might have been a way to do the franchise successfully.

And the Wurst brothers do all of those Lego movies, so everything could come full circle.

The *Fantastic Four* films have not been as successful as some of Marvel's other movies. What is the difficulty with successfully transferring the *Fantastic Four* from the page to the screen? One of the things we touched on is the theory then maybe the franchise needs to be done differently in some fundamental way. Maybe it just doesn't work as a live-action, action film.

As a lifetime fan of the Fantastic Four, the one of the three movies that I can live with is the very first big-budget one in 2005. I didn't have a problem with the cast, per se. They're clearly solid actors. It wasn't great, but a lot of times with superhero and science fiction properties, the first movie serves as more of an introduction like *Superman* and *Star Trek*.

Clearly, the second movies were really hitting their stride. The problem with the *Fantastic Four* is the second movie was horrifically disrespectful to the fans and the source material. Everybody universally hated their rendition of Galactus, who is such a great character that they just screwed up.

With this third film they were trying to tap into something new, but the results were mixed. There is a comic writer Jonathan Hickman who did a very successful run on the *Fantastic Four*.

I'm not familiar with that segment.

It was really cerebral, sci-fi and I just don't think you can do that for a movie with this property and with the superhero audience on these budgets of a gazillion dollars that have to earn a lot of money back. You've got to appeal to the mainstream. You've got to try to make a movie that's going to make a billion dollars these days if you're doing a superhero movie with a $200 million to $250 million budget. I felt Josh Trank's 2015 version was confusing and weird. It just never stood a chance. They need to find somebody almost a — I hate to say it — Steven Spielberg. His movies usually have a sentimentality and a sweetness that this series can use onscreen.

I maintain that the right way to do *Fantastic Four* is as a period film. Set it in 1961. Do it like a *Mad Men* but as a superhero movie with science fiction. Get a great cast. It's not that Jessica Alba isn't a good actress, but I think they were casting hot women — "let's find somebody who's gorgeous."

I'm looking on IMDb right now and for the 2005 version I see four actresses listed for the role of "Lusting Model" and one for "Sexy Nurse." The 2007 sequel has three actresses listed for "Hot Party Girl #1," "Hot Party Girl #2," and "Hot Party Girl #3."

Was casting Kate Mara as Sue Storm for the 2015 reboot a step in the right direction?

I actually liked Kate Mara as an actress better than Jessica Alba, but I didn't really feel that Kate Mara was good casting because of qualities, looks, and the role that that character needs to fulfill in that foursome.

Let's crunch some numbers from Rotten Tomatoes. The first is the Tomatometer and the second is the audience score. *The Fantastic Four* **(1994) — 29% and 27%.** *Fantastic Four* **(2005) — 27% and 45%.** *Fantastic Four: Rise of the Silver Surfer* **— 37% and 51%.** *Fantastic Four* **(2015) — 9% and 18%.** *Doomed!: The Untold Story of Roger Corman's The Fantastic Four* **(2015) — 83% and 64%. Well, done Mark and Marty! And I would imagine that** *Doomed* **has the lowest budget of all by many factors. These numbers suggest that the future of the franchise is not in making movies from the comics but in making documentaries about attempts to make movies from the comics.**

Please finish this sentence — referring to the unreleased version — "*The Fantastic Four* **is..."**

...one of the greatest Hollywood tragedies of all time. A lot of people think it's much worse than it really is because it wasn't released. Going back in time twenty years, I remember what everybody thought. We didn't see a *Fantastic Four* film for ten years. Nobody thought they trashed this movie and put it on a shelf because of how good it was. Everybody just assumed it was a terrible movie that couldn't be watched and that they did a really bad job on it because they didn't know the backstory and that's the only explanation that made sense. It's not a great movie, but it could have been released. For what they spent on it, it looked great. I think it would have made money. It wouldn't have gotten in the way of a film coming ten years down the road. It's just a tragedy.

Is this the worst thing that can happen to a film?
When you think of the worst thing that can happen to a film, this is it. You make it, you release it, everybody works really hard, a lot of people work for free, it never comes out, you never have anything to show for it, and everybody assumes it didn't come out because it was bad. I don't care, but I didn't get paid a dime to shoot that night on Hollywood Boulevard. I don't think anybody was getting paid. I'm not complaining. I would have done it again in a heartbeat, but the truth is there were a lot of other people who worked on that film way beyond what someone would do in a typical situation because they thought this was going to be a bigger film and a solid release for us. Of course, there's comments about the stretching effect and the invisibility effect. There's no question that the effects were flimsy, but the film deserved to be released. It still deserves to be released. Marty and I are committed to continuing to fight the good fight. We're sort of at an impasse because we obviously have no leverage over Marvel, but it is a tragedy.

What mysteries remain to solve regarding the making of the movie?
We were shocked when Lloyd Kaufman told the story about being approached by Bernd Eichinger. We're not even a hundred percent sure it's true, but since he said it and it happened to him firsthand, we let him tell that story. He's on record saying it. We never heard anything like that before.

Other than the Lloyd Kaufman revelation one of the other key pieces that we were trying to follow up on is the possibility that there were rumblings as early as productions that the movie might not come out.

I followed up on something you said in an interview and asked Carl about it. Carl told me that Oley told him that the movie might not come out.
If anybody else remembers that, they weren't talking. We asked every interview subject what the first sign was that the movie wasn't coming out. Once we interviewed Carl and he told us that Oley told him that the movie might not come out, then we were on a mission to get corroboration because that was a really huge reveal if we found that out.

It is such a big point. I asked Oley and he has no memory of that whatsoever. My aim is not group consensus but individual perspective, which is good because it's tough to reconcile their two accounts — one totally remembers it, and one does not remember it at all. It could just be a difference in each person's individual memory.

Oley vehemently denied it. He wasn't calling anybody a liar. Once he said absolutely not, that kind of killed it. If Oley denies it and Carl says he remembers it, what conclusion do you draw? I honestly 100% don't think for a minute that Carl is making it up. The only other possibility is — because it's so long ago — could Carl be remembering something that Oley said to him at a convention or when they were doing ADR, Automated Dialog Replacement, a post-production step? Could it have been something that didn't take place at the studio during production? Could he be a little mistaken in the timeline? One of the reasons Marty and I just never pursued it was because Oley was adamant that that didn't happen. It calls into question Carl's memory. It didn't seem like something that made any sense.

When I talked to Everett Burrell, he said there was a cool suit. He said it was separate from the Thing suit and would only have been used at the studio during principal filming. Carl said in our interview, other interviews, and his book that there was no cool suit, so I didn't ask him about this; he's already made it obvious that he did not recall one. I asked Oley who said there was not a cool suit.

Did you have a cool suit when you were in the Thing suit? Do you know of any existence of a cool suit?

A cool suit is news to me. I definitely did not have one. The suit was excruciating. I was dripping with sweat being in it for just ten minutes at a time and took the head off absolutely as much as possible. So, no, no cool suit.

Since your stint as the Thing was outside of the studio after principal filming, which is when Everett said that the suit was available, I didn't think so. And he said it was for use in the studio, and your shots were outside.

Everett, who made the suit, and Carl, who wore the suit, both made statements that cannot simultaneously be true, yet who would know better than them?

When people are trying to remember something from decades ago, sometimes there are differences in individual recollections of timelines, contexts, and the exact wording and expression of what was said or supposedly said. People can accurately and truthfully report their memories — or lack of memories — but those memories can be inexact or even wrong.

I don't know the details of what Oley might have heard. It could have just been something that came up in a conversation. Maybe Steve Rabiner said something to Oley like, "We're not even sure if this movie is going to come out." Steve wasn't responding to calls to be interviewed. Nobody knows what Steve knew and when, just like nobody knows what Roger knew and when. Maybe the idea circulating was just that this movie *might* not be released.

I don't have anything to back this up which is why I didn't say it in the documentary. Based on Carl's memory, I don't think that when Oley spoke to Carl — giving Carl the benefit of the doubt — that what he was saying was "I was just told that Marvel's buying up the film and the movie is not going to get released." I knew Oley back then and he wasn't nearly as mellow as he is today. He was a tightly-wrapped guy. I loved him. He would have blown a gasket if somebody had told him that there was a chance that people weren't going to see his movie. He would have walked off the set.

So it had to be something less. It had to be "Holy shit. Is there a chance this movie isn't going to come out?" The fact is that Carl is the only one that remembers this to this day. At the time, they might not have shared it. Twenty-five years later if there had been rumblings among other cast members about this information, they would have remembered it. Somebody would have remembered it. Alex Hyde-White and Michael Bailey Smith were really keyed in on this film and they spent a lot of their own money in 1993 when they were off promoting it.

Well, here's the thing about that. When I talked to Michael Bailey Smith, he told me that he thought Oley may have heard some rumors at the beginning of the film about it not coming out. But he told me that he thought Alex knew more. I didn't feel I could push him any further on these points.

It's occurred to me that people may have found out from multiple sources. If Oley did know — and I'm not saying he did or didn't — maybe he didn't find out from someone above but from someone below. What if a member of the cast told Oley first or just shared a concern, and then Oley repeated it to Carl? I suspect not, but it's not impossible. I find it more likely that he found it out from somebody above.

I believe that Steve probably communicated with Oley at some point during production something he probably wasn't even supposed to say. I wouldn't obviously know the context, but I could absolutely see there being news. Steve Rabiner was a lawyer, and he absolutely would have seen the contract between Corman and Constantin. I absolutely believe that it's possible that something was said to Oley. Who knows? Oley might have been talking about his plans for where they're going to take this home once they finished it — "We're getting great footage; this is going to get a big theatrical release." Steve might have rained on that parade a little just because he'd read a contract point that Oley had never seen. The point might have said something indicating Marvel had the right to buy the movie up. If you can get your hands on that file and that original agreement between Constantin and Corman, that document would be very telling.

Jay and I talked about how useful it would be to have that contract. The contract is not subject to memory. There may have been certain contexts, other understandings, deals made off the page, contingency plans, and so on, but the words on the page then are the words on the page now, and they tell would at least some of the story. Wouldn't that be fascinating material?

Yeah. Maybe Marty and I should have made a better effort to get our hands on that. I agree with you. Whether the film simply had to be going into production before the end of 1992, as we've all been told, or had to go into production by the end of 1992 and yield a finished product is a big difference. If there is a conspiracy, that would shed a horrifically bad light on both Eichinger and Corman and probably Rabiner. Eichinger might have said look, "This is someday going to be a $30 million to $40 million film at a studio. It's worth a million dollars to save the option." Try to think like Eichinger who had invested something like $400,000 in the option and shopped it around for what people say was about six years. As the option was dying, he was at risk of losing all of that $400,000, so he goes to Corman and says, "We've got to go into production." The plan on Eichinger's part all along could have been "I don't have any choices. This isn't originally what I wanted to do, but it's 1992, and I don't have a studio deal. I've got to get creative. I've got to go into production. If we do a really low-budget version and they want to do a big-budget version, they'll buy this out and keep us from releasing it. I'll keep my option and make at least a little money on this film."

That's why I don't feel that there was exactly a conspiracy because this film could have been released. I believe releasing it would have been his backup plan to at least get the money back they spent to make the film. And trust me, they didn't really spend the million dollars. Roger probably stuck it to Eichinger a little, too, by charging him for Laura Schiff and me. He racks up all these charges, but he's also charging three other films for the same people. He probably wasn't invested in this more than a quarter of a million and he got a million. We have that confirmed because Oley said Roger called him and told him that.

And that's also one of the tragedies. Everybody who worked on the film got paid, but nobody, of course, could earn residuals or the real money that would come with a sequel. It's sort of like that first professional sports contract. You get paid, but the bigger money is when you make that next deal.

A sequel was absolutely rumored. A theatrical release was never contractually promised. It was spoken about and spoken about and spoken about. They were handling this movie like no other movie. I'd never seen anyone on a Corman film take their own money, go travel, sign autographs, and meet the fans. These guys did not think this film was going direct-to-video. These guys thought this movie is going to get a theatrical release. It wasn't going to be *Jurassic Park* necessarily, but it would have launched or improved all of their careers. They would have gotten residuals.

I do lots of low-budget films. Experienced agents know this: When you negotiate, if you get an actor that is inexperienced, you say, "Look, here's how it works. You're going to get paid scale now — $2,000 or $3,000. You're going to get that same amount the first time it replays. Then, you're going to get that same amount when it goes overseas. So instead of $3,000 you're going to get at least $10,000." That's a negotiation point we use.

So they accept that because they believe they are going to end up making at least three times the scale amount down the line.

So these actors were working for peanuts. Really, they had no recourse, but if I had been Roger Corman in this situation with the way things went down, the way the movie was just eaten up, I would have done something for them. They took care of Alex Hyde-White, but I don't know if they ever took care of anybody else. I would have put Rebecca Staab as a lead in a movie in the next year. I would have put Jay Underwood as a lead in the next year. I would have kept these people. I would have at least been loyal and tried to help them out. I probably would have deterred them a little from all the stuff they were doing with appearances. "Let's wait. Let's wait. We're going to do that in 1994 once the movie comes out. We'll do that with you. Don't do it now." I think Rabiner was in a really awkward position. He wouldn't talk to us. There were a number of people who wouldn't talk. Craig Nevius wouldn't talk to us either and yet he's now come forward and really appreciates the documentary. He didn't want to do the documentary and possibly alienate Roger because I think he still thought he could work with the Corman family. A couple of people were concerned about that.

That's one of those kinds of psychological ironies. The people who have been mistreated are often hesitant to speak up about it for fear it will lead to further mistreatment of them or that they will be punished in some way for speaking out and just telling what happened. That's not the only reason some people don't want to talk and that's not the sole force shaping people's narratives, of course, but I think it may be a factor for some people.

The cast has nothing to lose. Roger has had twenty-five years to make it right, and he hasn't done it. They have nothing to lose by coming forward and saying, "Hey, this movie didn't get released, and we got screwed." Even future employers aren't going to say anything. Even producers look at that as a screw job. Producers can be some of the most jaded, cynical people in the business. The film doesn't get released and the actors to get screwed while the producer makes a ton of money? I think even the producers would say, "Wow. You couldn't give the actors each five grand or something?" I'm not going to give you a $100,000, but I made a million and probably $600,000 to $700,000 of that was profit. He could have slipped them a little money, given them a job a year later, and said, "It sucks that this movie didn't come out, but we want to use you on another film even five, six years later."

Rebecca did speak favorably of her experience as a lead in 1999's *Stray Bullet* produced by Concorde. Corman was executive producer for that. How much of that had anything to do with Corman trying to sort of help make things up to her because of *The Fantastic Four*, I don't know. My guess is that it's completely unrelated and that it was just right person, right price, right time, right job. Either way, that situation is much more the exception than the rule.

I think Alex Hyde-White was the only one he reached out to and that was probably because Alex was the greasy, noisy wheel. Alex is not afraid to do that. He used to show up at the office. I'm going back to 1993. Steve Rabiner just was in a very awkward position. I think it's probably part of how the news came down because Alex would literally, without an appointment, just come up and sit in the reception area wondering what was going on with the film, which was a justifiable question, but Steve didn't have an answer. Eichinger had to know before anybody else. I think he knew earlier than people think. The fact that he's passed away means we will probably never know exactly when he knew. Corman could have known, but we can't ascertain that. I can't remember who Carl said Oley talked to at the studio about the film maybe not coming out.

I didn't ask him if Oley told him where he got that information from. That would be interesting, though.

I think Oley was mostly in contact with Steve Rabiner. There was Steve Rabiner and Mike Elliott. Mike Elliott was in charge of some films. Steve Rabiner was in charge of others. And then Roger was Roger. Roger wasn't on the set checking production schedule and budget. Roger would see the info from Steve at the end of every couple of days or every week. Steve would have been responsible for letting Roger know if there had been any financial problems or issues. Steve may have known very early on that they had no intention of releasing it in theaters.

Back in those days what they did with a movie like *Carnosaur* is they did what we now call four-walling. They would rent a theater or find a theater that would take it for a night or two, put an ad in the Los Angeles papers and show the movie in Los Angeles for a couple of days, maybe even one day. They did this with *Carnosaur*, and *Carnosaur* wasn't even as big a movie as *The Fantastic Four*, supposedly.

And *Carnosaur* got a sequel! My understanding of four-walling is that it is a way to get a movie shown, generate attention, and maybe get some reviews. The studio is, in essence, paying to have the film shown in exchange for all ticket sales.

The cast may have been thinking "holy shit" when they heard it was getting shown.

So there's an inconsistency for the cast between hearing the movie is coming out and not being sure if it's finished and the special effects are done.

You can see it in the documentary. Are those done? Is that all they're going to do? Are they going to replace them? Why aren't they shooting this? Why do things seem stalled? For all we know, those things were all because Marvel and Eichinger were negotiating. They could have been negotiating for two months. They could have been negotiating for a long time between the lawyers to figure out exactly what Marvel was going to pay him and exactly what impact it would have on his option. We think it came down in a few days but those wheels could have been turning for a really long time. Avi Arad or whoever could have just said, "That movie is never going to come out." Then he realized they finished it. "Holy crap. He's actually planning to release this?"

The back and forth, the phone calls, and maybe even meetings could have been a process, perhaps even a lengthy, protracted one rather than a fairly compact event.

We all sort of think, for example, that one day Avi Arad steps forward and says, "We're going to exercise this clause in the contract, buy it all up, and cut you a check," and it's all done in a couple of days. Maybe the terms weren't so clear and concrete.

I just can't imagine that there is something in the contract that would establish an amount. I wonder if it had to be a mutually agreeable number, which would be weird. What rate though? Why would they even have that in the contract?

That seems a bit nonstandard, especially if Marvel doesn't anticipate that Eichinger is going to make a low-budget version. Why would you think you would need a provision for that possibility?

I would certainly never assume Roger isn't cynical enough to suspect that this could happen the whole time. I just don't know if he would understand the value of the property. Roger was in no way aware of comic books, and movies from comic books weren't making a lot of money back. I guess there was *Batman* and *Superman*. Well, maybe they did sort of hedge their bet. Getting that contract would be so cool. There's a few pieces of the puzzle we were never able to get ahold of, which is suspicious in and of itself.

Carl is convinced that Roger knew at an earlier point.

Oh, yeah. I think the cast would not exactly be shocked to find that out. It'll never be revealed because Roger would never cast himself as the bad guy. Roger walked out of the screening of *Doomed*. He came with his wife to Santa Monica. We had a screening at the Aero Theatre with 300 people in attendance. He walked out fifteen minutes in.

Did he ever explain why?

No, he didn't. I got a phone call from his assistant the next day telling me that Roger wants to talk to me. I gave him all my contact info, and I never heard from him. I just felt like I'm going to leave that one alone. Good Lord, the last thing I need is for him to sue us or to tell us, "Hey, I don't like the movie." I have to imagine there were things in the film that went a little too much behind the curtain. I don't think he's big on that stuff coming out.

Steve Rabiner didn't want to be interviewed about the movie. He is one of the people who would know some of the details. Roger at first declined to be interviewed as well. I know he's had some bad experiences with documentaries. I was able to take another route to getting him to talk. Did you interview him?

No, but I'm working on it.

I don't think he wants to talk about it. Evidently, he feels the documentary was unkind to him, so the film is probably a sore subject.

Roger Corman

Co-Executive Producer, Co-Founder of New World Pictures and Founder of Concorde-New Horizons

Ready to go. Ask me the questions and I'll tell you what happened.

Please tell us about Bernd Eichinger's initial pitch to you to make *The Fantastic Four*.

First, let me say this is one of the wildest projects I've ever been involved in. I think it was around September of 1992 that Bernd came to me and he said he had an option on *The Fantastic Four*. He had a $30 million budget, but the option would expire on December 31 of 1992 if he hadn't started the picture and he said he didn't have the $30 million. All he had was $1 million. He had a script and he said he had a proposal for me because he knew I had my own studio, my own staff, various editing departments, and so forth. He came with the whole plan worked out.

His proposal to me was he would give me a million dollars and I would make the picture starting before December 31. I said, "Well, that's a fair cut in your budget, Bernd — $30 million to $1 million." This was on a Friday. I said, "I'll tell you what I'll do. Let me send it down to the guys at the studio. They'll work on the weekend, and I'll look at it on the weekend. Let's all meet on Monday and see what we can do. Obviously, we're going to have to make a fair number of cuts. Without even reading your script, I know it's going to have to be modified slightly."

So we met on Monday, and I and the guys at the studio had made notes on what we had to modify. We actually felt we didn't have to change that much. It was just a matter of cutting some sequences out of it that clearly could not be made. We could make a simpler version of other sequences, so we came to an agreement.

When did production begin?

I said, "Bernd, this is September and this is a really complicated picture. You give up your option if you don't shoot on December 31. December 31 is essentially a holiday. I say we start shooting on December 30 to get one day in. I need every possible day to prepare this picture." Bernd said, "No, it'll be obvious what we're doing if we start shooting on December 30. Let's start shooting on December 26." I said, "Bernd, it's going to be obvious what we're doing either way," but I think we compromised on December 28 or close to then. We shot the film and it actually was a good little film. I was very pleased with it and so was Bernd. I thought, "This may be the chance, really, to score theatrically."

Did you ask for anything else beyond his initial offer?

I added one thing. This was the time in the early 1990s when the market for low-budget films was slipping, and I could see and anticipate it was going to be slipping more as the major studios took over and made more and more of the type of film we've been making. Frankly, *The Fantastic Four* was a big-budget version of what we'd been making. I said, "Here's what I'll do. If you'll give me money for distribution, I'll distribute the film." I thought this might be an opportunity to revive the low-budget market because I have a famous title that already has its own history, fans, and momentum. It might be a way to bring the market back and indicate a new way to go, so we finally worked out this deal. The deal was this: He gave me the million dollars. I made the film.

What happened after you made the film?

I think he had ninety days to shop around and see if he could make a major deal. If he could make a major deal, he would pay me $500,000 to give up my distribution rights. If he couldn't make a major deal, he would put up a million dollars for prints and advertising for us to distribute. I thought, "This is essentially a win-win deal." If I get to distribute it, we get a chance with a million dollars in advertising to really score. We agreed we would split the profits after my distribution fee. If he takes the film away, I get $500,000, so either way I could win. So we went ahead on that basis.

His ninety days were almost up. Halfway through that period we started making a trailer and a poster. We had a very nice poster. All around the office we have posters of some of our bigger films. In one of the back offices — because it was never released — we still have the poster for *The Fantastic Four*. What happened was that just before the ninety days were up, he made a deal with Fox. True to his word — Bernd was a nice guy and he's totally honest — he gave me a check for $500,000. I was happy to get the money but reluctant to have missed out on this experiment.

Bernd makes the big deal with Fox. What does that mean for the film you made?

I said, "Well, Bernd, what are you going to do now with the little film now that you have the $30 million budget for Fox?" The $30 million eventually turned out to be $100 million when he finally made it. He said, "Here's my plan. I'm going to release the big $30 million picture, and then afterwards I'm going to release the $1 million picture as a prequel, which will benefit from the publicity of the first one. I'll probably make more money off the $1 million film then I make off the big one."

Was there a strategy regarding who to cast or how to cast? Did you have someone particular in mind?

No. From the beginning we knew we knew we were not going to be able to get stars. Our feeling at that time — and Marvel later on has proved this — was that the star was the name *Fantastic Four*. We would rely on the name of the comic book to carry the film rather than a particular person's name. We had to go with unknowns in order to make it for a million dollars. We had to put our money into the production.

What was your initial investment in the film? Did you have to put money up front as well?

No. It was simply this: Bernd gave me the million dollars and I made the film for that million dollars. I had no investment.

Do you think Eichinger planned to release the film, or was making it just a way for him to hold onto the rights?

He was doing both things. He was first making certain that he held onto the rights. Secondarily, he planned to release the film if he couldn't make a bigger budget deal with a major studio. His first choice, which he ended up taking, was finally to put together the $30 million deal. If he couldn't get the $30 million deal, we would definitely release our $1 million version. We had a signed contract. He was going to put up a million dollars for prints and advertising to release the film. He felt and I felt as well that the film was really a pretty good picture. It's been pirated. The reactions were surprisingly good. People who saw the film said, "This is a good little film." We felt we could make some money with the release. It was sort of plan A: Make a deal for the $30 million picture, pay me my $500,000, and walk away. Plan B was just to release the film.

So how did Marvel get involved in terms of buying up the film?

Marvel Comics who owned the rights, heard about Bernd's plan. They knew what Bernd was trying to do and they did not want this to happen because they thought that although he might make a lot of money, it might damage the name to have this low-budget picture come out.

Do you know if anyone at Marvel ever saw the film?

As I understand it, they never even saw the film. They bought it away from Bernd sight unseen just to make certain that it didn't come out.

How much or how little did Eichinger have to do to hold onto the rights? We know he had to be in production, but did he have to have a finished film or did he just have to start production? What was the minimum he had to do?

He had to finish the picture.

(Note: In the recorded interview around 16:45 and in the previous draft, Roger Corman says, "All he had to do was start shooting — nothing else." After reviewing the draft, he changed that statement (that was the only significant change). That's important to keep in mind or else the next couple of exchanges don't completely make sense as they are based on his initial answer.)

Why do you think he decided to complete the whole thing?

I'm speculating here because I don't know the details; this is my assumption. If he didn't really complete the film, they could say, "You started this film on December 30 and you never shot more than the first day," or "You shot part of it." In other words, they would have had an argument that the starting of the film in December was just a ruse and that he never really intended to make the full film and, therefore, it wasn't truly the start of the film. To protect himself he had to really make the film. Otherwise, they would have a case that he was just pulling some sort of a con game on them.

I see. So technically he just had to start shooting it, but he thought, in your opinion, that filming the whole thing would be the best way to make sure that there wasn't any argument about it or opening for anyone to speculate about his intentions.

Yes, exactly. Plus, the fact that to start shooting, we really had to put a fair amount of money in the pre-production and if he didn't finish it, he'd lose the money already spent in pre-production. It was really more economical and would make more sense financially that if he started it, he would finish it and, therefore, have a real film that he could make some money with rather than write off an unfinished film.

I'm also thinking that if he's using the film as a bargaining chip with Marvel, he's going to have more leverage if he has the entire film shot out versus two or three days off raw, unfinished footage.

I don't think there was any bargaining chip involved. His option was just automatically picked up. He fulfilled the terms of his contract and so he continued to hold the option.

I see what you mean. I envisioned a scenario in which Bernd would use the film not just as a way to hold onto the rights but also as a way to put pressure on Marvel to help fund or secure a deal for the big-budget version because Marvel didn't want a lower-budget version to possibly lower the value of the *Fantastic Four* or other comic book films that they might make in the future. What you're saying is Bernd was never in a position, never had the ability to put that kind of pressure on them.

Yes.

There was nothing to negotiate with because Marvel always had the opportunity to buy up the film, bury the film, and eliminate any risk they felt it might pose to them. Bernd would still maintain his rights and could make another *Fantastic Four* film, but he would no longer own that particular *Fantastic Four* film.

That's right.

Very complicated.

Did you interact with Stan Lee?

I met Stan once. We had a very pleasant conversation. He knew of the script. He felt that the script had departed a little bit from his original thoughts. That's because we had to do a little bit of rewriting. I pretty much knew we were going to be shooting Bernd's script, but we discussed ways to slightly change it and bring it back into his original intentions, his original vision for the picture. It was really more of just a friendly discussion.

Why did you pick Oley Sassone as director?

Oley had directed two previous pictures for me. He had originally, I think, been doing some music videos but I'm not positive of that. I know he'd done two previous pictures for me and had done a good job. One of them was a very difficult picture and he brought it in right on schedule and on budget and did a good job. I felt this is going to be complicated and we had so little money and schedule to do an extremely complicated picture. I chose him simply because I thought he was a good director and would do a good job.

What did you think of the completed version of the film?

I was very pleased. For a million dollars with all the special effects and all the complications and other scenes that were very big that didn't even have special effects, I thought this is about as good as you're going to get. I was pleased with the film and so was Bernd. He congratulated me. He said, "This film has turned out better than I thought; we've got a good picture here."

When did you find out the film would not be released?

I was not aware Marvel bought it until much later. I don't even think I heard from Bernd. I don't remember how I heard it. I just heard later on that Marvel had bought it back from him.

What was the compensation they paid to you?

I got a small producer's fee out of the million dollars and, of course, it carried the overhead of our studio for a couple of months. That all came to us, so it took care of about a quarter of a year's overhead of the studio, which was a legitimate cost to the production.

When Marvel bought the film, did they pay you anything?

They paid me nothing. Bernd paid me the $500,000 to buy out my distribution rights. I had no real knowledge of the money involved in the deal between him and Marvel. I don't know what Marvel paid him, if they put pressure on him, or what they did. I don't have any information at all on that.

The director, cast, and crew were and are disappointed that the movie did not come out. What would you say to them now?

(*Pauses*) What I would say to them now which is what I said to them at the time, which is that they all did a good job. These were unknown actors, but they were all good. We all did a good job. We made the best film that we could make for the money and they should not take this as anything against them. It's just that we as filmmakers got caught up in the financial side of Hollywood. That had nothing to do with the quality of the filmmaking.

At the end of *How I Made a Hundred Movies in Hollywood and Never Lost a Dime* you wrote, "There are parts of me in all of my films." Are there parts of you in *The Fantastic Four*?

I think I wrote that before I made *The Fantastic Four*.

Yes, but I thought maybe it would still apply.

There isn't much of me in there because this is one of the few times where a script was given to me. Bernd developed the script totally on his own. I contributed some of my thoughts into the revision. I wouldn't even say that there was a rewrite. It was a slight revision of Bernd's script. We were primarily trying to stay true to the original comic book and still be able to do it on the budget that we had.

Over the years you've discussed your interest in Freudian psychology and offered Freudian readings of your films. Will you give us a Freudian reading of *The Fantastic Four*?

I'd rather not. (*laughs*) It's been so many years. I should probably steer away from that question.

How difficult was it to show the various powers of the Fantastic Four?

These were all difficult to do. For Reed it was the stretching of the body, and I thought of that as something that could be really great if we could do it on film. Johnny Storm had the ability to shoot flames. I thought that was very good, as shooting flames was one of the greatest looking things, and actually it was one of the easiest things to do because we'd worked with flames in so many films. That was easier to create then the stretching of Reed's body. Same thing with Sue Storm and her ability to turn herself invisible. That was very good visually, and yet again it was not that difficult to do from a technical standpoint. Ben as the rocky monster the Thing was not that difficult to do either because it was primarily a matter of makeup and prosthetics. I would say the most dif-

Craig J. Nevius and Roger Corman. PHOTO COURTESY OF CRAIG J. NEVIUS

ficult thing from a production standpoint was the stretching of Reed's body. The shooting of the flames, becoming invisible, and becoming a rocky creature were all good, but they were easier to do.

Reed Richards, Johnny Storm, Sue Storm, Ben Grimm, and Victor Von Doom — which of the film's major characters do you most identify with?

I would probably identify most with Reed himself. He's almost the perfect hero. At the same time, there are some problems within him, so I would also identify with him because of that. Maybe I would identify with Johnny Storm also because he's a more complex character. He's a flawed character. He's volatile. He's hot-tempered. He's rebellious.

What happened to the copies of the film?
Weirdly enough, some copies went out. It's not that difficult to tell somebody at the lab late at night when they're making prints, "Knock off a print of that picture for me, and I'll pay you some money." I don't want to get too deeply into that, but some prints went out. I don't know how many and they were all essentially pirated prints. There was no authorization, so I cannot tell you how those prints got out, but I would assume they had to come out of a lab somewhere and somebody must have been paid, or maybe somebody did it just for laughs to have a copy. I don't have any real explanation. I know there have been real film copies of it, and I know it's been on the Internet quite a bit. A fair number of people have seen this film even though it's supposed to be buried, and their reaction has been rather good according to comments on the Internet and so forth.

If it had been released, how well do you think it would have done in the box office?
I think we would have done well. I was very happy to get the check because I was getting money for doing nothing, but I was really more interested in the experiment. I liked the film and script. Obviously, nobody knows exactly what a film will do, but I've made enough films that I have a general idea, and I thought this film's going to do some business. I think we're going to have a nice little success and maybe more than a little success.

Do you think that the film will ever be released?
I would doubt it at this stage. Remember we made it in 1992. Here we are in 2018. That's a long time. The type of special effects that we could do then are dated today. Since then we've had computer graphics and other great advancements in special effects. I think the effects were adequate for their day, but today they would look a little cruder. I doubt there would be any particular point in releasing it. Although you might send the two pictures out as a double-bill in specialized theaters or maybe on Netflix. You could combine the two films on DVD as sort of an interesting thing to look at for aficionados.

So you don't really see it as a mainstream big-theater release, but you could see it coming out on DVD or as a double-billing or something more along those lines?

Yes. I don't think it could go out today on its own. It might go out on DVD on its own just as a curiosity.

Did Bernd ever express an opinion to you about the 2005 version that finally came out?

No. I never talked to him about it.

What did you think of the 2005 version?

I thought it was good, but, as with a number of these films, I didn't think it quite justified the budget. If you look at one of the guys who started with us, Jim Cameron, and the $100 million spent on *Titanic* and then the $200 million for *Avatar*, you say, "Yes, I understand. I can see it there." As we used to say, "It's all up there on the screen." When I saw the 2005 *Fantastic Four* for $100 million, I thought it was a pretty good film, but I didn't see where all the money was spent. It could have been a little better. I don't want to knock it.

Anything else you want to talk about, add, clarify, or elaborate on?

No. Your questions covered just about everything. The only thing I don't know about are the deals after Bernd bought it back. I know roughly what happened because I talked with him, but I don't know the details of all of that.

There been so many rumors about this film. I'm happy to have the chance to tell you what actually took place.

Bernd Eichinger
Co-Executive Producer, Constantin Film, Co-Founder of Summit Entertainment

This interview was originally conducted by Robert Ito, who interviewed Eichinger November 24 and November 25 of 2004 by telephone. He generously gave me permission to publish this previously unpublished interview.

If we could start from the beginning...
From the genesis! To start from the beginning, I am a big fan of the Marvel Universe, so to speak. And in 1983, I made my first move and met Stan Lee and told him that I want to have some of his Marvel comics, in particular *Fantastic Four* and *Silver Surfer*. So I met Stan Lee, and at that time, he said it was almost impossible that I could get the rights for the Fantastic Four because he sold the rights, or somebody from his company, Marvel, sold the rights for the film about one character, which was Johnny Storm, the Human Torch. And they wanted to make a movie about that.

And I think it was...the man who wanted to do it for his studio...You have to help me now, because I'm kind of coming from a different universe now *(laughs)*. I had my whole day full of stuff, a long day *(laughs)*! Who was the producer of *The Towering Inferno*?

Irwin Allen?
Irwin Allen? It was something with an "a," that I know. Anyway, it seemed like it still wouldn't fly, but I always thought that it's not likely that somebody would do a movie about the Human Torch only. I couldn't imagine that it was making it to the screen because — at least it was my feeling — it was not a real concept for a movie. And believe it or not, they never did the movie. So in 1986, I guess, if I'm not mistaken, we had

a deal on various characters, including Fantastic Four and Silver Surfer. And also, of course, as you know, this world of Marvel of Marvel comics includes quite a number of characters that have become interconnected over the years; there's the Sandman, there's the Mole Man, and so forth. And so in this universe of Silver Surfer and Marvel we decided to not only buy this but also buy the rights to quite a number of other characters within the universe who have something to do with the Fantastic Four and Silver Surfer.

So you bought all the secondary characters.

Not all! But quite a number.

And the villains too?

Yeah! Mole Man or Sandman or whomever. There's quite a number of characters. You need Alicia, the blind girl — quite a number. So we did package that and I think in 1986 we more or less had a deal with Marvel or with Stan. For me to meet Stan in 1983 was like meeting God *(laughs)*! No really, it was. I never imagined that I would meet Stan Lee. So it was very funny to suddenly see the man who wrote all this in person. I quite remember the day when I shook his hand. I was kind of wobbling *(laughs)*.

Where did you meet him?

L.A. I think it was at his house. I'm pretty sure I went to his house.

And how did he feel about somebody wanting to make these movies?

Oh, he's a very nice person. At that time, of course, Marvel characters were not so hot for the movies, so I think I was basically the person who really went out on this venture. I don't know if you know him, but he's a very, very kind person and has a great family, and he made me feel very good and I was very, very welcome. So when we met through all these years, we had a great time.

Did he give you any advice or pointers about how he wanted the characters done?

No. Not really, no. We were talking about it, and he realized that I really was into this whole system and world, so no. He was always talking to me on a very friendly basis, but never on kind of a tough basis and "I want this, I want that."

And then we tried several drafts of the script and this and that, and it's a very tough thing because at that time comics, they had not the routine to make comics into movies. So it's a very special thing to adapt a comic. At that time, we were not so clear on how to do it. So we worked our way through, and then it went to Warner, I think, first. Then it went from Warner to Columbia when David Puttnam was there. But I never sold it; it's just that I talked to the people. Tim Burton was at Warners then, and people were thinking about doing it with Tim *(laughs)*. That was before *Batman*.

Stan's done a lot of characters. Why Fantastic Four?

Uh, that's always a tough one! At a later point, I also had half of the rights to the X-Men, which I had to sell at a certain point. It was a joint ownership between Carolco Pictures and me. And Constantin. Whenever I talk about me, it always means the company, Constantin Films.

Was there something in particular that you liked about the Fantastic Four?

Yes, absolutely. What I really liked was that it was the first superhero subject which was a comedy, you know? The superheroes are one thing, but more or less, they're all kind of serious in a way. Even *X-Men*. If you look at it, it's serious. Now, of course, they know how to do it, so *Spider-Man* is not necessarily what you'd call a serious drama; it has some comic relief, but altogether it's not a comedy. If you see *Hulk*, it's not a comedy by any means. And *X-Men* is no comedy either. So the Marvel comics have always had a dark side to the characters.

Fantastic Four, for me, is family entertainment, if you understand what I'm saying, in the best sense because it's a comedy and the funny thing about it is that the superheroes are not happy with their powers in a way. They live in a normal world. They live in New York. They are considered freaks and they think of their powers, at least at first, as diseases. This makes the whole thing very funny because as Stan Lee always said, for him he likes this idea that superheroes are confronted with the normal world and have their problems. If the Thing is grabbing a cab, for instance, and sits in the back, the cab crashes down! Or he has no possibility to really use an elevator because he's much too heavy. Or he can't use a phone because his fingers are much too thick. So there are all kinds of really funny and entertaining stuff in it. To play along with superheroes who are not really controlling their powers, it's very funny. For example, the Human Torch is burning stuff.

How much did you pay at the time for the package deal of the Fantastic Four, the Silver Surfer, and other characters?

Oh, well, we don't talk about money. But it was, compared to today, certainly not that enormous.

Because it was an untried thing at that point, right?

Yeah, completely. As I said, there was nothing really there which you could compare it. Maybe in the B-pictures, there was something with superheroes, but not on a big scale. There was *Superman* pretty early on; I think that was the first A-movie, or big movie.

There was a feeling that you could do DC but not Marvel for some reason?

Yeah, yeah, exactly! I mean, Superman was certainly something that was there at that time, but, yeah, it was DC and not Marvel.

What kinds of reactions were you getting when you were trying to shop this around?

There was interest, but we all knew from the beginning that that was a pretty high-budget movie, and of course, this is always difficult. Just look at big-budget movies. But, no, no, there was interest, as I said, there was interest from Warner and from Columbia later, and then when David Puttnam left Columbia, I guess there was a moment, the heat out of it, in a way.

When did you have a script?

Oh, we had lots of scripts (*laughs heartily*). We had lots of scripts. Oh, boy, we had lots of scripts.

So from 1986, you had a script to shop around.

Not one script. Oh, no, no, I didn't shop scripts around. We tried to find our way with writers that would satisfy me in the first place. No, no, I didn't shop the scripts around. No, by no means. No, I was talking to people about the whole idea to make a movie about Marvel comics. It was the concept; it was very difficult to find a good concept.

Since the Fantastic Four are team, was it tougher because the story has to explain four different characters?

No, I don't think that. I think, if you look at it closely, you realize that this whole world of Marvel superheroes happens in a real world. It's quite a task, you know? I don't know whether it was more difficult or not, but what I remember at that time, a big writer was writing, a really big writer, Mario Puzo, was writing Superman for the screen. They took a real big writer.

Did you have a villain in mind that you were pitching?

Yes, here it was Victor Von Doom. It was always the concept, in a way, because Doctor Doom is a real bad guy. And he's very good for a very bad guy in a movie *(laughs)*. So many people in the movies are referring to Doctor Doom. I don't want to say that he stole it, but somehow his whole features are Darth Vader.

Oh, it's completely Darth Vader!

Yeah! So it's not just me saying that. But everybody who knows the comic knows that Darth Vader had something to do with Victor Von Doom. But I mean, look, I'm not saying these guys are bad guys who do that. It was around, of course. You could see that people used bits and pieces, and they obviously also were all fascinated by this bad character.

The first option was in 1986?

Yes, I was in and out of this, we were talking about three years more or less. I have a picture of the Fantastic Four on my wall which is signed by Stan Lee in 1983, so I know that was the year when I met him. And I think three years later, the other things were done, and in 1986 we had the contract.

Tell me what happened with Roger Corman.

Yes, what happened with Roger Corman is a funny little story. Because eventually *(pauses)* it was a different management from, at Marvel at the time. Now there's Avi Arad and he's a very good guy, so it's not Avi now I'm talking about *(laughs)*! There were people at Marvel at that time who managed Marvel who, when the option was rolling out, didn't want to prolong my contract. That was not an option. The rights had a certain limitation that in so many years I had to start principal photography.

Why didn't they want to prolong it?

(Pauses) Because I think they didn't…they, they hated the deal. Because in the meantime they realized that they could sell Marvel property much higher and much better, for better conditions. I *think* that was the real reason at the time.

They figured they could get more money at this point?

I would think so, yeah. I mean, they wanted to have a better contract, let's say. So the time was running out, and then I decided to start doing principal photography of a movie with the characters of Fantastic Four, for a low-budget. So what I did was, I went to Roger, and said to him, "What do you think about the idea that we do a real low-budget movie of the Fantastic Four?" And he liked the idea, a lot! Then what happened is that we, before the rights ran out, we made a movie together. And it's a funny little film! So consequently the rights couldn't fall back to Marvel because they had no further restrictions to the contract; it didn't say I had to make a big movie or whatever, so I made this movie, and it's a cute movie!

It was reported at the time that Marvel didn't want to renew. Did you know that, or did they tell you that?

No. I, of course, went to them and I realized that I could not have principal photography on a big-scale movie. So I said to them, early in advance, "Guys, let's talk about the prolongation of this time period because I've spent a lot of energy and a lot of money into the project, and I want to continue with it." And they didn't say, "Don't continue." They said, "But then we have to renegotiate the whole thing." Is that clear?

Yeah. So they might have wanted to prolong it, but it would have been for much more money.

Yes! Yeah. They wanted to have a much better contract.

So you hired a scriptwriter?

No, no. There were scripts, of course. There were constantly writers in the meantime, so the project was never sitting there. I always worked on the project. But of course, I realized that Marvel at that time didn't want to really prolong the contract as it was; they wanted to really renegotiate it, but on a big scale. And I said, okay, then what I will do is to make this on a lower-budget scale, which we financed and then I met Roger. He is a master of low-budget moviemaking. Plus, I like Roger a lot, and I thought this could be fun. And Roger had a distribution company and he said, "Well, let's go for it."

You mentioned that you can't talk about money, but I just wanted to run figures by you to see if it's in the ballpark. Roger said you had put up $1 million for the production and $900,000 for prints, trailers, and other things. Does that sound about right?

I don't talk about money *(laughs)*. Because it was a low budget I don't know what money he was ready to invest for release. That I don't know. But we knew that there were a lot of fans out there. We knew that we had an audience out there. That was clear.

So anyway, we did this movie and we were about to, in post-production, and we even finished the movie completely. Then when it came to release it, Roger had just started the promotion and the advertising and all of that, and it was just about to start. In the meantime, the management changed at Marvel. While I was shooting the movie and while I was in post-production with Roger on the movie, the whole management of Marvel changed. And there was a new guy coming up whose name is Avi Arad, and he's also co-producer and executive producer on many of the movies which were done from the Marvel Universe like *X-Men* and *Spider-Man* and *Hulk*.

So here's a very fine guy and he called me up and said, "Listen, I think what you did was great; it shows your enthusiasm for the movie and for the property, and I tell you what. I mean, I understand that you have invested so-and-so much, and Roger has invested so-and-so much. Let's do a deal." He really didn't like the idea that a small movie was coming out and maybe ruining the franchise in his eyes.

So he was thinking big.

Yeah, he was thinking big. And I think he was right in doing that, and that he would give me back the money we invested, both to me and to Roger, and we don't release the film.

So everything went to him, the film, everything.

Yeah, exactly. You see? *(conference call coming in)* Perhaps could talk tomorrow.

The Next Day

Your meeting with Avi. When did that take place?

That's a tough one. I think I forgot to say before that Chris Columbus came in when we were still in negotiations with the prolongation of the contract. He said he was interested in being attached to this.

So that was before you started the film, then?

Yes, it was sort of overlapping. But I couldn't give him an okay because I didn't know whether or not I had the rights. I think what happened was that Chris contacted me and that was a certain process, that was a time when I had to renegotiate the contract, so I couldn't give him a stiff okay on that one because I didn't want him to spend time on a movie where I have problems with the rights.

And afterward he said, somehow it was maybe too difficult for him, but also he said he didn't want to go in the way of a filmmaker who did the small movie; he didn't want to ruin his career or something like that. So basically we were talking to Chris and Chris was talking to me, but it didn't happen because we had to shoot this movie in order to save the rights. And later on he probably had other ideas, I think *Mrs. Doubtfire*, maybe. So he was into another movie, and he was not available any more. I think that's more or less what happened.

So your meeting with Avi was after the film was already completed?

Exactly, yes. Absolutely, because he was talking to me about not releasing the movie.

What did he say to you at that meeting?

What he said to me was he is now in charge of Marvel, and that he wants to give me back the money that we spent on the movie, and that we should not release it.

And how long did it take for that deal to be made?

It was not such a difficult deal because there was a clear accounting of what we spent on the film. We didn't want to make a profit, really. It was really to say, "Fine, okay, we get back our money and the effort was, of course, this and that," but, in a bigger picture, so to speak, we decided to give him the movie, to sell him the movie.

Did Avi see the film?

No, I don't think so. I don't know. I mean, ask him (*laughs*)! No, it was not so much a matter of see it or not see it. He knew it was a small movie, and of course, he didn't buy it to release it; he didn't buy it not to release it.

So it wasn't because he thought it was a bad movie?

No! No, no. Of course, we always thought about a big movie with all the possibilities of a big commercial movie, and, of course, he was worried about the franchise.

Did he mention he might want to release it in the future, maybe after the big movie?

(Laughs heartily) No, we were joking about it. He said he'd probably make more money with the small movie than with the big movie. No, but today, well, we'll see. For the time being, of course, we are thinking about the big movie. The deal was made to give us back our money and not release the movie. It's not the quality as such, because, you have to understand, if you do a movie for so and so million and then you want to mount a movie, say seventy, eighty, ninety or something like that, of course, then, you think it might hurt the bigger movie.

Were they thinking seventy to ninety million at that point?

I don't know.

Because that's what it is now, in 2004 dollars.

Yeah, yeah. But, you have to talk to Fox about it. The thing is, back then, I don't know what numbers we were talking, but it was a big-budget movie. In my eyes, when I bought it in the first place, I always had a big commercial movie in my head. Of course! I never wanted to make a B-movie; I just did that in order to make sure that I didn't lose the rights.

What did you do next? You called Roger?

No, Roger was not the problem. He said, "Let's sell it," and that's that. So, to make a long story short, we did this deal, and he was okay.

So Avi and Marvel got the film. What happened to the actual film after that?

I don't know! I don't think they did anything with it.

So it's probably in storage somewhere?

Yeah.

So when did you see the finished film?

I produced it, so I saw it many times *(laughs)*! I edited it and all of that, you know. It was not meant to be a bad movie; we made a low-budget B-movie, but we took our energy into it, absolutely.

So what did you think of the finished product?

Well, it's a B-movie! You know. But it's a funny film.

I saw a version of it.

You saw it!

Uh-huh.

How could you see it?

It's all over eBay.

You're kidding.

Yes, it's all over eBay. So I have to confess I saw an illegal copy *(laughs).*

The official story seems to be that the movie was never intended to be released.

No, that's not true. That's definitely not true. No. No. There was a release budget attached, and we were about to release it. And I think that's also the reason why maybe there was a copy, which somebody at that time simply took from the screener. I don't know.

But had you heard that story? Even Stan Lee told me that the film was never intended to be released.

No, it was not our intention to make a B-movie, that's for sure, but I mean when the movie was there, we wanted to release it.

Yes, Roger said he would never had put money into the promotion of it if he (Note: the transcript says "I" not "he" but that doesn't make sense. The spacing of the transcript I received and the flow of the conversation suggest that this is Ito and not Eichinger speaking) didn't want to release it.

Yes, of course! It was about to be released, no question about it. And at the last moment, Avi came in and said, "Let's do a deal and not release it."

Now, how did the Fox deal come about?

Yes, that was a couple of years later, I think. Because of the fact that Chris, when he was at Fox, or was he at Fox at that time? I'm not sure anymore. I think his production company, 1492, yeah, they were still on the Fox lot. That's for sure. Yeah, yeah, and I received a phone call from Bill McKoenig, who was then running Fox, and he asked me whether or not I would be interested in making the movie with Chris Columbus for Fox. And I said, "Yeah, sure!" I mean, I knew Chris for many years by then, and knew that he was very interested in doing that, so what happened was, we started the whole thing again. We sat down together with the Fox people and made a deal to produce the movie. At first it was planned that Chris and some writers would write the script and Chris would direct.

So this was around 1995, 1996?

I really don't know because I don't have my stuff here. I could check it, or somebody from his production company 1492 would certainly know. Or even Fox would know.

So what happened with that?

Then some time passed. There were several scripts, and then Chris got some interesting offer, I think, during that time period. I think it was, was it *Mrs. Doubtfire*, or was it already the first *Harry Potter*? I don't know. He was working on *Home Alone 2* when I first met him, so this was later. I remember I was on the set for *Home Alone 2*, and that was the first time I met him. Definitely. That was when I was trying to make sure I had the rights.

How far did you get with that?

I don't know exactly the reason, but I think it was because of a picture he could jump right into, which was a very interesting proposition for Chris, and he says he wants to produce it rather than direct it. And from then on, we had a lot of different drafts until we were all satisfied and started to shoot.

After Chris decided to produce, you started looking for other directors?

We looked at a lot of directors. We came in with quite a number of directors and writers, in and out and in and out, and eventually we found the right package and did it.

Was this something that was always in motion?

Yeah, pretty much so. Sometimes not on a daily basis, because when writers are writing, then you have to wait *(laughs)*. But again, there were quite a number of writers on it.

For you and for Constantin, this must be one of the longest productions?

It was by far the longest! Altogether I was counting, I was looking back, I thought, "Oh, my God, now it's 2004", and it was around 1983, which is 20 years altogether when I first started it.

You were mentioning lots of scripts. Can you tell me about the previous scripts?

The basic concept was pretty much always the same. The basic concept was, of course, the struggle from the Fantastic Four and Doctor Doom as the villain. So that was always the structure of it. Because that's also the Fantastic Four, the first segment of it, which is true also for the comics. If you see the genesis of the comics, this is how they go into space to do some kind of research and experiment, and the experiment goes sour and they all go down and Doctor Doom is also infected, but he goes to the dark side, so to speak. It's the genesis of the Fantastic Four.

I spoke with Nevius, the original screenwriter, and he said because of the limited budget he started with the origin and wanted to keep the action sequences to a minimum.

(*Laughs*) Yeah. In this one, we start with them going to space. That was, of course, not possible in the lower-budget movie.

You also considered a lot of different actors?

Yes, as a team, you always have to have in mind that it is a team, and if you pick one, that the character then matches with the others. So when you have an ensemble piece you have to be very clear about who is matching who. They have to fit together, and, therefore, it was a lot of testing and a lot of asking around. But I did that from a distance, I must say. I was at that time not available because I was shooting another movie, and I had just the names and then we discussed the names on the phone.

Were there people you were hoping to get for this?

I thought it was fine. I think it's fine.

How much are you targeting the hardcore fans?

(*Laughs*) I think the fans are very important because the fans are the building of an audience. If you do a mistake in not satisfying the fans, I think already you have a problem. Of course, you don't want to limit it to the fans, but you have to really make sure that the fans are not annoyed. Because I know how annoyed I am if something changes. If I'm very familiar with the comic, and then I see the comic onscreen and the comic, say, doesn't care about these things, then I get annoyed. Absolutely.

Another movie I produced was *Resident Evil*, which is not a comic but a video game. And there also we had to really make sure that we didn't annoy the fans because people are playing a lot and they're living with the characters and they go deep into this whole world, you know? And if you don't make sure that they recognize things, or you do things wrong, then you annoy them.

As a producer, I'm a fan. And that's the main thing about it: the source material and the movie don't conflict. In order to get a big audience, you have to be true to the characters.

Long before *Batman* came out, fans said Michael Keaton is not Batman.

Yeah, but that's different. You always hear things like that, but then you have to be convinced at the end of the day. What counts is the screen, and onscreen he was convincing.

You have always discussions before a movie comes out. That's clear. If you have a fan audience, the audience is buzzing and doing it now with the Internet, and it's a huge thing, but it's fun. But they didn't see the movie, so they're guessing.

What about Jessica Alba as Sue Storm?

The comic was already out in the early 1960s, so women changed in the meantime. You like cool women today. At that time, yes, they were cool, too, in the comic, but somehow it was a different role. It's a different role, and nowadays the audience wants a cool lady. And this is not in conflict with the character.

Is the Fourth of July the release date?

I hear that, yes *(laughs)*. That's something you have to inquire about more precisely at the studio. Yeah, that was the plan.

That's a huge vote of confidence, right?

Yeah, of course, but it's the Fantastic "Four" *(laughs)*. No, that question has to go to the studio. It sounded great, and I think it's a great plan.

How does this feel over twenty years later?

Well, I'm happy. I think the people at Fox do a great job, and I really must say, they were really finally into it, so for me, it's quite relaxing *(laughs)*.

Does it seem real to you?

Good question! Yeah! It does. It does. But it's a Fox production, and it's fun to watch.

How involved are you?

Not much. Not much, I must say. To be honest, I could lie to you, but I don't want to lie, so I'm not really hands-on. I was hands-on, believe me! I was hands-on for many, many years.

Now you're watching it like a...father?

Yes, exactly *(laughs)*!

Have you visited the set?

Actually, I'm not a big set man because in my opinion nowadays it's so easy to see something. You don't have to sit around on a set where a producer has to be around, but it's in good hands, so, on a movie like that, it's done. The moment that they really started shooting it, it's okay. Now, good luck *(laughs)!*

Ivan Kander
Lucky 9 Studios

According to the credits, you wrote, directed, edited, produced, and were responsible for the visual effects of *Von Doom* (all on a budget of $11,292.83 along with some donations of time, skills, and equipment). Can we add anything else to that list?
I edited the film, too. Anytime you direct an indie film project, you have to wear a lot of hats. That's often why you see one person's name in the credits so much. It's less about this weird need to do everything and more about being the only person to step up that's going to actually do it. I had tons of amazing help to put that film together, but just to get it going you have to wear all of those hats.

Your short films cover a wide spectrum of ideas, scenarios, and categories. What made you decide to focus on comic books in the form of 2015's *Spider-Man Lives: A Miles Morales Story* and 2017's *Von Doom: A Dr. Doom Origin Story*?
I'm a big comic book fan and have been since I was a kid. Because comic book movies are so popular nowadays, I don't feel like I'm unique in that aspect. I wanted to make something that I thought people would be more inclined to watch than my normal talkie, dramedy type stuff, so I figured that would be a good way to get my name out there. Also, I thought that if I was going to make a comic book movie, I wanted to do it on characters that either I hadn't seen onscreen or create something that I feel is better than what currently exists.

I see a lot of fan films that feel like cinematic cosplay to me. It's really fun to make a movie in this world that we love. But if I was gonna make a movie in a comic book world with existing properties that weren't my own, I wanted to make sure that I had something to say.

Spider-Man is a hero and staple of comics. Doctor Doom is a less obvious choice. You mentioned wanting to focus on a character that doesn't receive as much attention. Are there other reasons why you picked Doom as the central character for a film?

You probably had the same reaction; correct me if I'm wrong. After watching the most recent *Fantastic Four* movie, weren't you just mad (*laughs*)? It was basically anger. I was being a spiteful, annoying guy when I watched it. How many times have you watched a movie and been like, "Oh, I can do better than this?" That was my initial reaction. This character is not being treated right. Plus, I just love this concept of a hero who is the villain in his own story. I think that's just a really compelling idea. I thought that would be a great way to tackle a Doctor Doom movie.

Doctor Doom reminds me a lot of the movie version of Magneto. Like Magneto, Victor has a tragic backstory. When I spoke with Joseph Culp who played Doom in the 1994 movie, he expressed a kind of pity and sympathy for Doom while also recognizing his totalitarian tendencies. Is Doom a hero, a villain, an anti-hero, or something else?

The reason he's such an interesting character is that he's both. There's a lot of iterations of Doom that show him as both a hero and a villain. That character has been around since the 1960s so he's been portrayed in all kinds of ways. At one point, he was a cheesy, stereotypical, stock villain. As the comics go on, Doom becomes a more nuanced character. The one thing I really like about Doom and that really attracts me to him is that he's the hero in his own story, which I think is really important. Beyond that he's right or almost right a lot of the time. If Doctor Doom just ran everything, things would probably be more efficient and go a lot better.

That's the plotline of *Emperor Doom*. He takes over the world and makes a lot of changes that benefit everyone, but, of course, everyone lives underneath a global dictatorship.

You have to get over the fact that you have to be a really evil person to do that. It's interesting that we're in this post *Infinity War* stage right now because the Thanos that was created for the cinematic universe holds a lot of similarities with what I picture to be a great Doctor Doom. The Thanos that was created for the movie is very different than the one that was created for *The Infinity Gauntlet* comic book series. I feel like they're just cribbing from some of their better stuff with other villains and giving it to this villain we haven't seen onscreen before.

What were your sources or guideposts for the story and for Doom's character?

My first introduction to the Fantastic Four as characters was the 1990s Saturday morning cartoon series. For this particular film, the *Books of Doom* run was the thing I was trying to capture. *Books of Doom* is a really excellent run that makes Doctor Doom a nuanced and interesting character who is compelling. When a lot of people think of Doctor Doom, they think of this mustache-twirling, very comic booky villain. But the *Books of Doom* is something that does a lot to go against that notion. Obviously, I had to condense a lot. I didn't do a fully accurate depiction of his backstory, but I was trying to get the feeling of his backstory right.

More so than the long films, *Von Doom* brings out a lot of the science and sorcery that Doom uses as powers. Why did you decide to focus on that instead of the other characteristics of Doom such as Doom as tyrannical madman (though there are shades of that part of him in your film)?

To do Doctor Doom accurately you can't shy away from the aspect of magic. He's also a genius on the same level as Reed Richards. In that sense, you need to both embrace the comic bookness of it but still give people a grounded thing to latch onto as well so that they're not wondering what all this gobbledygook science fiction stuff is. Doctor Doom is this really perfect combination of Doctor Strange and Iron Man. I wanted to reflect that and what he would look like as a character.

***Von Doom* packs a lot action, story, and ideas into its fourteen minutes. I don't want to give too much away for readers who may not have seen the film, but *Von Doom* is full of themes such as "finding the right balance is key," the interrelationship between science and magic, timing, struggling against oneself figuratively and literally, death cannot be cheated, destructive manifestations of grief, the past determining the future, the impossibility of changing the past,**

and the importance of fate or destiny. Are these accurate? What others can we add?

I think you covered it. That's what the movie is going for. I love time travel stories.

One of my favorite movies is *12 Monkeys* because it's all about the futility of trying to change what's already happened. I thought that would be a fun way to approach this comic book story, which would also allow Doom to be both the protagonist and antagonist in his own story.

I'm glad you brought up the time travel aspect because I think that too much of the time when movies or television shows start getting into and using time travel, they really unravel. I thought the use of time travel helped undo the *Heroes* series, but the German series *Dark* integrates time travel in a very complex and intricate, but successful way. *Dark* demands a lot of attention, but it works well. *Von Doom* uses time travel really well and uses it in a clever and novel way without it becoming too confusing or the plot disintegrating.

Thanks, I appreciate that.

Colin Cassidy voiced Doom. Blake Night built Doom's mask. Rebecca, your wife, made Doom's robes and cloak. What instructions did you give to each of them? In other words, what was your vision for how Doom would sound and look?

I think we did okay. I think everyone worked really hard. If we had more money and time, I would have spent more time on his look, overall. I knew I wanted him to be big and imposing. I really like this idea that's he's both an imposing figure, but also not a clunkily moving figure. I didn't want him to be like a robot that struggled to move. I wanted him to have a certain grace but also be this large, imposing figure. If had more time, I would have spent time adding more texture to his cloak and making it larger. The fabric needed to sleep a lot more and feel more...I'm trying to think of the word.

Regal?

Regal. That's it. Perfect. Thank you. I learned a lot about texture and fabrics, and I learned that cosplay is really hard *(laughs)*.

I wanted to mention that I think that having the fur on his costume was a really good touch because, again, it shows that tension or dichotomy because you've got the suit of armor, which is electronic and very advanced, and you've got the fur, which is more organic and primitive. I thought that was a really neat and effective combination.

I think it captures his aesthetic really well.

What's your opinion of the unreleased 1994 *Fantastic Four*?

Out of all the movies that have been made about the Fantastic Four, it's definitely the best one. It's cheesy, but I appreciate it. The original spirit of the 1960s Fantastic Four feels very Buck Rogers, 1960s World's Fair, anything-is-possible, we're-all-going-to-travel-to-space-and-be-in-flying-cars. The 1994 movies captures that sensibility. In an idealistic way, it's a little cheesy but at least feels accurate to what the initial comics were like. While it's not my favorite iteration of these characters, which I think comes from the comics, it's definitely the best that's been put to film by an actual crew of people *(laughs)*.

What do you think of the rest of the *Fantastic Four* films?

I think they're just bad *(laughs)*. I don't think I've seen *Rise of the Silver Surfer*. I've only seen the first one all the way through. It's kind of weird to think how far we've come with superhero movies. It's weird we live in a world now where Chris Evans can only be associated with Captain America when he played Johnny Storm. It felt like comic book movies were apologizing for being comic book movies in the late 1990s and early 2000s. We've come away from that and now we're in this strange, amazing place where there's a cinematic universe with twenty plus movies that people all over the world understand, and they understand this really comic booky stuff. The reason I think the Marvel Cinematic Universe has been so successful is they've never apologized for being comic book movies, so they have a sense of humor about themselves, but they're also very serious about being true to the feel of a comic book. It's really important that they've figured out where to exist. The original Tim Story *Fantastic Four* movies just didn't know what they needed to be. Are we going to be super-goofy and stupid? They were unwilling to commit to the goofiness of themselves without being dumb.

They were struggling to find themselves and figure out their own identity.

You get to the most recent one. That film does the opposite. It's too weird and dark and doesn't know what it wants to be. Everyone talks about how the first *Incredibles* is the best *Fantastic Four* movie ever made. It's about family. Its embraces its comic book nature, and isn't afraid to be a comic book film.

If you were making a big-budget full-length *Fantastic Four* movie, who would you cast in the roles of the Fantastic Four and Doctor Doom?

It's hard, right? I feel like I need to spend weeks thinking of the right people. Do you have a dream cast list in your mind?

No. Luckily, I haven't been asked that much (laughs). I was talking with someone else who said there is an online petition to get Emily Blunt and John Krasinski...

...to play Susan Storm and Reed Richards.

Right. That's a very interesting combination.

I could see that. I think that's actually pretty good casting. Off the top of my head, for the Thing I'd cast David Harbour from *Stranger Things*.

I can see that. He kind of has that tender interior but rough exterior quality.

For Reed Richards, I'd cast Lee Pace. Do you know who that is?

No, I do not.

He did a show called *Halt and Catch Fire*. He's great in it. He could be a potential Victor Von Doom. He's just a great actor. You're going to think I'm crazy but for Victor Von Doom, I would cast Robert Pattinson. He's probably too young. I'd cast him even if it's just for a young Victor. Robert Pattinson was in a movie called *Good Time* last year. He is just incredible in it. It proves that he's way more than the horrible *Twilight* movies. I feel like I want to give him a chance to stretch in that direction.

For Johnny Storm, I'd cast an actor named Billy Magnussen. Most recently, he was in *Game Night*, but he was also in a movie called *Ingrid Goes West*, which I really enjoyed from last year.

For Sue Storm, you're going to think I'm crazy, but I'd cast Gillian Jacobs from *Community*.

I can see these people playing those characters. I think about stars like Robin Williams who was Mork from Ork and then later on is doing *Dead Poets Society* and *Good Will Hunting* or Jamie Foxx going from *In Living Color* to *Ray*. I don't know if anyone saw those coming. Sometimes we see folks make what seem at the time like leaps, but in hindsight it makes total sense and looks like a natural progression.

I tend to think that comedic actors in dramatic roles have a certain depth. I think it would be really interesting in this case because I think to do the Fantastic Four right it needs to capture that wide-eyed, Tomorrowland aspect of what the future can be. I feel like if you make *Fantastic Four*, I would make it a period piece like I did with *Von Doom*. I'd make it about these people coming together in the 1970s with that kind of technology. I think it'd be really interesting to do it from that perspective. You have to capture both the seriousness of it but also the wide-eyed, comic bookness of it.

What is the future of comic book movies? Is the future in shorter, lower-budget pieces like yours? Is the future in focusing on villains or anti-heroes? Is the future in creating more story and depth of character and relying less on special effects?

It's tough, man, because we're superheroed out right now. Where else can they go from here? They're on TV. They're making all the money at the box office. I think the only way that the movies are going to do well is if they figure out their characters first and worry about all the other stuff second. The reason the Marvel Cinematic Universe is so successful is people genuinely care about those characters. They mean something to us. The DC movies haven't been successful because we just don't care about Cyborg as a character. In the future in order for these movies to be successful, they need to tell character-based stories. I don't need to see one more laser beam that's coming through the sky that's going to destroy the earth. I don't care about that. The reason that a movie like *Logan* is really good is that it's a character piece that happens to be a superhero movie. The reason I like *Infinity War* so much is that I actually care what happens to Steve Rogers, Tony Stark, and whatnot.

With some of the people that I've been talking with I've asked them if they've seen *Logan*. Even though it's not really a kid's movie, in some ways I think maybe that's the direction for superhero movies, these sorts of darker and more serious films. I thought it was an excellent movie.

It's a great movie. It's not necessarily the darkness of it. I think it works for Wolverine as a character to be dark. I think that they figured out that how to make a character story and a smaller story with him. We're so CGIed out that seeing a building fall down means nothing anymore, so we need the stakes to be large. You make stakes larger by making them smaller, if that makes sense.

Maybe some of it is to make bigger movies you need larger characters instead of bigger effects and plotlines that try to do too much or operate on a global scale.

Something like that. I think so.

Stan Lee
Co-Creator of the Fantastic Four, Co-Founder of POW! (Purveyors of Wonder) Entertainment

This interview was originally conducted by Robert Ito who interviewed Lee November 3, 2004 at the POW! Offices in Beverly Hills, California. He generously gave me permission to publish this previously unpublished interview.

Don't hesitate to make me sound better whenever you can.

How were you involved with the first film?

Not at all *(laughs)*. I really had nothing to do with Marvel's movies. I haven't had anything to do with them for years. I'm like a friend of the court, but I'm not actively involved in the movies. But I'm aware of what happened with the first movie, and it was a very interesting thing. That movie was never supposed to be shown to anybody.

The reason that the movie was made — and you can get these details from Marvel — was that the fellow who had the option to do the *Fantastic Four* movie had that option, I think, for fifteen years and somehow never found the story that pleased him. And finally the option was due to lapse, I think in November of whatever year it was that they did the movie. If he hadn't begun principal photography by November or December, then he would lose this option that he has had all the years. And he still wanted to make the movie! He didn't want to lose that option. So he figured he'll bat out a fast movie for a $1.98 budget or something, just to be able to say, "Hey, principal photography started, so now I keep the option." And that's what happened with that movie.

I think the tragic thing about it is that the people involved in the movie weren't aware that it was never gonna be; it was never supposed to be seen by any living human beings. Or dead ones. And they did their best, struggling with a *miniscule* budget, and trying their best to make a movie that would be their entrance into stardom. "If people see us in this movie, or they see how I direct it, or they see how what we can do, this is our big chance." But nobody was supposed to see it. And it's really a shame. Another thing that's kind of sad about it is that so many people did see bootleg copies because those things always pop up, so there were videotapes. People would see them and say, "What a lousy movie!" not realizing that it was done for almost no budget, and it wasn't supposed to be shown ever.

As far as I know, that's the whole story.

So they selected Roger Corman because he's fast?

Yeah, right. On a shoestring.

Any idea what the budget was?

No. I would just be guessing. Maybe five dollars *(laughs)*. I'm kidding. But I don't know. Somebody had to wonder, how do you do Fantastic Four on a shoestring budget? Well, they just tried to do it to keep that option, just to show, look, we've started principal photography.

You're the creator. How did you feel when this was happening?

Well, I was kind of friendly with the fellow who directed it, Oley Sassone. And I was glad that he had a chance to do something. He was enjoying it. He had been doing television before that — he's very talented — and I thought at least he'll have something later on that he can show people and he was happy, and I was. I was... caught up by the enthusiasm of the people working on the movie. They were all enthusiastic about it. And they were doing their best, considering the... the limitations that they had to work with. No budget, really. I think they did a great job, but nobody realizes that.

So he would have something nice for his portfolio, and you wouldn't have to worry about it going out with the Fantastic Four name or the Marvel name?

Well, we *shouldn't* have had to worry about it, if the bootlegged videos hadn't come along.

You've seen the film?

Yeah.

When did you first see it?

Oh, as soon as the illegal videos were around, somebody showed me one.

So you never saw the actual film?

I don't think it was ever shown in a theater. If it was, I'm not aware of it. Remember, it wasn't supposed to be.

So you saw a bootleg at somebody's house?

Yeah! That's all I ever saw.

What did you think?

Well, I thought it's a shame that it didn't have a big budget.

What were some of the problems with it?

Well, if you can imagine the Fantastic Four done where there's not enough money for special effects, those were the problems.

And you can't do the Fantastic Four without special effects.

It's impossible. Now, the new movie is totally different. I was on the set of the new movie, and I think the special effects are going to be mind-boggling. Especially the way they have the Thing, his makeup and his acting. I was so impressed with...

Michael Chiklis?

Yeah, Michael Chiklis. What a nice guy! We became very friendly. But he told me that he had wanted to play the Thing since he was very young. He said he was an actor when he was young, had always read the *Fantastic Four*, and as a youngster he had said, "I want to be the Thing." And I understand that a year ago, he called whoever it was at Marvel and he said, "When you do that movie, I want to play the Thing." And it's a good thing that they got him to do it. I can't imagine anybody doing it better, or even as well. He's perfect. It can't be fun to wear the costumes he wears. It's very difficult. In fact, there's a space in the back of the head and in the back where they have to blow air, with a hair dryer or something. They blow air in there every few minutes. It's really difficult. But he's wonderful.

The cast is terrific. All of them. And the director, Tim Story, I wondered, well, gee, he hasn't done this kind of movie, but he had everything under control. It was a very happy crew. Everybody is happy with everything. It was a wonderful cast and a great director and I think, with luck, the movie will be a big hit.

Was there anything you liked about the first film?

I liked the effort that they put into it *(laughs)*. To me it was fun to watch because it was still the first time that I had seen the Fantastic Four done cinematically as a movie. So even though it wasn't the movie I would have wanted it to be, it was fun to watch it because I wasn't expecting *Spider-Man*, you know?

And they stayed pretty close to the original story?

Yeah! *(pauses)* I can see this interview is really just about the early movie. I wish I knew more about it.

Do you know what happened to the original film?

No idea. No. I was never really involved; I just happened to walk by a few times when they were shooting, and I would talk to the cast. I wasn't part of the production company.

You went down to the set, though?

Yeah, I think they were shooting it around here somewhere.

You're happy it wasn't released?

(Pauses) It wasn't terrible. It couldn't compare to the movies you have today. And it was obviously done on the very lowest budget. It was obvious. It was almost like a bunch of kids in college got together and got a few cameras and said, "Let's make a movie." But they worked hard at it, and they did the best they could. They did a great job for what they were doing.

How were these bootlegs created?

I don't know. But has there ever been a movie where there weren't bootlegs?

But often they go into the theaters.

Oh, is that how they do it?

The really cheap ones.

Oh, you're right. I don't know that this was ever in a theater, but they must have put it on film at some time, and someone must have gotten ahold of it. Or maybe it was in a theater, and I didn't know about it. Maybe part of the contract said it had to be shown somewhere *(laughs)*. I don't know. I'm not aware of that. All that I knew was that they had to begin principal photography by a certain date. That much I know. And what else the contract said, I don't know.

What took so long, from then until 2005, to get the film made?

Well, don't forget it had been around fifteen years that they hadn't come up with a story he liked. So it took another little while, but they finally got a script they liked and they went to work.

Was the script the primary thing?

Yeah. As far as I know, it was always the script. I'll be honest with you, I don't know why it was so hard to get a script over these years.

Because your story was great!

I thought so! Funny thing, I said to them one day, years ago, years ago. I think in the late 1980s or the early 1990s, I said, "Gee, you're having so much trouble getting the right story, I'll write a story for you!" And he said "No." And I said, "Why not?" And he said, "No, no, don't you do it, Stan." So I couldn't understand that, so later I said to one of the guys at the production company, "How come you never wanted me to try to write a script?" And he said (*laughs*), "They thought if they didn't like it, how could they tell you?" I was so surprised, because I figured, hell, if they didn't like it, I'd write another one. It's not hard to come up with stories. But it's probably just as well because the story that they got for the new movie is really a good one.

Who told you this?

You know, I don't want to mention his name. But one of the producers.

That's funny. Because as a writer, sometimes people like the stories and sometimes they don't.

No, no, they always like them *(laughs)*.

No, you know what I mean? You're a businessman, you're a creator, they thought they couldn't tell you.

I was surprised. I had never heard that before. "He wouldn't have known how to tell me if he didn't like it." But I love the guy, and I appreciate it. In a way I can understand them. If he thought that I'm a good friend and he had a lot of respect for me, and he said, "Gee, if I don't like it, how can I say, 'Stan, this isn't right for the *Fantastic Four*?' How can I tell the guy who created the Thing?" I thought it was silly of them; he could have told me and I would have done it again! Because he knows more about movies than I do. But I still respect what he meant.

As creator, what is it that you hope they get right with the film?

Well, the main thing — and I think they did get it right, so I'm happy — is the characterization because I don't worry about the special effects, and I don't worry about the action because you know they're gonna be good because people know how to do that today. They know how to do great special effects. In a big-budget movie, they know how to get action and suspense and all of that. But it's the characterization that makes the story work. And as I say, from what I've seen of the movie, they have the characterization down pat. I'm talking about the new one.

Were you worried that they might not take it seriously or do something campy?

Not at all. The fellow from Marvel, Avi Arad, he takes these things very seriously. I have worked with him in the past, and he understands the characters and he feels about them the way I do, and he just wouldn't let anybody do a movie that wasn't true to the characters. So I have a lot of confidence. As far as the Marvel contingent is concerned, I know that they ride herd on these things. And another thing, almost always, these are directed and produced, and even acted, by people who have been fans of the Marvel comics and of these characters. And nobody has any desire to change anything. They just want to try to depict these really colorful characters in the best possible light.

I don't have maybe that many talents, but I think one talent I have is that I'm able to think like a fan. I think I understand the mentality and the makeup of fans. And I know that almost everything Marvel does will end up pleasing the fans. For example, with the *X-Men* movie, they changed the costumes. Instead of these colorful costumes they wore, they gave them the black ones. And I knew the fans would understand. They would like that because it was more realistic. They would have looked like idiots running around with brightly-colored suits, you know what I mean? So most of the fans are pretty intelligent. It's just they're a little bit nuts in one area: They're fanatical about the characters they like (*laughs*)! But they're not dumb. This wasn't the case fifteen or twenty years ago, but most of the fans today have learned a lot about movie making, cinematography, what makes a good movie, and what works, and what doesn't.

And the people involved in the movies usually log onto those websites and see what the fans say. And there's a bond! You don't want to do anything that the fans are gonna think is stupid, or wrong, and we generally don't. The fans are pretty much on our side on most of the things we do.

I loved movies when I was young.

And Jack Kirby...

Oh, he was the greatest. He and all the guys, John Romita, John Buscema, Steve Ditko, Gil Kane, Gene Colan — they all thought movies. The way they laid out the panels, it was like watching a storyboard for movies. It isn't even difficult for them anymore. I was talking to a director some months ago. He said, "Stan, there is nothing you can imagine — nothing! — that we can't put on the screen today." And it's really true.

How does the Thing look?

So good I can't tell you. It's the comic book come to life but in a very believable, credible way. I'll make a prediction. Next Halloween, the Thing costume is gonna be the most popular by far, the way Spider-Man was this year. Every kid, and a lot of the grownups, are gonna want Thing costumes.

They're all exciting for me. The X-Men, Spider-Man, Daredevil, the Hulk, sure. But this particularly because of all the Marvel characters that I did, the Fantastic Four was the first. So it means a lot to me.

Like a dad?

In a way, yeah. My firstborn.

To put you on the spot...

Don't ever put me on the spot!

What was your favorite Marvel film?

Oh, *Spider-Man*, I think. Especially *Spider-Man 2*. I loved the first *Spider-Man*, but I thought *2* was even better. I loved the first *X-Men*, and I thought *2* was even better.

I already did my cameo in the *Fantastic Four* movie. I hope they don't cut it out. It's unfortunate because if the movie runs too long they can omit it, and nobody would miss it. It's not key to the movie, but Reed Richards is coming to the Baxter Building. The whole FF are coming to the Baxter Building after having done something heroic, and there's a whole crowd outside cheering them as they walk in, and they walk to the elevator, the doorman greets them, and I'm Willie Lumpkin, the mailman.

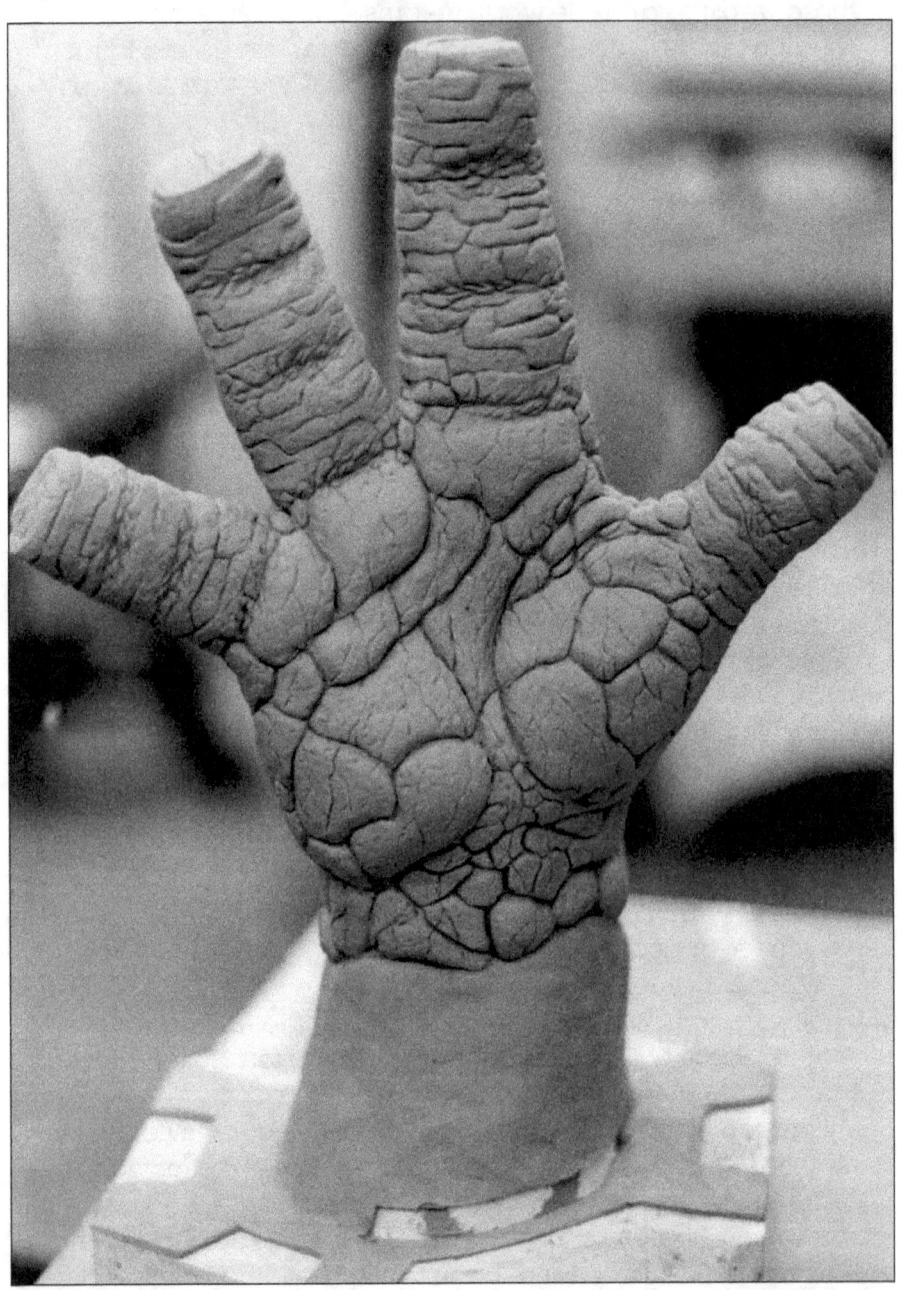

The Thing's hand. Looks like a wave goodbye. Or a hello. PHOTO COURTESY OF EVERETT BURRELL

Conclusion

Who knew what when? And why was the movie never released?

These are still the central questions.

Certainly, one piece of information that these interviews have uncovered is that there was something brewing from the start. According to Corman, Eichinger never intended to release the film in 1994. Instead, it would come out after the first big-budget *Fantastic Four* movie appeared (Eichinger and Corman probably didn't anticipate it taking until 2005 to get the big-budget version out).

Multiple people involved with the film knew something was strange. Some of them had an idea from the very beginning such as Mick Strawn who said several times he had been told from the start that only half of the movie had to be made. Chris Walker says he heard something from Scott Billups who, in his estimation, picked up on something being off in the early stages of making the movie. John Vulich also mentions hearing whisperings during production or perhaps post-production — he doesn't seem quite sure — that the movie's real purpose was to maintain and extend Eichinger's rights. Michael Bailey Smith believes Alex Hyde-White knew something and that perhaps that something may have been more of a sense of unease that came from experience with and an understanding of how the business works or should work compared to what was actually happening with the film.

Others such as Oley Sassone began to get a sense of things further down the line. As Mark Sikes and I discussed, it's doubtful Sassone knew the truth from the very beginning. Buying up comics and assembling the cast at his house to discuss the movie, as various actors said he did, seems more of the actions of an excited and energetic filmmaker determined to make the best film he possibly can rather than a seasoned player holding his cards close to his chest and perpetuating a lie from the beginning of production until the end of filming. The intent and the actions don't match up. Also, why would he continue to work on the film on his own time if he knew it wouldn't come out? Yes, perhaps he was just determined to see it finished and see the project through no matter what, but that seems doubtful and somewhat pointless. It's more likely that even though he may have sensed something wasn't right perhaps at the end of filming and definitely during post-production, he still hoped for the best, for a release, and thought that was still possible. He and Carl Ciarfalio may have had a conversation about the film possibly getting shelved, but as Sikes and I discussed if it did occur, Sassone did not make a definite statement that film was not coming out. To paraphrase, Ciarfalio says that Sassone said that he heard something that *maybe* the film wasn't coming out.

Approximately a quarter of the people interviewed in this book knew something, heard something, and/or believe someone else had information or got wind of something before, during, or shortly after production about the movie not coming out. Eichinger says that his primary motivation for making the first version of the film was to retain the rights and that making a low-budget version was never his aim or true vision for the movie. And, of course, Corman admitted knowing from the beginning that there was a good or strong possibility that *The Fantastic Four* was not going to come out.

One of the biggest questions concerns Corman. Did he know? What did he know? When did he know it? His interview corroborates the basic backstory everyone seems to agree upon: Eichinger's option were going to expire very soon, so he had to start production with a limited budget. However, Corman also made a deal with Eichinger to cut him in on distributing the film. This is important for several reasons. It indicates at that stage of development, Corman thought it was possible that the film would be released. That deal also demonstrates that Corman believed in the marketability and profitability of *The Fantastic Four*; this wasn't just a professional favor to an associate or a private, pet project.

Corman also believed that the film potentially pointed to a new direction, or, as he says, "It might bring the market back and indicate a new way to go." Although Corman had more than made his reputation at this point, to an extent he was in a similar position as some of the actors and crew who were hoping The Fantastic Four would take them to the next level. In Corman's case, he hoped to return to a higher level. There are numerous stories about Corman's thriftiness. It's difficult to believe he would have made a trailer and spent the money on physical items for promotion unless he thought there was a strong possibility — not just a possibility — that the film would come out.

Incidentally, this promotion along with what Alex Hyde-White and Michael Bailey Smith did may have worked against the release of the film by making Marvel feel threatened that this "little" film was going to be become a bigger film than they wanted it to be, and, therefore, the best way to stop that from happening was by killing its release.

Although The Fantastic Four did not revive the market, it did indicate a new and unexpected way to make money. Corman says that he made half a million dollars on, essentially, not doing anything but getting Eichiner to agree to let him distribute the movie if it did come out and agreeing to pay him if it did not. That's a brilliant move. If it had come out, Corman would have had a million dollars in backing for prints and advertising. We don't know what would have happened if Eichinger and Corman had not agreed on those terms. Perhaps Corman would have still made the movie for the amount they discussed. Maybe he would have asked for more and gotten it. Maybe the whole deal would have fallen through.

Eichinger was running out of time, stood to lose a lot, so he had to make something happen. This might also explain why Lloyd Kaufman doesn't remember being offered much money. Perhaps Eichinger didn't make the same offer to Kaufman that he eventually made to Corman because he felt he didn't need to. At some point discussion stops between Eichinger and Kaufman, and Eichinger then knows he must make a deal that much more quickly and no longer has as much room for negotiation so he raises the financial incentives.

Also, as Craig J. Nevius talked about, Corman's company, although also low-budget, brings a higher level of reputation and service, a bigger brand, to the project. The lack of time and Corman brand may be the main reasons Eichinger made an increased offer to Corman. While the extra time and increased budget exceeded what was available for the average Concorde-New Horizons film, they were not *that* out of line with their budgets and timelines at that point. In other words, if Eichinger had $10 million and six months to start the movie, he probably would have gone somewhere else.

Why make Eichinger's motivation for making the movie such a big secret? Well, it seems no one — not even Eichinger and Corman — were sure what was going to happen. No one seemed to have known absolutely that *The Fantastic Four* wasn't going to come out, only that it *might* not come out. If Marvel had not stepped in, it seems Eichinger would have released the movie in some way and Corman prepared for that possibility.

Keeping the primary goal of securing the rights a secret was also important in order to recruit cast/crew and summon their fullest effort. Some of the interviewees have said they would have still worked on the film, and others have said they would not have worked on the film. And some, like Glenn Garland, have said that they would probably have still done the movie but probably not with the same energy and enthusiasm. If you are going to release a movie, you want the final product to be as good as possible relative to your resources. If you are going to make a movie for some other purpose, but you still need it to look like a releasable, "real" movie that might even find itself offered as evidence in a course case, you still need — maybe even more so — the finished film to be as strong as possible. You are already limited by time and finances and now the situation is compounded by suddenly trying to find talent at one of the worse times of the year when Hollywood is closing shop for the holidays. You can't afford to run the risk of anyone holding back or, even worse, saying no and spreading the word that this movie may not even be released. And, you can tell yourself, it's always possible this movie will come out someday, if not the following year, so maybe it will all work out in some way. So no, keeping folks in the dark is not a good model for how to treat people, but, as some have said, it was a good business move.

It's strange that Concorde-New Horizons is simultaneously promoting the movie but pulling back resources for putting the final finish on it. The entire film was essentially shot, and enough of it was made to satisfy Eichinger. Corman felt confident that he could promote it and that it was in his best interest to do so. If the film gets pulled, no need to waste extra resources (i.e., money) putting the final touches on what doesn't need it. Following Corman's account, Eichinger had ninety days to make a deal. If the main shooting is completed somewhere in the middle or end of January, Eichinger has until the end of April to make a deal. If Eichinger doesn't reach a deal at the end of April and the film is slated for a Labor Day release in September of 1993, that leaves four full months — more than four times what everyone had to shoot the film — to finish it. January 19, 1994 is another date that has been given as the release date. That date doubles the time to eight months if Eichinger takes the full ninety days to make a deal. Since Eichinger and Corman would split the profits of a release, it's worth it to Corman to pay for putting the finishing touches on the film — but only if it's going to be released. If indeed Eichinger's plan was to release the film after the first big-budget *Fantastic Four*, Corman had more time to complete it. He may have thought that special effects would be both better and cheaper in a couple of years, so waiting to finish them on *The Fantastic Four* might make the best sense from both an artistic and financial standpoint. It if only appears on video, what's there may already be good enough. If it doesn't come out at all, then there is no point in dumping additional resources into it.

The reason could also be as short and simple as Corman was satisfied with the special effects whether the movie went to video or the theater.

This may also explain the initial special effects from Scott Billups. As Walker has explained, Billups had the sense that this may not have been a project that would actually see the light of day. If so, Billups may have felt it was somewhat pointless or unnecessary to devote his full effort to something that would never come out or come out only video. In other words, he may only have given the effort needed for the job and produced what amounted to placeholders or suggestions — a rough draft. However, if Sassone and others don't know that the film may not come out — and Billups and anyone else who knows this plays it smart by not telling them — it seems that Billups is not living up to expectations because they are not the same expectations. He may not have anticipated pushback and critical comments from, for example, Sassone, and he probably didn't anticipate anyone outside of the film's immediate circle ever seeing it if he thought from the beginning that it wasn't going to see a release. Thus, if no one ever sees it who isn't directly connected to it, and it is never released, he could have thought that the professional impact — positive or negative — would be negligible. Perhaps Billups was holding back, didn't fully know what he was doing, or a combination of both as many have speculated. He did make a career in Hollywood somehow whether through skill, luck, and/or some other quality or qualities, so perhaps his work on *The Fantastic Four* is an early anomaly.

There's another oddity in this whole situation: There are call sheets, logs, notes, and even original photographs documenting the process of making this movie, but it seems that there is not one shred of legal paperwork memorializing the terms of the agreements between and among Eichinger, Corman, and Marvel that has been made available. In his interview, Corman says, "We had a signed contract." Although I did not directly ask Corman for it during our interview, I made several requests to Concorde-New Horizons for copies of contracts between Corman and Eichiner using the same contact information I used to request and communicate about the interview before and after, but as of this writing, I have not gotten any response.

That contract might help answer lingering questions and verify or give specifics to some of the answers. In the various interviews there are different recollections and speculations about how much of the movie had to be made. Did they just have to shoot one day? Did half of the movie need to be completed? All of it? Could there be something in the paperwork that would contradict Corman's narrative? The only real thing one would imagine Corman would want to conceal would be

CONCLUSION

his prior knowledge that movie might not come out. However, Corman has already clearly stated he had that information from the very start and that might or might not be evident from the contract anyway. So what else could it be?

We can speculate endlessly, but a few possibilities come to mind.

Maybe Corman's understanding was that the movie wasn't going to get a theatrical release but it was going to get a home video release. The real surprise came not when it didn't get the former but when it didn't get the latter. Could Corman have expected the real payoff to come through the home video market? The trailer, the announcement of a theatrical release, and the public relations work Hyde-White and Smith did would also have promoted a home release. This might also explain why the rough edges of the movie were never smoothed. Corman deemed it good enough for the home market.

Is it possible the Corman didn't get paid from the buyout? The man whose biography is titled *How I Made a Hundred Movies in Hollywood and Never Lost a Dime* would seem to be very concerned about money and profit margins. While Corman may not have lost a dime on *The Fantastic Four*, is it possible that he may not have made one either?

Maybe he wasn't aware or didn't see the possibility of a Marvel buyout and so there was nothing in any contract about it and what he would gain if Marvel bought the movie. Could Corman have been outmaneuvered in some way? It's especially difficult to believe that Corman would not have known the movie might or wasn't going to come out when so many other people have explained that they knew or heard something.

Given Corman's business acumen and vast experience in the business, I felt these were outside possibilities, but I decided to share some of these hypotheticals with Sikes since he knows both the story and the business so well. He said that "If Roger didn't get a payout, there would have been a lawsuit and it would have been very public. I was close with Roger's attorney at the time and there is zero chance Roger got screwed." Regarding the lack of response to the request for a copy of the contract, Sikes offers, "I would imagine that is not something he does. Why potentially stir things up when there is nothing in it for him? And perhaps there are other deal points having nothing to do with the payout that he wants secret. Or perhaps he just doesn't wish to officially make the deal points public. Or perhaps he is under a non-disclosure agreement." Whatever the reasons may be, Sikes said that he "firmly believes that Roger got his payout." He went on to say that "In all of 1992 and 1993 I never heard even once the possibility that Roger didn't get his pound of flesh. No way it wouldn't have come up and no way Roger would have signed on in the first place if he wasn't 100% guaranteed to make money." While Sikes is "certain that Eichinger was in control," he is "equally certain Roger was guaranteed either way to come out of it in the black. Roger did co-productions all the time and he was well-versed in how to come out on top no matter what." He concludes by proclaiming that "When it comes to making money, Roger truly is one of the greatest minds in the history of the entertainment industry."

All of Sykes' explanations make sense. Perhaps it's as simple as Corman gave the interview, has said what he has to say, and that is it. He doesn't feel obligated — and/or perhaps legally able — to offer contracts and so forth for inspection, publication, and analysis. Whether a contract would or wouldn't have yielded anything of interest, I don't know, but I am just grateful that he agreed to talk with me.

We have explored the possibilities as to why Corman didn't disclose the whole story prior to making the film. He wants everyone to put their full effort into the film, doesn't want them asking for more money since they know this is a one-shot deal and they won't earn residuals, and he doesn't want to look like a bad person for not being upfront about knowing the film might never appear (keeping quiet at the time about his buyout, though, might have helped bolster people's perception of him, but he was probably quite proud of the bonus). However, there's another very important reason why he might have not let everyone in on what happened at the time.

When the film was shot in 1992 and Corman knew it wasn't coming out, he was much younger and knew or hoped that he would be in the business for years, and, as it turned out, decades to come. Perhaps he concealed what he knew because he had to preserve something money cannot buy:

trust. He needed people to keep trusting him. You can work for people who are cheap. You can ever work for people whom you dislike. Can you work for people whom you do not fundamentally trust? If he had later said that he knew before filming even began that there was a good chance it wasn't going to come out, then going forward how does anyone who might work on another movie for him or become a business partner know that he will be straightforward with them? He had a reputation to protect if he wanted to keep making movies. Saying, "By the way, your work may never be seen and the quality is completely irrelevant to a greater and completely different goal" is not a great way to earn trust, interest talent in your projects, and positively motivate people to give their best. Creating a reputation for making movies that no one will see doesn't strike me as a career builder.

Why talk now?

At the time of our interview, he was ninety-two and in a different phase of his life. He knows he is probably not going to be making movies for decades to come and perhaps wanted to set the record straight once and for all.

If we compare Corman's and Eichinger's respective filmographies, we discover that while Corman found sustained success with making movies such as *Sharktopus* and *Piranhaconda* for the Syfy cable channel, Eichinger had huge success with theatrical releases such as the first four *Resident Evil* movies, *Downfall*, and *Perfume: The Story of a Murderer* (Summit Entertainment, which Eichinger co-founded has its own impressive list of cinematic successes). Of course, we cannot forget the two big-budget *Fantastic Four* movies he co-produced. While they not be critical highlights, they were lucrative. In some ways, this is not surprising as Corman had always tended to work in the low-budget film arena, while Eichinger had experienced mainstream success before 1994 with such films as *The Neverending Story* (1984) and *The Name of the Rose* (1986). In a sense, both went on doing what they had always done. Nonetheless, it seems that making *The Fantastic Four* ultimately led to more of a boost for Eichinger than it did for Corman, though it is not the only factor in their post-1994 careers.

I still wonder if *The Fantastic Four* was a bargaining chip for Eichinger to use with Fox. That's another reason Corman might promote but not finish a movie he wasn't sure was coming out. He was confident Marvel would give in first in an elaborate game of cinematic chicken. Marvel can see the promotion, but they can't see the finished/unfinished film during that ninety-day window. Corman refuted that idea. Why would he misrepresent the truth of what happened? What would be the advantage to him? I don't know. Let's keep in mind, too, that Hyde-White and Smith are the ones putting most of the time, money, and effort into the promotion; Corman is only paying for some promotional items and that may come out of the promotional budget provided by Eichinger. Advertising and promoting the movie months ahead of a potential debut both cost Corman little to nothing.

Eichinger's interview, while not giving specific numbers, indicates Corman did get something from the buying up of the film. Eichinger recounts that "he (Avi) would give me back the money we invested, both to me and to Roger, and we don't release the film." While Eichinger doesn't get into the details with Ito as much as Corman does later on with me, what Eichinger does say generally supports what Corman says. However, Eichinger also says that "It was not such a difficult deal because there was a clear accounting of what we spent on the film. We didn't want to make a profit, really." Although Eichinger does not explain who the "we" refers to, it cannot be Corman. Corman didn't want to see a profit from *The Fantastic Four*? That's impossible to believe. Also Eichinger makes it appear that he spoke with Corman about the deal before it was made and Corman gave his consent. My impression from Corman's interview is that he knew Eichinger might make a deal and they had a provision or understanding in place if he did, but Corman was not involved in making the deal and was informed by Eichinger of it after the fact. Details matter, of course, but these are essentially details.

Still, I think the bottom line is that the essential shapes of Eichinger's and Corman's interviews match and that their interviews are basically true. However you arrange the pieces, not all of them fit smoothly together. Time changes the shapes of things. Finally, there is the imprecision of human memory. If you've read all of the interviews, you've probably seen little contradictions here and there about, for example, what somebody made for their work or if they made anything at all. No one is exempt from that. The bottom line is that in any narrative you believe, remember, or construct, *The Fantastic Four* remains without an official release and this is still the one Roger Corman movie that didn't come out. This is the one that got away.

With *Doomed* and this collection of interviews, we have, if not the final words on the making of *The Fantastic Four*, then most of the words on its making. Steve Rabiner and Avi Arad won't talk. Bernd Eichinger and Stan Lee can't talk. I made several attempts to contact Stan Lee through people who knew him but I was unable to talk with him. My understanding is that he probably would not want to talk about the movie due to it being a sore subject with Marvel. My plan was instead to ask him about some of the creation and evolution of the Fantastic Four. While I don't think we would have gotten much, if any, insight into the movie — maybe I could have asked him about his early film treatment — and my questions about the Fantastic Four have probably already been asked, I, of course, wanted him to have a voice within these interviews. And what comic book fan wouldn't have wanted to talk to Stan Lee?

Stan Lee's interview is particularly interesting because he is in somewhat of a delicate position. He is aligned again with Marvel and promoting their movie. He doesn't want to say anything bad about it and knows they don't want to discuss it, and, therefore, probably don't want him saying much of anything about the old movie or bringing attention to it. Ito points out in his article, for example, that Stan Lee declines to be a part of a photo shoot with the original cast because, as Stan Lee himself explains, "With the new *Fantastic Four* movie coming out, I'd rather not be associated, in any way, with the old one." Yet, Stan Lee does not refuse to talk about "the old one" and he doesn't trash it during the interview; in fact, he makes some positive comments. You can reach your own conclusions, but my impression is that he recognizes its limitations within the context of the budget but doesn't think it was horrible. For him not to declare it a complete failure suggests that he thought a lot more of it than he lets on because he knows that the politically correct thing to do is to speak of it only in highly critical and negative terms. His comments about the film not being meant to be seen by anyone are not, I think, an opinion of the film itself. Instead, those comments are a recognition that the film was made first and foremost to preserve Eichinger's option.

Stan Lee is not the villain in this drama.

It's significant that a lot of the discussion in these interviews focuses on the Thing and Doctor Doom — the two characters that are the most physically disfigured and that have the largest emotional loads to carry. The future of superhero movies may be in exploring imperfect characters such as the Joker, Dark Phoenix, Logan, and Magneto. In *X-Men: Apocalypse* the scenes with Magneto saving a fellow worker from dying at the risk of exposing his powers and the scenes when he and his family are confronted later by the townspeople are the most powerful part of the film. Consider *Watchmen* with its world of neurotic heroes, imploding and dysfunctional hero collectives, and characters threatening the world in order — in their eyes — to save it. There is a narrow, gray space in which heroes are not always heroic and villains are not always villainous. This complicated space of anti-heroes and anti-villains is complex and rich. Jamming movies full of special effects may sell movies but may also sell the public short. I think we can handle serious comic book films that challenge us, disturb us, don't provide us with easy answers, and leave us with lingering questions pertinent to our own lives. You can illustrate and contemplate the universal by focusing on the local.

And there will always be and should be a space for comic book movies that are just fun or oriented toward kids. That doesn't always have to be an either/or choice. These movies can always respect audiences of any age by being smart and not just flashy.

This book is a story about many things: the future of comic book movies, comic books; Stan Lee; Jack Kirby; the Fantastic Four as a group, a comic, and as a film; the many people who worked on or were involved in some way with the film; the movie business; memory; and the ways that people deal with disappointment. It's also about the purpose of heroes. Yes, a good comic book like any other good story helps take us out of whatever negativity is going on right now and gives us some relief. There is an element of entertainment and escapism to all forms of art. However, good art also brings us into the core of our beings. It drives right into the messy heart of the world and brings us right along. Comics don't make us want to be someone else, somewhere else. They show us not only who else we can be but also how to be the best versions or ourselves right here, right now. We realize that other person, that hero, is just a reflection of us. You can't be anybody but yourself with all of your imperfections, but you can be the best version of you. Villains fascinate us, but we strive to be and want to find heroes. Comics show us that great things can come from difficult or flawed origins. It's what happens afterward that counts.

You can't rewrite the past. Nothing will change what happened with the shelving of *The Fantastic Four*, but releasing it now is a meaningful action — not just a gesture — that would help ease that pain. Place it in one of the eight — more to come, I'm sure — compilations of Marvel films that include *Fantastic Four* (2005). It's already bought and paid for. People know it exists. We also know that good copies of the film survive. Locate one of those film reels and play it in the arthouses, midnight theaters, and such. The film franchise is failing. Wouldn't it be something if this low-budget film from over a quarter of a century ago helped show the way forward and reignited interest in the Fantastic Four?

Once there was a kid who shared a bedroom with his brother while his parents slept on a foldout couch in a one-bedroom apartment at 1720 University Avenue in Bronx, New York. He wished for windows and, instead, made his own vision of what he wanted to see. He saw and made a world no one could have dreamed of but him. His name was Stanley Martin Lieber. Wherever he is, I bet he still believes in comic books, the Fantastic Four, the heroic potential, and the power of individual imagination.

APPENDIX ONE:
Who Created the Fantastic Four?

Although it is not the purpose of this project to finely detail and debate who created the Fantastic Four, a very brief and incomplete summary of decades of history and hundreds of pages of legal filings and court findings feels appropriate. In one sequence of events, Stan Lee came up with the concept and characters of the Fantastic Four, wrote the story for the first comic, and handed it off with a series of notes to Jack Kirby who contributed just the artwork. Then, Stan Lee got it back and put in the dialogue. That process describes what came to be known as the Marvel Method, which was used for a number of Marvel comics at the time. In another account, the creation of the Fantastic Four was either a much more collaborative event in which both men had a more or less equal part in the Fantastic Four's creation and discussed the characters, plot, and other significant elements. In a third scenario, Kirby essentially reversed Stan Lee's remembrance and came up with the story, characters, and art and *then* handed it off to Stan Lee who did the dialogue. Kirby maintained the second and third versions were closest to the truth, and Stan Lee held to the first and second versions. Both men's perspectives shifted around over the years depending, to some extent, on their relationship with Marvel and/or their individual relationships with each another.

Though credits would be more finely distinguished in some later issues, the first page of the first issue of the *Fantastic Four* shows the four members at the top and says, "Stan Lee + Jack Kirby," which strongly suggests the two co-created the comic. At one point, Stan Lee published a typed synopsis in issue 358 of the *Fantastic Four* in 1991 that shows his original vision for the Fantastic Four. However whether he wrote that before involving Kirby, after involving Kirby, or with Kirby remains an open question.

Kirby died in 1994, and in 2009 his heirs began legal proceedings over credits and copyrights to the Fantastic Four, X-Men, Thor, and many other Marvel characters. Marvel responded with the argument that Kirby's productions were "works made for hire." In such a situation, the employer and not the employee is legally considered the author of the work. Consequently, Kirby had no legal rights to what he produced whether or not he created them in part or in whole, Marvel argued. Rulings in the lower courts had been favorable to Marvel. Still, Marvel stood to lose a lot if they lost in court and they didn't know what other lawsuits they might face in the future if this precedent was set. Kirby's family persisted and advanced through the court hierarchy. On September 26, 2014, just three days before nine Supreme Court justices were scheduled to hold a conference to decide if they would actually hear the case, both sides released a joint statement that read, "Marvel and the family of Jack Kirby have amicably resolved their legal disputes and are looking forward to advancing their shared goal of honoring Mr. Kirby's significant role in Marvel's history." The terms of the settlement were not publicly disclosed. The prevailing theory is that Marvel wrote a big check and the common understanding is that Jack Kirby is the co-creator of the Fantastic Four.

APPENDIX TWO:
A Brief History of The Animated Fantastic Four

There's another point worth exploring that no one seems to have talked much about. On September 24, 1994 the *Fantastic Four: The Animated Series* debuted. It was the third cartoon series about the Fantastic Four. *Fantastic Four* came out in 1967 and contained twenty episodes. *The New Fantastic Four* came out 1978 with thirteen episodes. The series features the robot H.E.R.B.I.E. (Humanoid Experimental Robot, B-type, Integrated Electronics) in place of the Human Torch. The reason is that Universal Studios was not involved in the cartoon but they had the rights to the Human Torch and would not allow him to be used because they were trying to develop a live-action movie or series of some sort. However, the exclusion of the Torch gave rise to an urban legend that he was left out because of concerns that children would see the cartoon and set themselves on fire. That story may have originated from *Fantastic Four* issue 285 (1985) in which a socially ostracized boy named Hanson sets himself on fire to emulate the Human Torch and ultimately dies.

Fred and Barney Meet the Thing, a 1979 crossover cartoon between the Flintstones and the Fantastic Four, reversed that situation by featuring just a single member of the Fantastic Four. In this particular version, Benjy Grimm transforms into the Thing by touching two magic rings together and shouting "Thing ring, do your thing!" To add insult to injury, when the Shmoo was added, the show was retitled as *Fred and Barney Meet the Shmoo*.

The 1994 cartoon version, which drew heavily from the comic book, features all four members and contains twenty-six episodes and is important for several reasons. Notably, Avi Arad and Stan Lee were two of the executive producers. Lee, in fact, appeared before various episodes providing brief introductions to the episodes and characters. The opening voice introduces him as "Mister Marvel himself." Stan Lee's relationship with Marvel seemed to be secure or at least renewing itself.

This series also had an accompanying toy line produced by Toy Biz. Besides vehicles such as the Fantasticar — a version of which appears in the 1994 movie around the 1:15:30 mark — and action figures including the core Four and other characters and villains such as Doctor Doom ("Dr. Doom") and the Mole Man ("Mole Man"). Incidentally, the Mole Man appears in all three animated versions, so perhaps his appearance in 1994's *The Fantastic Four* movie shouldn't be so surprising.

So in 1994 we have or would have had a live-action movie, an animated series coming out a few months after, and a toy line that overlapped with both. Of course, the live-action film and the cartoon would have cross-promoted one another. In fact, that's what would eventually happen — but with another *Fantastic Four*. Within just a few days of the July 8, 2005 release of the live-action *Fantastic Four*, Walt Disney released the 1994 cartoon series on DVD on July 5. A fourth, and to this date, final cartoon version with twenty-six episodes appeared in 2006 titled *Fantastic Four: World's Greatest Heroes*. And, yes, rest assured that the Mole Man appears yet again. Eight episodes appeared, the series stopped airing, and then more episodes began airing just a few days before the premiere of *Fantastic Four: Rise of the Silver Surfer*. The co-existence of the cartoons with the live-action movies demonstrates that multiple onscreen versions of the Fantastic Four could complement and not compete with another. While the 1994 *The Fantastic Four* is not a cartoon, it could have stood and could still stand with the big-budget Goliaths.

Index

Numbers in **bold** indicate photographs

12 Monkeys 332
1492 Pictures 324, 325
24 159
Action Heroes Inc. 38
Adventure Inc. 146
Adventures of Superman 13
Aero Theatre 143, 303
Alba, Jessica 157, 289, 294, 327
ALIAS 85
Allen, Irwin 315
Allen, John 91
Altered Carbon 136
The Amazing Spider-Man (television show) 13
Amazon 22, 199
American Shaw Festival 254, 256
Angelfist 146, 282
Apple 199
Arad, Avi 17, 34, 142, 146, 167, 168, 188, 206, 229, 243, 287, 288-290, 291, 302, 303, 319, 321, 322, 323, 324, 342, 355, 362
Archie 161
Argyle 277
Armstrong, Louis 147
Arrested Development 290
Arriflex 122, 136, 137
Attack of the Crab Monsters 27, 232
Audible 230
Avatar 314
The Avengers (comic book) 131
The Avengers (film) 131, 167, 188, 239, 290
Avengers: Infinity War 52, 66, 189
Babylon 5 105
Badenov, Boris 247
Baker, Rick 109
Bashore, Juliet 85
Basil the Bingo Bassett 91
Batgirl 38, 276

Batman 38, 41, 128, 272, 276, 277, 327
Batman (film) 13, 128, 136, 162, 164, 173, 216, 303, 317, 327
Batman (film soundtrack) 128
Batman (television show) 13, 39, 40, 41, 163, 271, 272, 276
Batman & Robin 159
Batman Begins 14
Batman v Superman: Dawn of Justice 272
Battle Beyond the Stars 128, 283
Battlestar Galactica 221, 224
Beheshti, Macky 85
Belthazor 207
Beverly Hills 90210 191
Big Apple Comix 73
Bill Bixby 53, 159
Billups, Scott 49, 50, 59-61, 77, 81-84, 88, 93, 116-117, 134, 266, 345, 349-350
Binks, Jar Jar 229
Bixby-Brandon Productions 15
Black Crowes 130
Black Panther 75
Black Panther (comic book) 131
Black Panther (film) 242
Black Scorpion 40, 276
Bloodfist (films) 133, 146, 282
Blood Shot 204
Blunt, Emily 189, 334
Bonomi, Pietro 85, 91
Books of Doom 331
Bowie, David 147
Boxcar Bertha 7
Braille Institute 215
Breathtaker 277
Broccoli, Robert R. 35
Buck Rogers 313
Buck Rogers in the 25th Century 221, 224

Buechler, John 109
Buffy the Vampire Slayer 136
Bullock, Sandra 193
Burrell, Everett 10, 49, 77, **94**, **106**, 107, 109, 136, 296
Burton, Tim 136, 271, 276, 317
Buscema, John 343
Butler Brothers 196
Butterfly in the Typewriter 146
Byrne, John 95
Cameron, James 36, 224, 314
Cannom, Greg 109
Cannon Films 15
Captain America 76, 79, 333
Captain America (1944 serial) 53
Captain America (television movie) 13, 162, 264, 291
Captain America II: Death Too Soon (television movie) 13, 162, 221, 264
Captain Kirk 38
Captain Nuke and the Bomber Boys 252
Carnosaur 47, 283, 286, 302
Carolco Pictures 317
Carradine, Robert 177
Casino 159
Cassidy, Colin 332
Catch Me If You Can 230
Cavill, Henry 271
Chabrol, Claude 27
Challengers of the Unknown 292
Chaplin, Charlie 25
Charmed 207
Cheers 191
Chekhov, Anton 248
Chiklis, Michael 79, 289, 339
Children's Miracle Network 202
CIA Code Name: Alexa 195
Ciarfalio, Carl 31, 97, 98, 100, 11, 137, 146, **150**, 176, 179, 180, 176, 197, 198, 210, 280, 295, 296, 297, 298, 301, 303, 346
   See also The Thing
Class of Nuke 'Em High 19, 253
Cohn, Steve 129
Colan, Gene 343
Colossus (character) 144
Colossus (cosmic power) 45, **64**, 120, **121**, 240, 252, 272
Columbia Pictures 317, 318
Columbus, Chris 50, 207, 226, 285, 321-322, 324-325
Comcast 229

Community 334
Concorde Films / Concorde-New Horizons 14, 15, 28, 56, 90, 108, 119, 122, 141, 279, 301, 348, 349, 350
A Confederacy of Dunces 147
Connery, Sean 35
Constantin Film / Constantin Film AG 14, 19, 34, 36, 40, 43, 44, 55, 114-115, 123, 135, 137-138, 142, 144, 147, 201, 216, 227, 248, 263, 264, 268, 274, 279, 281, 285, 298, 317, 325
Contamination (convention) 183
Coppola, Francis Ford 36
Criminal Minds 192
CSI 159, 192
Culp, Joseph 37, 43, 96, 100, 144, 159, 171, 178, 179, 182, 205, 210, 213, 230, 250, 267, 330
   See also Doctor Doom
   See also Victor Von Doom
Culp, Robert 37, 231
Cyborg 335
Dallas Cowboys 197, 199
Damme, Jean-Claude Van 202, 282
Daredevil 343
Dark 332
The Dark Half 104
Darkman 71, 76
Dark Phoenix 356
Dark Shadows 190
Davison, Jon 282
DC Comics 107, 130, 131, 134, 162, 272, 292, 318, 335
Dead Poets Society 335
Deadpool 24, 160
The Deer Hunter 175
Demme, Jonathan 36, 221
Demolition Day 252
De Niro, Robert 36
Desperate Housewives 192
Dexter 192
Die Hard 21
Di Franco, Paul 129
Disney 52, 76, 171, 229, 258, 362
Disney Channel 292
Disney Imagineering 76
Ditko, Steve 73, 74, 75, 107, 343

Doctor Doom 7, 30, 42-43, 44, 45-46, 47, **48**, 49, 51, **54**, **65**, 78, 84, 95, **96**, 97, 100, **101**, 102, 108, 110, 120, 136, 140-141, 144, 168, 171, 178, 192, 192, 205, 206, **206**, 207, 213, **214**, 215, 225, 226, 231, 233, **234**, 235-236, 238, 239, 240, **241**, 242, 243, 247, 248, 249, 250, **251**, 256, 257, 272, 287, 312, 319, 325, 326, 330, 331, 332, 334, 356, 362
  See also Victor Von Doom
Doctor Strange 13, 76, 331
A Doll's House 249
Dolphin Man 23
Donovan, Tate 193
Doom Patrol 292
Doomed!: The Untold Story of Roger Corman's The Fantastic Four 7, 9, 10, 19, 27, 50-51, 93, 106, 137, 146, 158, 165, 167, 176, 177, 180, 207, 208, 230, 242, 267, 280, 287, 294, 303, 355
Doom, Victor Von 7, 43, 51, 168, 192, 225, 226, 242-243, 251, 252, 272, 312, 319, 330, 334
  See also Doctor Doom
Downfall 353
Dragonfest 159
The Drew Carey Show 191, 362
Dr. Hauptmann / Dr. Hauptman 43, 253, 254, 256, 257
Dr. Strange (television movie) 13
Efron, Zac 272
Eichinger, Bernd 14, 16, 18, 19, 20, 23, 24, 25-26, 27, 28, 29, 31, 33, 34, 35, 36, 37, 38, 39, 41, 42, 43, 44, 138, 144, 154, 165, 166, 167, 184, 201, 202, 211, 226, 227, 228, 237, 269, 270, 274-275, 279, 284, 285, 286, 295, 298-299, 301, 302, 303, 305, 306, 307, 308, 309, 310, 311, 314, 345, 346, 347-348, 349, 350, 352, 353, 354, 355, 356
The Elephant Man 137, 140
Elfman, Danny 14, 128
Ellen 191
Elliott, Mike 93, 98, 105, 142, 301
Elongated Man 292
Emperor Doom 330
Evans, Chris 79, 333
Evil Dead (films) 79
Evil Dead III: Army of Darkness 49
Extant 159
Fangoria (magazine) 76, 104

"Fantastic Faux!" 17
Fantastic Four (animated cartoons) 272, 292, 331, 361-362
Fantastic Four (comic book) 11, 40, 47, 72, 74, 81, 95, 134, 231, 257, 292, 293, 294, 325-326, 356, 359
The Fantastic Four (1994) **222**
  Budget 22, 36, 56, 84, 122, 136, 139, 144, 156, 162, 163, 165, 257, 286, 299, 301, 305, 306, 307, 310, 320-321, 338, 348
  Buyout 22, 138, 264, 286, 351, 353
  Effects 46, 49, 50, 52, 59, 66, 69, 70, 81, 82, 83, 85, 93, 97, 98, 113-114, 116, 134, 141, 142, 155, 162, 168-169, 175, 182, 183, 184, 207, 223-224, 243, 245, 258, 261, 262, 265-266, 272, 274, 276, 291, 295, 302, 310, 311-312, 313, 339, 349
  Fee for Roger Corman 21, 23, 264, 310
  Message, Meaning, and Theme 44, 140, 158, 167, 181, 188, 205, 228, 229, 239-240, 286
  Music and Soundtrack 127-129, 135, 266, 273
  Negative and Copies 28, 122, 138, 141, 142, 159, 168, 188, 206, 243, 287, 288-289, 313, 324
  Premiere 16, 123, 124, 164, 166, 202, 228, 270
  Prequel 307
  Promotion 15, 124, 138, 155, 201-202, 203, 269, 288, 306-307, 321, 324
  Script and Screenplay 15, 33, 39, 40, 41, 42, 45-46, 108, 112, 119, 134, 161-162, 226, 252, 286, 305, 310, 311, 313, 316-317, 318, 320, 340-341
  Sequel 36, 40, 104, 139, 157, 181, 184, 215, 227, 249, 257-258, 275, 299
Fantastic Four (2005 film) 16, 17, 27, 51, 52, 55, 71, 77, 79, 95, 138, 144, 192, 207, 212, 218, 229, 237, 260, 270, 289, 291, 293, 294, 314, 334, 339, 340, 343, 345, 349, 353, 355, 357, 362
Fantastic Four: Rise of the Silver Surfer (2007 film) 77, 266, 294, 333, 334, 353, 362
Fantastic Four (2015 film) 52, 55, 109, 294

Far and Away 159
The Fast and the Furious 159
Fat Man and Little Boy 109
Feige, Kevin 52
Fennell, Geoff 85
Ferrigno, Lou 159
Fight Club 159
Film Threat (magazine) 15, 16, 47, 49, 50, 164, 264
Final Embrace 133
Firebrand 292
Fist of the Dragon 282
The Flash (comic book) 292
The Flash (1990 television show) 153, 159
Fleischer, Max 87, 98
FotoKem 122, 141
Fox (media) 34, 72, 144, 226, 228, 229, 237, 268, 269, 275, 323, 324, 325, 327, 328
Fox Searchlight 22
Foxx, Jamie 335
Friends 77
Frost, Mark 129
Full Moon Entertainment 284
Gable, Clark 169
Galactus 293
Game Night 334
Gardner, Tony 76
Garland, Glenn 88, 89, 124, 141, 142, 267, 348
George, Roger 98, 99, 100
Gilligan's Island 229
Glee 191
Gods and Generals 230
Golden Apple Comics 134
Goldsman, Akiva 23
Goldsmith, Jerry 128
Good Time 334
Good Will Hunting 335
Google 199
Gorshin, Frank 277
Gosnell, Raja 71
Gossett Jr., Louis 15
Gotham 146
The Greatest Showman 273-274
The Green Hornet (2011 film) 159
Green, Kat 230
    See also Alicia Masters
Grillo, Glen 85
Grimm, Ben 43, 44, 45, 50, 51, 69, 140, 141, 168, 178, 179, 180, 197, 198, 199, 205, 208, 211, 240, 273, 312
    See also The Thing

Groundlings 254
Guardians of the Galaxy 24, 131, 244
Guiding Light 191
Gunner 256
Gunn, James 24
Hallmark Channel 192, 218
Halt and Catch Fire 334
Hammond Lumberyard 53, 55, 95, 100, 104, 105, 142, 224, 253
Harbour, David 334
Harry Potter 168, 325
Hart, Jonathan 38
HBO 284
Heathers 75
Hefner, Richard 21
H.E.R.B.I.E. 361
Hercules (television show) 146
Heroes 332
Herz, Michael 21, 24, 27
Hickman, Jonathan 239
The Hills Have Eyes 198
Hollywood Boulevard 282
The Hollywood Reporter (magazine) 15, 123
Home Alone 2 325
Hook 109
Horner, James 128, 135
Hosack, Mark 210
Howard the Duck (film) 13
Howard, Ron 36, 290
How I Made a Hundred Movies in Hollywood and Never Lost a Dime 311, 351
The Hulk 112, 268, 343
Hulk 317, 321
Human Bomb 292
Humanoids from the Deep 7
Human Torch 44, 70, 79, 98, **222**, 291, 315, 318, 361
    See also Johnny Storm
Hunger 242
Hyde-White, Alex 15, 41, 43, 100, 138, 144, 151, 159, 175, 178, 179, 180, 196, 200, 201, 203, 204, 210, 212, 219, 267, 268, 273, 297, 300, 301, 345, 347, 351, 354
The Incredible Hulk (television show) 13, 53, 159, 291
The Incredible Hulk Returns (television movie) 15, 53, 291
The Incredibles 291, 292, 334
Independence Day 59, 266
Independent Film Channel 22
The Infinity Gauntlet 331

INDEX

Ingrid Goes West 334
In Hell 202
Inhumans 75
In Living Color 335
Invisible Girl 171, **172**, **222**
The Invisible Man 292
Invisible Woman 171, **172**, **222**
Iron Man 76, 144, 331
Iron Man (comic book) 11
Iron Man (film) 87, 160
Ito, Robert 17-18, 315, 324, 337, 354, 355
Jackman, Hugh 189, 273, 274
Jackson, Michael 78
Jacobs, Gillian 334
Jay Jay the Jet Plane 87
The Jeweler 43, 50, 102, **103**, 108, 144, **145**, **185**, 239, 247, 254, **255**
  See also Mole Man
Johnston, Dietrich 204
Joker 356
Jurassic Park 47, 70, 207, 283, 299
Justice League 131
Kander, Ivan 30, 286
Kander, Rebecca 332
Kane, Gil 343
Kaufman, Lloyd 14, 34, 36-37, 295, 347
Keaton, Buster 25
Keaton, Michael 327
Kidman, Nicole 15
Kikumoto, Jan 141
Kinmont, Kathleen 195
Kinnevik 91
Kirby, Jack 8, 17, 51, 52, 69, 72, 73, 74-75, 107, 108, 343, 356, 359-360
Kirby, Roz 72
Kragdstadt 249
Krasinski, John 189, 334
Krogstad, Nils 249
Kronos 235
Krueger, Freddy 195
Kruger, Diane 147
Kulzer, Robert 142, 144, 147
Kutchaver, Kevin 116
Lamas, Lorenzo 157, 195
Langford, Marty 7, 10, 31, 51, 106, 165, 176, 281, 294, 295, 296, 298
The Laughing Sutra 274
Leedarson 209
LEGO Hero Factory 131
Lieberman, Ilona 49
Life of Pi 86, 90
Lifetime 283
Lightning Dubs 142

Little, Frank 85
Little Lotta 171
The Little Shop of Horrors 232, 284
Live by the Fist 282
Logan 160, 189-190, 244, 272, 335, 336, 352
Looney Tunes 129
Lord of Latveria 43
Los Angeles (magazine) 17, 289
The Lost Boys 109
Love Potion No. 9 193
Loyola Marymount University 120
Lucas, George 223
Lumpkin, Willie 343
Lundgren, Dolph 15
Luthor, Larry 85
Mad (magazine) 161
Mad Men 242, 293
Magneto 330, 356
Magnussen, Billy 334
Majors, Lee 38
Malcolm X 161
Mall of America 16, 123, 164, 202
Mallrats 152
Mann, Thomas 147
Mara, Kate 294
Marshall, Garry 223
Martial Law 146
Marvel Animation 72
Master-Bater 23
Masters, Alicia 45, 168, 211, 213, **214**, 215, 216, 316
Masters of Sex 192
McClory, Kevin 35
McKoenig, Bill 324
McMahon, Julian 192, 207
Measmer, Mike 102, 104
Mego 39, **39**
The Mentalist 192
Meredith, Burgess 277
Microsoft 199
MIDI 129
Millennium (film company) 15
Miracle Desert 210
Misalliance 256
The Misfits 169
Mission: Impossible 159
Mister Fantastic 97, **222**, 232, 292
  See also Reed Richards
Mitty, Walter 268
Modern Cartoons 91
Mole Man 43, 57, 61, 62, 63, 66, 97, 102, 108, 144, 239, 316, 362
  See also Jeweler

Monroe, Marilyn 169
Moore, Roger 35
Mork from Ork 335
Morris, Garrett 277
Morton, Marlena 129
Mouthpiece 292
Moviola 261-262
Mr. Film 77, 78, 81, 85, 90, 91, 134, 262, 266
Mrs. Doubtfire 226, 322, 325
Mulholland Drive 60
Mutant X 146
Namco 24, 25
The Name of the Rose 353
Natural Born Killers 159
NCIS 192
Netflix 22, 102, 147, 290, 314
Neue Constantin Film. *See* Constantin Film
The Neverending Story 353
Never Say Never Again 35
Nevius, Craig J. 8, 10, **37**, 144, 277, 286, 300, **312**, 326, 348
New Constantin. *See* Constantin Film
New Horizons. *See* Concorde
New Line Cinema 55
Newmar, Julie 277
New World International 15
New World Pictures 9, 10, 14, 15, 28, 56, 61, 282
New World Television 15
Nicholson, Jack 27, 221
Nickelodeon 291
Night, Blake 332
A Nightmare on Elm Street (films) 63, 71
A Nightmare on Elm Street 5: The Dream Child 195, 195
Night of the Witch 26
Nip/Tuck 192
Oasis 130
Octopussy 35
Optic Nerve 49, 77, 78, 80, 93, 104, 106, 233
Orion Pictures 14, 15
Osram Sylvania 209
Pace, Lee 334
Pan's Labyrinth 136
Patten, Dick Van 133
Pattinson, Robert 334
Percy, Walker 147
Perfume: The Story of a Murderer 353

Phantom Lady 292
The Phantom of the Opera 141, 235
Pipes, Ron 104
Piranhaconda 353
Pixar Animation Studios 86, 292
PixelMonger 83
Plastic Man 292
PM Entertainment 158, 281
Poe (movie cycle) 27
Police Comics 292
Port Charles 190, 191
Pretty Woman 221
Prince 14
Professor X 190
Pterodactyl Woman from Beverly Hills 60
Punch Audio 230
The Punisher 15
Puttnam, David 317, 318
Puzo, Mario 319
Rabiner, Steve 16, 33, 37, 38, 41, 42, 223, 275, 277, 279, 280, 281, 297, 298, 300, 301, 302, 303, 355
Raimi, Sam 71, 76, 290
Ray 335
Ray, Fred Olen 109
Ray, Scott 156
Reeve, Christopher 271, 272, 273
Reeves, George 271
The Reflecting Pool 242
Renegade 196
Resident Evil (films) 326, 353
Revis 262
Rhythm & Hues 89
Richard III 235
Richards, Reed 42, 43, 45, 71, 97, 120, 168, 171, 178, 188, 189, 205, **222**, 223-224, 226, 228, 229, 230, 240, 242, 243, 252, 272, 273, 311, 312, 331, 334, 343
See also Mister Fantastic
Richards, Reve 136
Richie Rich 171
Rock, Kevin 40, 41
The Rocky Horror Picture Show 218
Rogen, Seth 159
Roger Corman Presents 276
Rogers, Steve 335
Romero, Cesar 104
Romero, George 277
Romita, John 343
Ronald McDonald House 164, 202
Rotten Tomatoes 294
Roundtree, Richard 133

INDEX

Saltzman, Harry 35
Sandman 316
Sarandon, Susan 147
Sassone, Oley 8, 10, 16, 28, 59, 61, 63, 67, 69, 70, 71, 81-82, 84, 88, 95, 100, 102, 104, 108, 116, 117, 120-121, 123, 124, 126, 127, 128, 129, 151, 153, 154, 155, 158, 159, 161-162, 163, 164, 167, 168, 169, 173, 184, 196, 202, 203, 210, 223, 232, 248, 250, 252, 253, 254, 256, 258, 261, 263, 264, 265, 266, 267, 274, 275, 279, 280, 281, 286, 295-296, 297, 298, 299, 301, 310, 338, 345, 346, 350
Sassoon, Catya 146
Sassoon, Vidal 146
Savini, Tom 104, 109
Schiff, Laura 279, 299
Schwarzenegger, Arnold 203
Scooby-Doo 71
Scorsese, Martin 229
The Seagull 248-249
Secret Identity: The Real and Not So Real Lives of Stan Lee 268
Seinfeld 191
The Sentinel 146
Sgt. Kabukiman N.Y.P.D. 19, 20, 23, 24, 25, 35
Shangraw, Howard 247, 249, 250
Sharktopus 353
Shatner, William 38
Sheen, Martin 253
Shipp, John Wesley 159
Shmoo 361
Sholly, Pete Von 67, 68
Showtime 276, 284
Shrine Auditorium 285
Sid and Nancy 67
SIGGRAPH 89
Sikes, Mark 10, 30, 31, 51, 100, 106, 107, 137, 165, 173, 176, 253, 294, 345, 346, 351, 352
Silver Surfer 40, 52, 75, 89, 316, 318
Silver Surfer (comic book) 315
Silver Suzy 89
Simpson, O.J. 196
Six Million Dollar Man 38
The Skateboard Kid 105, 111
Sleepstalker 79-80
Smith, Doug 85
Smith, Michael Bailey 15, 50, 151, 155, 164, 178, 180, 238, 297, 345, 347
See also Ben Grimm

Snowpiercer 79
Sony Classics 22
Spectral Motion 78
Spider-Man 38, 44, 76, 133, 157, 268, 330, 343,
Spider-Man (comic book) 73, 94
Spider-Man (films) 14-15, 87, 104, 159, 224, 268, 269, 290, 317, 321, 340, 343
Spider-Man Lives: A Miles Morales Story 329
Spielberg, Steven 50, 155, 223, 283, 294
Springer, Odette 129
Staab, Rebecca 37, 66, 159, 169, 196, 209, 210, 300, 301
See also Invisible Girl
See also Susan Storm
Stalling, Carl 129
Stallone, Sylvester 36
Stark, Tony 335
Star Trek (film) 128
Star Trek (television show) 39, 163, 293
Star Wars 127, 283
Steinberg, Flo 73-74
Stepmonster 33
Storm, Johnny 51, 59, 82, 85, 161, 168, 175, 176, 205, 216, **222**, 229, 240, 273, 311, 312, 315, 333, 334
See also Human Torch
Storm, Susan 163-164, 171, **172**, 173, 184, 189, 191, 192, 199, 205, 213, **222**, 239, 240, 243, 273, 294, 312, 327, 334
See also Invisible Girl
Story, Tim 334, 339
Stranger Things 334
Strawn, Mick 10, 136, 345
Stray Bullet 177, 301
Summit Entertainment 353
Sundance Film Festival 22, 224
Super Freddy 195
Supergirl (film) 13
Supergirl (television show) 272
Superman 38, 87, 98, 157, 271, 272, 319
Superman (comic book) 74
Superman (films) 13, 15, 128, 162, 164, 238, 271, 273, 293, 303, 318
Swamp Thing (film) 13
Syfy (cable channel) 353
Terminator 2 85
Terror T.R.A.X.: Track of the Vampire 79

The Thing 31, 45, **48**, 68, 72, 78, 79, 94, 95, 97, **98**, 99-100, 102, **103**, **106**, 108, 110, 112, **113**, 120, 136, 137, 141, 144, 149, **150**, 151, **152**, **157**, 160, 164, 168, **172**, 176, 179, 180, **185**, 186, **187**, 188, 197-198, 199, 206, **206**, 207, 213, 215, 216, **217**, **222**, 229, 240, **255**, 270, 280, 296, 312, 317, 334, 339, 341, 343, **344**, 356, 361
Cool Suit 98-100, 146, 149, 153, 296, See also Ben Grimm
Thor 360
Thor (comic book) 75
Thor (film) 160
Thriller (television show) 108
Thunderball 35
Tin Man 235, 236
Titanic 238, 314
Tomorrowland 335
Tomorrow's Realities 89
Toole, John Kennedy 146-147
Toxic Avenger 24, 34
The Toxic Avenger 19, 23
The Towering Inferno 315
Toy Biz 362
Trank, Josh 293
The Trial of the Incredible Hulk (television movie) 15, 53, 291
Trigger, Ian 66, 144, 254, 256, See also The Jeweler
Trigorin 247, 248, 249
The Trip 27
Troma Entertainment 14, 19, 20, 21, 22, 23-24, 25, 26, 27, 28, 29, 34, 36
Troma's War 21
Tromeo and Juliet 24
True Blood 191
Turner, Cole 207
Twilight 334
The Umbrella Academy 102
Underwood, Jay 37, 175, 176, 178, 196, 210, 298, 300
   See also Human Torch
   See also Johnny Storm

Universal Pictures / Universal Studios 76, 221, 258, 361
USA Network 283
Vader, Darth 235, 319
Variety (magazine) 133
Ventura, Jesse 196
The Vibrator 23
Viper 146
Von Doom: A Dr. Doom Origin Story 286, 329, 331-332, 335
Vulich, John 49, 77, 93, 95, 97, 102, 104, 105, 106, **106**, 136, 345
Wagner, Robert 38
Walker III, Chris 78
Walker, Chris 78, 80, 262, 345, 350
Walker, Peter 147
Warner Bros. 317, 318
Watchmen 160, 356
Welcome to the Men's Group 242
Wells, H.G. 292
West, Adam 39, 41, 271, 276, 277, **277**
Westworld 159
Williams, John 128
Williams, Robin 335
Wilson, Don "The Dragon" 133, 283
The Wizard of Oz 235
Wolverine 190, 336
The Wonder Years 191
World's Finest Comics 272
Wurst Brothers 135, 266, 273, 293
Xena: Warrior Princess 146
The X-Files 136
X: The Man with X-Ray Eyes 26
X-Men (comic book) 44
X-Men (films) 13, 45, 87, 104, 245, 268, 269, 274, 317, 321, 342, 343, 356
The Young and the Restless 191
Zargarpour, Habib 85

Bear Manor Media

Classic Cinema.
Timeless TV.
Retro Radio.

WWW.BEARMANORMEDIA.COM

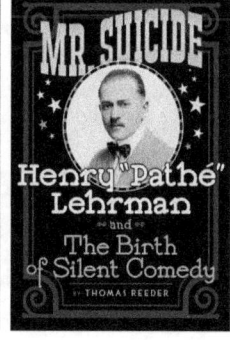

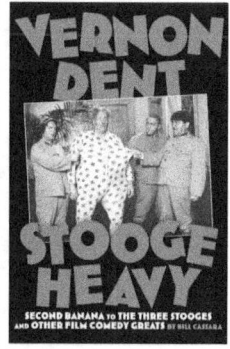

www.ingramcontent.com/pod-product-compliance
Lightning Source LLC
Chambersburg PA
CBHW050159240426
43671CB00013B/2184